Interdisciplinary Studies in Human Rights

Volume 7

Human rights are one of the normative cornerstones of contemporary international law and global governance. Due to the complexities of actual or potential violations of human rights and in light of current crises, new and interdisciplinary research is urgently needed. The series Interdisciplinary Studies in Human Rights recognizes the growing importance and necessity of interdisciplinary research in human rights. The series consists of monographs and collected volumes addressing human rights research from different disciplinary and interdisciplinary perspectives, including but not limited to philosophy, law, political science, education, and medical ethics. Its goal is to explore new and contested questions such as the extraterritorial application of human rights and their relevance for non-state actors, as well as the philosophical and theoretical foundations of human rights. The series also addresses policy questions of current interest including the human rights of migrants and refugees, LGBTI rights, and bioethics, as well as business and human rights.

The series editors are Members of the Centre for Human Rights Erlangen-Nürnberg (CHREN), an interdisciplinary research center at Friedrich-Alexander-University Erlangen-Nürnberg. The Advisory Board brings together human rights scholars from a wide range of academic disciplines and regional backgrounds. The series welcomes suggestions for publications of academic research falling into the series subject matter.

More information about this series at http://www.springer.com/series/15339

Lutforahman Saeed

Islam, Custom and Human Rights

A Legal and Empirical Study of Criminal Cases in Afghanistan After the 2004 Constitution

Springer

Lutforahman Saeed
Islamic Law Faculty
Kabul University
Kabul, Afghanistan

ISSN 2509-2960 ISSN 2509-2979 (electronic)
Interdisciplinary Studies in Human Rights
ISBN 978-3-030-83085-4 ISBN 978-3-030-83086-1 (eBook)
https://doi.org/10.1007/978-3-030-83086-1

This Springer imprint is published by the registered company Springer Nature Switzerland AG.
The registered company address is: Gewerbestrasse 11, 6330 Cham, Switzerland

I dedicate this book to my wife, Hosna Saeed, and my children for their endless support without whom I would not have been able to complete this research. In addition, I dedicate this research to my deceased parents, who paved the ground for me to reach this stage, though they were unable to see the completion of it.

Foreword

This book deals with a topic of outstanding relevance from both scientific and practical legal perspectives. It combines thorough empirical research with a sound study of legal documents and literature. The author had to tackle considerable obstacles, given the extreme form of legal and cultural normative pluralism in Afghanistan and the factual shortcomings in the Afghan judiciary and administration. It is extremely difficult to figure out which normative setting was and is to be applied in general and in the exemplary criminal law cases the author has researched and evaluated in detail.

The complexity of the topic is already demonstrated in the introductory remarks: while there are no provisions in Afghan criminal law dealing with the acts committed by the culprits, courts sentenced these persons on the basis of very general constitutional provisions enabling or demanding the application of Islamic law, while these outcomes are disputed both under Islamic law and human rights principles on the necessity of appropriately clear criminal law norms (*nulla poena sine lege*).

I highly appreciate the initiative of the author to engage in this research due to his extraordinary knowledge of the Afghan legal and social situation and his equally extraordinary capabilities to get access to information, which is usually not available to Western researchers. In his work, he successfully links more theoretical and general reflections on the applicable norms, including the intricate issues of interpreting Islamic norms, with concrete case studies. The book provides a wealth of information, observations, and very plausible evaluations of the Afghan legal scene, its extraordinarily complex normative basis, its institutions, and the interplay between societal expectations. It enables deep insights into the challenges for formulating and implementing laws, which are broadly accepted and apt to be implemented in a highly multicultural country with limited means for the state administration and judiciary, not to mention the intricate security situation in many provinces.

The book also sheds light on the widespread superficial application of Sharia rules, be it due to a lack of sound knowledge or under the pressure of public opinion.

Furthermore, the author obviously counts among the very small number of Afghan legal scholars digging deeply into the international theoretical debate on the reasons and emanations of legal pluralism in the context of Islam-related legal issues. Thus, for the first time, the tensions between traditional approaches to the application of legal norms and the rule of law, which clearly limits the scope of discretion for administrations and courts alike, are discussed and commented on in detail. Furthermore, the author has developed sound suggestions for reforms enabling the implementation of human rights standards in coherence with the country's culture.

In sum, this book is a milestone, which will set standards for a long time regarding the topics it covers, ranging from Afghan constitutional and ordinary law, the legal pluralism in Afghanistan, and the ways of interpreting Islamic norms up to the socio-legal context within which normative issues are dealt with. This is why the book is a "must" not only for all those interested in Afghan law, culture, and life but also for everyone who is interested in deep exemplary insights into the interplay between Islamic law and local customs, as well as the dynamic potential of Islamic normativity in search for an overlapping consensus in human rights issues based on respective legal cultures and societal conditions.

Erlangen, Nürnberg, Germany Mathias Rohe

Preface

A third-year student of the journalism department at Balkh University, Saīd Parwīz Kāmbakhsh, printed an article from the Internet, including insulting words to the Holy Quran and Prophet Mohammad (PBUH) and distributed it among his classmates. He was arrested and convicted of the death penalty by the primary court of Mazar-e-Sharif city. In addition, a truck driver was arrested and sentenced by the primary court of Kunduz city because of carrying 1000 donkey skins in his truck. Besides that, the primary court of Herat city sentenced two people to 13 years in prison because they slaughtered a dog and intended to sell its meat in the market. Not all these acts are criminalized in the law of Afghanistan. The courts have decided based on Article 130 of the Afghan Constitution, which allows courts to use the doctrine of the Ḥanafī School in the case of a legal lacuna. The courts' decisions regarding these cases caused huge debates among the legal experts and civil society activists; even in some cases, the court decision received political backlash and drove international community involvement.[1]

This research will answer the main question of how the Afghan courts use the provisions of the Ḥanafī school of thought if the law is silent regarding a case under consideration in the courts. To find an answer for such a question through a case study, it would be better to shed light on the legal framework and legal pluralism, along with the legal norms and standards in Afghanistan.

The legal framework for the use of Sharia, particularly the Ḥanafī school of thought, in the legal cases in Afghanistan is chiefly based upon the social structure and dominant beliefs of Afghan society. As a majority Muslim country (99.7% Muslim and 0.3% others),[2] Islamic principles influence and are reflected in the Afghan social structure, sources and interpretations of law, cultural practices, social

[1] As in Parwīz Kāmbakhsh case, during president Karzai, he got help from the high-ranking Norwegian and Swedish officials to leave the country. He was smuggled out of Afghanistan by a Swedish government airplane with the help of Swedish Foreign Minister Mr. Carl Bildt in 2015.

[2] https://www.cia.gov/-library/publications/the-world-factbook/geos/af.html, accessed at 6:15 pm date 06/01/2019.

values, and more generally the worldviews of Afghan individuals. To clarify the role of Sharia in judicial decisions, it is necessary to discuss the role of Islam and Sharia principles in Afghan society, particularly in the legal system of Afghanistan. The book has two main parts, each of which consists of several chapters.

The first part provides information regarding the legal framework and conceptual analyses of the role of Sharia principles in the legal history of Afghanistan. Since Islam has been considered as a general framework that covers almost all aspects of Muslim life, especially the legal aspects, it is also necessary for this study to clarify the role of Islam and religious leaders in Afghan society. This clarification will help us have a better understanding of the legal system and the role that Islamic principles and religious leaders play in Afghan society. To this end, the first chapter will demonstrate the root of religion in the field of law in Afghanistan, especially as it deals with criminal matters. Indeed, the power of law mainly derives from Islamic principles and has its foundations in the belief systems of the people it governs and is well connected to the values that are respected in Afghan society, including custom and morality. Due to the differences between the Afghan society and other majority Muslim countries, it is also important to explain the meanings of the terms Islam, Sharia, and *fiqh*. This explanation will prevent a misunderstanding of the precise meaning of these terms in the legal context of Afghanistan. As such, the chapter will shed light on the exact meaning of these terms in the context of Afghanistan.

To explain why and under which circumstances the Afghan courts disregard codified law and use Ḥanafī provisions, and sometimes customary law standards, it is necessary to focus on the role of Islam and Sharia in Afghanistan and what it means in the context of Afghan society.

The second chapter of this book addresses legal pluralism in Afghanistan and discusses the main players in the legal field. It discusses the three pillars (Sharia, customary law, and statutory law) of the legal system of Afghanistan and explains the ancient and complex system of customary dispute resolution in Afghanistan. Furthermore, it speaks about legal education and the role of the most effective field of legal knowledge, as well as some aspects of the judiciary of Afghanistan.

Chapter 3 of Part I analyzes Article 130 of the Afghan Constitution, including its historical background, particularly how judges have turned to Article 130 to justify applying Ḥanafī provisions in the case of a legal lacuna. Additionally, the chapter discusses the main source of Article 130 of the Afghan Constitution and provides a historical background that when this article appears in the Afghan Constitution and how its concept has developed through the constitutional history of Afghanistan.

Chapter 4 explains the implementation of Article 130 in practice and discusses the legal norms and standards guiding criminal procedures. In addition to the applicable norms and standards under Afghan law and Sharia, the chapter examines the concept of *taʿzīr* (discretionary punishment) and how it should be applied. This chapter also discusses how the Afghan courts apply the concept of *taʿzīr* in the light of Article 130 of the Afghan constitution.

Part II of this book is devoted to a case study and demonstrates how the Afghan courts apply Sharia principles, particularly the provisions of the Ḥanafī school of thought, to cases. Although there are a huge number of cases that Afghan courts had made decisions on in the light of Article 130 of the Constitution, I have tried to choose a number of important cases from different parts of the country with different facts that illustrate the usage of Ḥanafī school's doctrines in the case of a legal gap. The copies of court decisions regarding such cases have been collected from different courts across the country with the permission of the Supreme Court of Afghanistan. Having access to the cases is very difficult in Afghanistan. Luckily, acting on the official request to the Supreme Court, the Chief Justice, Mr. Yusuf Halim, issued a letter to all courts to provide me a copy of some cases. In addition, my relationship with many judges helped me have access to the copies of such cases because since I graduated from the Kabul Sharia Faculty and have taught there for around 25 years, I know so many judges at different levels of the courts.

Chapter 5 of the book examines the apostasy case of Parwīz Kāmbakhsh, a man who downloaded and printed an article from the Internet and distributed it to his classmates. This article included insults to the Holy Quran and Prophet Mohammad. He was sentenced to capital punishment by the primary court of Mazar-e-Sharif city, but the Kabul appellate court overruled the decision and instead sentenced him to 20 years in prison. The Supreme Court affirmed the Kabul appellate court's decision.

Chapter 6 analyzes the "Selling of Dog Meat Case" from Herat province in the western part of the country. Three people slaughtered a street dog and cut its meat into small pieces to sell in the market. The police arrested them, and the Herat city primary court sentenced them to 13 years in prison. The appellate court of Herat province and the Supreme Court affirmed the decision.

Chapter 7 discusses the "Trafficking Donkey Skins Case," where a defendant was convicted for trafficking donkey skins. The Kunduz police arrested a truck driver who had around 1000 donkey skins in his truck while he was traveling from Mazar-e-Sharif city to Kunduz province. The primary court of Kunduz city punished him by imprisonment and issued an order to confiscate the truck. The appellate court and the Supreme Court affirmed the decision.

In each of these cases, the defendants were convicted for actions that are not described as crimes by the penal code in Afghanistan; nonetheless, Afghan courts have made decisions based on Sharia, namely the Ḥanafī School's doctrine, which caused a huge debate locally and internationally. Through these case studies, finally this research provides tentative answers to the question as to how Afghan courts implement Sharia principles in criminal cases in the absence of statutory law.

The last chapter consists of an overview of the dissertation, its major findings, recommendations, and a conclusion. After the overview, the chapter lists some major findings of the research and follows up with some recommendations. The last part of this chapter briefly concludes the whole book.

Kabul, Afghanistan Lutforahman Saeed

Acknowledgments

First, I am thankful to God for letting me live to see this book published. In addition, I would like to express my sincere gratitude to the Hamida Barmaky Scholarship Program, funded by the German Foreign Office, implemented by the Max Planck Foundation for International Peace and the Rule of Law, for letting me be a part of the Ph.D. candidates. Further, I would like to say special thanks to my supervisor, Prof. Dr. Mathias Rohe, for his thoughtful comments and recommendations and boundless support, which made this research an exciting experience for me. I am also thankful to the members of my dissertation committee, Prof. Dr. Safferling and Prof. Dr. Krajewski, for their contribution and kindhearted support. My thanks must go also to the entire staff members of the Faculty of Business, Economics, and Law School of Law at Friedrich-Alexander-University Erlangen-Nurnberg for all the support and considerate guidance.

I am grateful to the Max Planck Foundation, particularly the Ph.D. project team, Dr. Tilmann J. Röder, Mr. Patrick Kuebart, Mrs. Maria Karimzad, Dr. Elisa Novic, Dr. Ghazaleh Faridzadeh, Dr. Astrid Wiik, and other colleagues at the foundation, for their support and the facilities they have provided me through my period of study in Germany and Kabul.

Furthermore, special thanks to many people, especially Dr. Shamshad Pasarlay, Mrs. Alice Stocky, Mrs. Elizabeth Baldwin, Ms. Rebecca Alhadef, and Miss Farida Razaqi, for their support regarding the language and structure of the book.

I also wish to thank those judges who have been a great source of support and for access to relevant cases to my research, which are not easily accessible in Afghanistan. To conclude, I cannot forget to thank my family, especially my wife, children, and friends, for all their unconditional support in these very hard and extreme academic years.

Contents

Part I
The Legal Framework and Historical Background

Chapter 1
The Legal Framework

1.1 Introduction

Afghanistan's legal system is basically dominated by Islamic law, particularly the Ḥanafī school of thought. For instance, Article 1 of the 2004 Constitution defines Afghanistan as an "Islamic republic."[1] Defining the country as an Islamic republic shows and reiterates the importance of Islam and its impact on the legal system of the state, just as Islamic values are also reflected in people's daily lives. More importantly, Article 2 of the Constitution declares Islam as the official religion of the state. The Constitution says:

> The sacred religion of Islam is the religion of the Islamic Republic of Afghanistan. Followers of other faiths shall be free within the bounds of law in the exercise and performance of their religious rituals.[2]

This constitutional provision carries many implications that are reflected in different policies of the government, especially in the legal system.

Moreover, the Constitution provides that state laws will be invalid if they contract the basic principles of Islam. The Constitution says:

> No law shall contravene the tenets and provisions of the holy religion of Islam in Afghanistan.[3]

In fact, this provision of the Constitution has a direct impact on the legal system of Afghanistan. It declares that law shall not contradict the beliefs and provisions of Islam. Although the terms "tenets" and "provisions of . . ." are very broad and could

---

[1] The Constitution of Afghanistan (2004), Art. 1. Available at http://www.afghanembassy.com.pl/afg/images/pliki/TheConstitution.pdf. Accessed 6 Nov 2020.

[2] The Constitution of Afghanistan (2004), Art. 2. Available at http://www.afghanembassy.com.pl/afg/images/pliki/TheConstitution.pdf. Accessed 6 Nov 2020.

[3] The Constitution of Afghanistan (2004), Art. 3. Available at http://www.afghanembassy.com.pl/afg/images/pliki/TheConstitution.pdf. Accessed 6 Nov 2020.

L. Saeed, *Islam, Custom and Human Rights*, Interdisciplinary Studies in Human Rights 7, https://doi.org/10.1007/978-3-030-83086-1_1

be interpreted in many ways, it shows the vital role of Islam in the legal system of Afghanistan. This article is relatively short but has a lot to be discussed in a separate piece of writing.

Moreover, the Constitution indicates that the government shall implement a unified educational curriculum based on Islamic principles, common culture, and scientific principles. The Constitution says:

> The state shall devise and implement a unified educational curriculum based on the tenets of the sacred religion of Islam, national culture as well as academic principles, and develop religious subjects curricula for schools on the basis of existing Islamic sects in Afghanistan.[4]

The above provision obliges the state to develop a unified curriculum based on Islamic beliefs and emphasizes teaching Islamic principles systematically to school children. The very common issue among Afghans, even from childhood, is to know what's legal and illegal (*Ḥalāl* and *Ḥarām*) in accordance with Islam. This appetency for understanding what is legal and what is not legal in the light of Sharia will increase the Islamic knowledge of the citizens on the basis of their daily lives. Furthermore, Afghanistan takes the position that Islam has a significant impact on the culture of Afghans, and the majority of Afghans think that their culture is mostly Islamic. So Islam systematically impacts the mind of Afghan citizens through educational curricula and the cultural norms that have been followed in Afghan society.

In addition, constitutionally, the president,[5] the ministers,[6] and the Supreme Court justices[7] are obliged to pledge fidelity to Islam and take an oath before they take their office. The Constitution gives priority to Islamic values and principles and puts an obligation on the president, ministers, and justices of the Supreme Court to respect and protect Islamic values and fulfill their duties within the limit of Islamic principles. Therefore, it seems that Islamic principles play a normative role in the legal framework of governmental activities, especially for the justice sector of

[4]The Constitution of Afghanistan (2004), Art. 45.

[5]The Constitution of Afghanistan (2004) Art. 63, "Before assuming office, the President shall take, in accordance with special procedures set by law, the following oath of allegiance: In the name of Allah, the most Gracious, the most Merciful, I swear by the name of Allah Almighty that I shall obey and protect the Holy religion of Islam, respect and supervises the implementation of the Constitution as well as other laws..." Available at http://www.afghanembassy.com.pl/afg/images/pliki/TheConstitution.pdf. Accessed 6 Nov 2020.

[6]The Constitution of Afghanistan (2004) Art. 119, "Before assuming office, the Ministers shall take the following oath in the presence of the President: In the name of Allah, the most Gracious, the most Merciful, I swear by the name of Allah Almighty that I shall protect the Holy religion of Islam, respect the Constitution and other laws of Afghanistan..." Available at http://www.afghanembassy.com.pl/afg/images/pliki/TheConstitution.pdf. Accessed 6 Nov 2020.

[7]The Constitution of Afghanistan (2004) Art. 119, "Members of the Supreme Court shall take the following oath of office in the presence of the President: In the name of Allah, the most Gracious, the most Merciful, I swear in the name of Allah Almighty to attain justice and righteousness in accordance with tenets of the Holy religion of Islam, provisions of the Constitution as well as other laws of Afghanistan..." Available at http://www.afghanembassy.com.pl/afg/images/pliki/TheConstitution.pdf. Accessed 6 Nov 2020.

Afghanistan. Thus, it is necessary to shed light on the role of Islamic Sharia and its significant impact on the legal system of Afghanistan throughout history.

1.2 Islam in Afghanistan

As mentioned above, the Islam religion has played a significant role in Afghanistan, particularly in the field of law. Because of the high rate of illiteracy in the country and the low level of knowledge regarding Islam and Sharia, people mostly rely on religious leaders. This situation gives more power to religious leaders and has a significant impact on the population.

Religious leaders are highly respected and play an important role in Afghan society. In rural Afghanistan, where more than 80% of the population live,[8] there are three bodies that play a main role in the community—*shūrā*,[9] *malik*,[10] and mullah—and power is divided among them. *Shūrā* is the main council body of the village, *malik* is considered the executive branch of the village, and mullah is the judiciary and religious division of the community.[11] The *mullā imām* (religious leader) is the spiritual leader of the village and traditionally plays the role of a judge, a teacher, and, in the absence of a medical professional, even a village doctor. The *mullā imām's* power is derived from the religious and judicial character that he exercises on a daily basis. Mullahs, *as religious leaders*, are strongly supported by the public and have an impact on the other bodies when they make a decision.[12] It is not easy for any individual, including powerful people in the community such as *zamindār* (village landlord) and *qaryadār/malik* (village headman), to confront an imam in public.[13] Of course, there are exceptional cases, but in general it is very difficult to oppose the leadership of an imam in a village in Afghanistan.

Afghanistan has many sayings about how to treat religious leaders. For example, it is said, "[c]onfront anyone you want, but never confront a mullah, because every powerful person needs to secure their blessing before they exercise their power."[14] Afghan history has many examples showing that even powerful people cannot stand against the power of religious leaders. King Amānallāh Khān, who forced the British colonial government to recognize Afghanistan's sovereign authority, was ousted

---

[8] Murtazashvili (2016), p. 3.

[9] *Shūrā* is an Arabic term that refers to council. Almost in all villages, there is a council that composed of elders and religious leader that they are considered as main decision-makers in the village.

[10] *Malik* is also an Arabic word that refers to king. *Malik* in the context of Afghanistan refers to the person considered as the head of the village and who represents villagers in the government and vice versa.

[11] Murtazashvili (2016), p. 4.

[12] Murtazashvili (2016), p. 9.

[13] RaḤmānī (2006), pp. 8–9.

[14] *Id.* at 8–9.

from power by a group of religious people led by a famous mullah (*mullā-i lang*) in 1929.[15] Another example is the collapse of the Communist party and regime due to the actions of jihadi leaders, who were Islamic religious leaders.[16] Since the majority of Afghans are followers of the Ḥanafī school of thought, most mullahs have been trained in Ḥanafī jurisprudence, and the majority of legal issues are addressed according to the Ḥanafī school of thought.[17]

However, there is a minority Shia sect (10–15%)[18] that is divided into two major groups: one is a group of 12 imams (*jaʿfariyya*), and the second one is called *ismāʿīliyya*. Although they have different perspectives on imamate (the leadership of ʿAlī, the fourth caliph, and his family and descendants) and jurisdictional issues, they are categorized under the Shia sect in general. The Constitution of Afghanistan recognizes their jurisprudence as a source of law for the courts. The Constitution says:

> The courts shall apply the Shia Jurisprudence in cases involving personal matters of followers of the Shia sect in accordance with the provisions of the law. In other cases, if no clarification in this Constitution and other laws exist, the courts shall rule according to laws of this sect.[19]

Based on this provision of the Constitution, the law on personal matters of Shia followers was drafted by a famous Shia scholar, Ayatollah M. Āṣif MuḤsinī, and enacted in 2009. Although the above provision mentions that in case of a legal lacuna the court should make a decision in accordance with the Shia sect, as far as my research is concerned, practically, with the exception of personal matter cases, there is no other case in any field that is to be adjudicated based on Shia jurisdiction.

Due to the dominant role of the Ḥanafī school in Afghanistan throughout history, Afghan scholars have played a substantial role in developing a legal system based on the Ḥanafī school of thought. For many centuries, Sharia has been used as the main source of law in Afghanistan. Islamic law, particularly the Ḥanafī school of thought,

---

[15] Farhang (1992), pp. 577–578, also see Ghubār (2015), pp. 1074–1075.

[16] The movement of *jihad* (holy war in its traditional understanding) in Afghanistan started in the 1970s. There were seven Sunni jihadi parties in Pakistan and 8 Shia parties in Iran; the majority of those parties were led by religious leaders. Even though one of the leaders, Gulbuddīn Ḥikmatyār, was a student at Kabul Civil Engineering Faculty, but he always put himself forward as a religious leader. This demonstrates the importance of religious leaders and the impact of their ideas on Afghan society.

[17] The majority of the Afghan citizens follow the Ḥanafī school of thought, which is one of the four main Sunni schools of thought in the field of jurisprudence. It was founded by Imam Abū Ḥanīfa (699–767) and developed by his two famous students, Imam Abū Yūsuf (738–798) and Imam Mohammad al-Shaybānī (749–805). The Ḥanafī followers mostly live in Afghanistan, Turkey, western Middle East, the western and Nile river regions of Egypt, Central Asia, Pakistan, Bangladesh, parts of Southeast Europe, India, China, and Russia. Based on estimation, one-third of all Muslims worldwide follow the Ḥanafī school of thought.

[18] See Central Intelligence Agency (2020) The World Fact Book available at https://www.cia.gov/-library/publications/the-world-factbook/geos/af.html. Accessed 6 Nov 2020.

[19] The Constitution of Afghanistan (2004), Art. 131. Available at http://www.afghanembassy.com.pl/afg/images/pliki/TheConstitution.pdf. Accessed 6 Nov 2020.

together with traditional or customary law, is considered the foundation for the modern justice system of Afghanistan[20] because the Ḥanafī doctrine is followed by around 85% of the population.[21] Generally, Muslim scholars and particularly Afghan religious leaders believe that Sharia provides a complete collection of legal sources to address every single issue in a Muslim's life. It can be applied to almost all aspects of life in society and could be developed within a specific framework to answer new issues that may arise in society. Thus, Afghan religious leaders have a central position in society and are considered an important source when addressing most societal questions.

Ruling according to Allah's will is a key expectation to meet when governing an Islamic society. In Afghanistan, the general expectation is that legal issues will be solved according to divine law because the majority of Afghans think solving problems in the light of divine law is the best approach. A common belief among Muslims is that divine law must be used when solving a problem; otherwise, they would go against the will of Allah. For instance, in the Holy Quran, there is a verse stating, "Those who do not rule according to what Allah revealed, they will be considered as the unbelievers (*kāfirūn*)."[22] This is followed by two other verses saying, "Those who do not rule according to what Allah revealed, they are considered as the evildoers" (*ẓālimūn*)[23] and "Those who do not rule according to what Allah revealed, they are considered as the Sinners" (*fāsiqūn*).[24]

Generally, there are two kinds of interpretations regarding these verses: one is the classical perspective, and the other is the contemporary Islamic scholars' view. In the classical interpretation, most Islamic scholars believe that these verses are talking about Jews and Christians (*ahl al-kitāb*), not about Muslims.[25] They claimed that the concept of these verses includes only non-Muslims because they do not follow the genuine Torah and Bible and obey the falsified version of these books; thus, based on Islamic principle, they are considered unbelievers *kāfir*.

In contrast, most modern scholars interpret these Quranic verses according to their context and explain that the texts have a clear message that must be followed.[26] They interpreted these verses very broadly and included Muslims in the concept that demands judges to make decisions based on divine law. The second interpretation is mostly accepted in the case of Afghanistan, and it has been a common understanding between Afghan citizens and some Islamic scholars, especially those who have a Sharia background. This interpretation gives more authority to the religious leaders

[20] Johnson et al. (2003), p. 25.

[21] Sirat (1969), pp. 217–219.

[22] The Holy Quran, Sura al-Mā'ida (5:44) وَمَن لَمْ يَحْكُم بِمَا أَنزَلَ اللَّهُ فَأُوْلَئِكَ هُمُ الْكَافِرُونَ.

[23] The Holy Quran, Sura al-Mā'ida (5: 45) وَمَن لَمْ يَحْكُم بِمَا أنزَلَ اللَّهُ فَأُوْلَئِكَ هُمُ الظَّالِمُونَ.

[24] The Holy Quran, Sura al-Mā'ida (5: 47) وَمَن لَمْ يَحْكُم بِمَا أنزَلَ اللَّهُ فَأُوْلَئِكَ هُمُ الْفَاسِقُون .

[25] See Tafsīr al-Ṭebarī (2000), p. 324; Tafsīr Ālūsī (1994), p. 500; Tafsīr FatḤ al-Qadīr (1994), p. 312; 7 Tafsīr al-Rāzī (1999), p. 132; Tafsīr al-Khāzin (1994), p. 282; Tafsīr al-Jāmiʿ li-Aḥkām al-Qur'ān = Tafsīr Qurṭubī (1964), p. 1704; Tafsīr RūḤ al-Maʿānī (1994), p. 314.

[26] Tafsīr fī Ẓilāl al-Qur'ān, p. 365, also see ʿAbdallāh ibn Bāz fatwa.

in society to have a greater role and deal with legal issues very broadly, especially in the provinces.

For more than three decades of war, the establishment of jihadi parties in the region, supporting extremists outside the country, along with a strengthening movement of Wahhabism,[27] has a strong effect on Afghans' interpretation of Islamic texts. In addition, many Afghans have been trained in Arab countries, and now they serve the religious sector in Afghanistan. These scholars could also be the main reason that led Afghans to the second interpretation and implement Sharia as the only source of law when they make a judgment. Ḥanafī school scholars do not allow the imitator (*muqallid*) followers,[28] who lack sufficient knowledge and qualifications regarding Islamic jurisprudence, to issue opinions directly based on the divine law sources.

Recently, some Afghan scholars have been referring directly to the main sources of Islamic law (Quran and Sunnah) when making judgments in a case without considering what the Ḥanafī school provisions would say regarding the case. However, according to Ḥanafī school's principles, the imitators cannot deduce a legal opinion based directly on the sources.[29] This might be the impact of the Wahhabi sect movement, which has been recently growing in the Afghan religious community. In general, the Wahhabi sect does not believe strongly that a Muslim should be a follower of any school of thought. They recommend that, rather than following other schools, Muslims should refer directly to the main sources of Islamic law, the Quran and *Sunnah*, in disputed cases. This idea contradicts the Ḥanafī school principle that says if a Muslim does not have enough knowledge regarding Islamic jurisprudence and does not know about the principles of *ijtihād*,[30] he must rely on other scholars and be a good follower. Regardless of these differences, Islam is the main feature of Afghan society and has a strong influence on almost every aspect of life in Afghanistan, particularly on legal issues.

---

[27] Wahhabism refers to the belief of the followers of Mohammad ibn ʿAbd al-Wahhāb (1703–1791), a Ḥanbalī scholar, reformist, and revivalist for the reconstruction of Muslim societies in terms of faith. Arguably, he claimed that Muslims have gone astray and must return to the ideal path of Islam by following those who live during the era of Prophet Mohammad and his successors (*salafi*). They prefer to strictly follow the Islamic main texts, Quran and Hadith, rather than pondering on and using rational reasons in their interpretations. They reject medieval interpretations of Islam and jurisprudence; thus, they call themselves "*salafi*." They proclaimed *tawḤīd* (uniqueness and unity of God) as its primary doctrine and seriously reject *taṣawwuf*, philosophy, and the Shia sect. History of Islamic Sects, Mohammad Abū Zuhra, p. 177.

[28] The term imitator (*muqallid*) refers to those Muslims who do not have enough knowledge and skill to infer rules from the main sources of the Sharia (particularly the Quran and Sunnah). Since they lack this capacity, they must rely on other scholars who are capable of doing *ijtihād* (making rules independently from the main sources of Sharia).

[29] Al-Dihlawī (1995), p. 56.

[30] *Ijtihād* is an Arabic term that means hard work and effort, but in the field of jurisprudence, it refers to independent reasoning while consulting and interpreting the respective Islamic relevant sources. For further information on this, please see Islamic Law in Past and Present by Mathias Rohe.

1.3 The Role of Sharia in the Legal History of Afghanistan

The Ḥanafī school of thought (madhab)[31] has been practiced as the main source of law for hundreds of years in Afghanistan. Azizudeen Wakily Popalzaey observed that judgments in Afghanistan have been made according to Ḥanafī jurisprudence from the era of Imam Abū Ḥanīfa (eighth century) up to the present.[32] It means that throughout history, since Islamic law had been introduced as a legal system in this region, the Ḥanafī school of thought has been considered as law in Afghanistan. Imam Abū Ḥanīfa's son, grandsons, and students have applied Ḥanafī jurisprudence to all cases in all courts in Afghanistan since the time Islam arrived in this region.[33] Rulers and Islamic scholars in Afghanistan have relied on the Ḥanafī school of thought and have made decisions according to this school's doctrine because the majority of the population, around 84%, follows the Ḥanafī madhab.[34] The Islamic law "Sharia," *ʿulamāʾ* religious leaders, Sharia faculties,[35] and imams have been considered as the main sources of law in the country. Almost all powerful rulers in Afghanistan have considered the Sharia principles, specifically the Ḥanafī school of thought, as the main source of law, and religious leaders (mullahs or *ulamā*) have worked as judges in their courts and made decisions in accordance with these principles.[36] The first article of the second Afghan Constitution stated that the official religion of Afghanistan is the holy religion of Islam and the official school of thought is the Ḥanafī school.[37]

Reviewing Afghanistan's history, in the early eleventh century, Sultan MaḤmūd Ghaznawī, who ruled most of south and central Asia from Ghazni[38] for many years, built a big mosque in Ghazni city and called it *ʿArūs al-falak.* Beside this mosque, he built a madrasa (religious school) and provided facilities for Islamic scholars to stay and teach there. Notably, there was a specific place for judgment that was used as a court, and a staff (slaves) served for judges during their duties. It shows that a form of court system with specific governmental employees (the judges) existed in that era. Commonly, judges worked in their houses or mosques and usually did not have any specific office. The religious scholars were working as judges and using Ḥanafī

[31] Madhab (Arabic: مذهب) is an Arabic term that refers to an Islamic school of thought.

[32] Wakily Popalzaey (1990), p. 41.

[33] Wakily Popalzaey (1990), p. 47.

[34] Mahmoudi (2004), p. 871.

[35] In Afghanistan, there are two faculties that train legal experts: (1) the Sharia Faculty and (2) the Law and Political Science Faculty. The majority of judges have a Sharia background, and most of the law graduates work at the Attorney General Office as prosecutors and defense attorneys. The legal education and educational institutions in Afghanistan would be discussed in more detail later.

[36] Wakily Popalzaey (1990), pp. 47–48.

[37] The Constitution of Afghanistan (1952) Art. 1.

[38] A province in central Afghanistan and southwest of Kabul, 100 km from Kabul.

doctrine as law, and there was only one judgment with no right of appeal to the Supreme Court for review in case of oversight.[39]

Likewise, in the era of *Tīmūryān* (the Timorese), at the time of the successors of Genghis Khan, under King Shāhrukh (1376–1447), the son of King Timur (Tamerlane), Sharia was the main source of law and religious leaders worked as judges in the courts. King Shāhrukh initially established courts operating in two systems: in one system, decisions were made based on Mongolian customary law and a code of conduct (*yāsā)* dating back to Genghis Khan, which was strictly implemented by his successors;[40] in the others, decisions were based on Islamic Sharia. *Yāsā* was the main source of law for a while in Genghis's territory, and its violators were severely punished. After some time, King Shāhrukh revoked *yāsā*, and the only law source remaining was Islamic Sharia. At that time, the highest rank of the judiciary was called *ṣudūr*, and Islamic scholars were in charge of the judicial branch of his government. All judges made decisions according to the Ḥanafī school of law.[41]

Islamic Sharia and Islamic scholars were the main sources of law when AḤmad Shāh Durrānī (1722–1773) established modern Afghanistan in 1747.[42] Imam Darbāri, a courtier religious leader, examined and introduced judges to King Ahmad Shāh and then appointed them as judges of their own courts. A position was created for a judge in the capital of his territory, Kandahar City, called *khān ʿulūm* or *qāḍī al-quḍāt*, or "Chief Justice," who was in charge of the judiciary branch of his government. A famous religious scholar, Mullah Idrīs, worked as chief justice and had eight assistants and a clerk.[43] A collection of scholarly legal opinions (fatwas) based on the Ḥanafī school of thought, called *Fatāwā AḤmad Shāhī*, was written in the Pashto language by Mawlawī ʿAbdallāh Kandahārī, a famous Afghan scholar, and later published in 1904. The judges used the *Fatāwā AḤmad Shāhī* as a code of law in all courts.[44] Islamic law, especially the Ḥanafī school of thought, also continued its role as the primary source of law after AḤmad Shāh.

Following AḤmad Shāh Durrānī, his son, Tīmūr Shāh, moved from Qandahar to Kabul and made Kabul the capital of his territory in 1776.[45] For the first time, he established a court in the western part of Kabul city, and an Islamic scholar, Mawlawī ʿAbd al-RaḤīm, was appointed as chief justice. He established two places, *bāgh-i shāh* (King's Garden) and *bāgh-i qāḍī* (Judge's Garden), where people could submit their petitions for justice.[46] In addition to the courts, there was another place,

---

[39] Hussami (2009), p. 24.

[40] Hussami (2009), p. 26.

[41] Hussami (2009), p. 28.

[42] See Supreme Court of Afghanistan, http://supremecourt.gov.af/fa/page/620/2958. Accessed 7 April 2014.

[43] Hussami (2009), p. 32.

[44] The History of Ministry of Justice of Afghanistan, http://moj.gov.af/fa/page/7943/16571664. Accessed 7 April 2014.

[45] The History of Ministry of Justice of Afghanistan. http://moj.gov.af/fa/page/7943/16571664. Accessed 7 April 2014.

[46] The History of Ministry of Justice of Afghanistan, http://moj.gov.af/fa/page/7943/16571664. Accessed 7 April 2014.

called *tasbīḤ khāna* (House of Praise), where religious scholars and judges could conduct research, meet to discuss legal topics, and find solutions for new legal problems in accordance with Sharia.[47] Tīmūr Shāh's followers, including Shāh Zaman, Shāh MaḤmūd, Shāh Shujāʿ, Amir Dūst Mohammad Khān, and Amir Shīr ʿAlī Khān, continued to use the Ḥanafī school of jurisprudence as a main source of law, and *ʿulamāʾ* religious leaders served as judges and chief justices in their governments.[48]

For the first time in the history of Afghanistan, Amir ʿAbd al-RaḤmān Khān (1891–1901) started a reform in the judicial sector of his government.[49] Before Amir ʿAbd al-RaḤmān Khān, there were two main sources of law: Islamic Law and local custom (*ʿurf*). There was no central court system, and judges worked either in their houses or in a mosque and applied Sharia provisions to all cases, and they also solved disputes based on custom if there were no contradictions between Sharia and *ʿurf*. In addition, there was no guidance for judges to formulate their judgments.[50] When ʿAbd al-RaḤmān Khān came into power, he centralized the court system and appointed judges paid by the government. The judges worked full time in their offices, like other state employees, and were prohibited from conducting any other business, including teaching in the madrasas (religious schools). Islamic *ʿulamāʾ* religious scholars, who had a specific level of knowledge regarding Islamic jurisprudence, were chosen by the King as judges and worked in the new court system.[51] Having Islamic scholars as judges is still common in Afghanistan, and the majority of Afghan judges graduated from Sharia faculties.

At that time, Afghan religious scholars were mostly trained in India and Central Asia (especially in Samarqand, Bukhara, and Tashkent).[52] Since all judges were chosen from Islamic scholars who were teaching in religious schools, it was a revolutionary decision to prevent the *ʿulamāʾ* from participating in their main business of teaching, a profession that is highly rewarded by Islam. This change in the judges' position was part of a set of rules that were codified in a book called *Asās al-Qużāt*, written by a famous Islamic scholar, AḤmad Jān Alukūzay, in 1885 in Dari.[53] This is significant because the main language of Islamic jurisprudence, particularly the legal texts, was Arabic. Even most non-Arab scholars wrote their books in Arabic. Arabic had also been accepted as the main language for all court judgments for hundreds of years in Afghan society. Thus, it is important that an Afghan scholar changed the legal tradition by writing a legal text in the local language.

---

[47] Wakily Popalzaey (1990), p. 174.

[48] Hussami (2009), pp. 32–37.

[49] Barfield (2003), p. 1.

[50] Hussami (2009), p. 37.

[51] Ghani (1983), p. 354.

[52] Sirat (1969), pp. 217–219.

[53] Ghani (1983), p. 354.

Making judges government employees not only separated them from their historic primary duty of teaching Islamic jurisprudence, but it also controlled their workplace and limited their time and daily activities.[54] According to Islamic jurisprudence, judges were permitted to operate a court in a mosque or in their homes and formulate judgments concerning their people, but based on concerns about corruption and the carelessness of the people regarding the truth, the "qadi" judges were required to perform their duties in the office of the governor.[55] From that period until today, judges have been considered state employees and have been paid by the government.

In conclusion, Sharia, and particularly the provisions of the Ḥanafī school of thought, has been used in Afghanistan as the main source of law for many centuries. The majority of the public and private religious schools (madrasas) and faculties in the universities have trained legal scholars based on the Ḥanafī doctrine and have trained a considerable number of religious scholars to work in the justice sector. These scholars also deal with legal issues in informal community-based institutions, which are normally accepted by the majority of the population, specifically in rural areas. Thus, Islam and Islamic scholars have played and continue to play a significant role in the Afghan legal system and are considered the main source of law of Afghanistan.

1.4 The Meaning and Scope of "Sharia"

There is no consensus among Islamic scholars, modern or classical, Muslim or non-Muslim, regarding the exact meaning of Sharia and its usage in the field of Islamic legal studies. Rohe states in his book, *Islamic Law in Past and Present*, that the term "Sharia" is ambiguous.[56] In addition, the legal scholar ʿAlī Khān claims that the comprehensive scope of Sharia has created confusion in the field of Islamic legal studies.[57] Additionally, the authors of *The Sharia from Mohammad's Time to the Present* said that Sharia is "a long, diverse, complicated intellectual tradition" rather than a "well-defined set of specific rules and regulations that can be easily applied to life situations."[58] Some scholars claim that Sharia has never been collected and codified in a specific law book to easily understand its clear-cut borders.[59] Commonly, there are multiple interpretations of the same concept according to Sharia. This ambiguity regularly causes misunderstanding about the nature of Sharia and its usage in the Islamic legal culture, especially in western academia.

[54] Alukūzay (1885), Art. 26.

[55] Alukūzay (1885), Art. 8.

[56] Rohe (2014), p. 10.

[57] Khan (2003), p. 344.

[58] Hunt and Kahlmeyer (2007), p. 3.

[59] Vikør (2000), p. 2.

Most scholars believe that the term Sharia literally refers to a straight path[60] or "path to be followed."[61] According to Rohe, Sharia means "the path which has been prepared or the divinely appointed path."[62] Some classical scholars have said that Sharia means a clear statement and expression; it means Sharia is a clear and understandable set of rules.[63] Some other scholars have claimed that Sharia literally refers to right religion "madhab" and religious community *milla*, which allows the followers to reach their goals.[64] Irshād ʿAbd al-Ḥaqq states: "*Sharia* literally means in original usage '*the road to the watering place or path leading to the water.*'"[65] Similarly, some scholars believe that Sharia means the path to the water source or spring, where water is always directly available to drink without needing any objects like twine, a well, or a bucket.[66] In other words, Sharia means implicitly the path to the source of life that will lead believers to be prosperous in this life and afterlife.

Bassiouni states that the term "Sharia" refers to that which Allah ordained in the Quran. He believed that the term Sharia includes general principles, guidance, and prescriptions in the light of the Quran.[67] Another prominent modern Islamic Scholar, Muṣṭafā al-Zarqā', believes that the term Sharia refers to the verses of the Holy Quran sent down to Prophet Mohammad as well as "hadith" (his sayings) and "Sunnah" (his deeds), which are considered additional explanations complementary to the Quranic text and containing practical performance, obligations, and prohibitions.[68] Some scholars believe that Sharia is a "jurists' law" that has been established and expanded by *fuqahā'*. Islamic jurists (*fuqahā'* and muftis) have exclusively played a role in expressing the will of Allah, and others must obey them. Thus, they believe that Sharia is a set of religious moral rules that have gradually developed and transformed into the legal field and are continuously imposed on society.[69]

Naturally, the concept of Sharia refers to a variety of sources in Muslim societies and has been used to address various kinds of issues in its long history. Generally, Sharia addresses multiple problems in society, including Muslims' personal and social matters. It intervenes in the life of Muslims from birth to death. This broad scope of Sharia draws an ambiguous picture and makes it difficult to provide a widely accepted and clear definition of Sharia. Thus, Muslim and non-Muslim scholars have defined Sharia in different ways throughout different periods of time. However, the term Sharia has been used differently in the concepts of Afghanistan. Generally, there are two perspectives in the Islamic legal culture regarding the

---

[60] Iṣfahānī (2008), also see, Tafsīr al-Rāzī, vol. 6, p. 74.

[61] Mahmoudi (2004), pp. 1–2.

[62] Rohe (2004), p. 325.

[63] Al-Khāzin, ʿAlī ibn Mohammad (1994) Tafsīr al-Khāzin, vol. 2, p. 293.

[64] Al-Qurṭubī (2003), p. 5111.

[65] Abdalhaq (2006), p. 16.

[66] Ibn Manẓūr (1994), also see Tafsīr al-Lubāb, vol. 6, p. 105.

[67] Bassiouni (2014), p. 39.

[68] Al-Zarqā' (1988), p. 65.

[69] Layish (2004), p. 87.

usage of the term Sharia: (1) the classical Islamic scholars and (2) the modern Islamic scholars. To exemplify this, the following will assess some of the definitions belonging to these two perspectives. Different factors, such as time, place, school of thought, and culture, have prevented the formation of a single clear definition of Sharia acceptable to most, but not all, Islamic legal scholars in the long history of Islamic law.

According to classical Muslim scholars, the scope of Sharia is very broad. Some of them even consider Sharia to be a synonym to religion. For instance, the famous Islamic scholar al-Ṭebarī said: "Sharia means *Religion*" (Arabic: *dīn*).[70] He believed that the concept of Sharia includes all issues that could be discussed within the area of religion. Another famous Islamic scholar, al-Qurṭubī, believed that Sharia includes all divine orders sent down by Allah and revealed by the prophets. Al-Qurṭubī claimed that Sharia includes faith and believing in one Allah, the five pillars of Islam, crimes and punishments, good ethics, being kind even to animals, etc.[71]

Currently, neither Sharia nor *fiqh* terms have the same meaning as they have been used in the main sources of Islam: Quran and Sunnah. ʿAbd al-Mannān ʿUmar, in his book *Dictionary of the Holy Quran*, believes that the word Sharia is derived from the Quranic root *Sh-R-ʿ* and refers to the law or institution prescribed by God, the right way, a clear highway, and so on.[72] Also, Dr. Hashim Kamali, in his book *Sharia Law*, states that the term Sharia is used only once in the Quran; nevertheless, both the terms Sharia and *fiqh* have not been mentioned in the Quran and Sunnah and have been used in their common meaning after the era of Prophet Mohammad and his caliphs.[73] Ibn Qayyim al-Jawziyya believed that Sharia is a composition of justice, mercy, wisdom, and good things that guarantee the success of a human being in his life and afterlife:

> The foundation of Sharia is based on the interests of the human being in this life and the afterlife. Sharia is all about justice, mercy, wisdom, and good. Thus, any ruling that replaces justice with injustice, mercy with its opposite, common good with mischief, or wisdom with nonsense, is a ruling that does not belong to Sharia, even if it is claimed to be so. Sharia is mercy of Allah and his justice among human beings. Sharia is source of all good things, and all Evil and bad things derive from lack of implantation of Sharia.[74]

Therefore, according to most classical scholars, Sharia comprehensively deals with all aspects of Muslim life and can address any problems related to Muslims' personal and social lives.

Modern Islamic scholars, however, narrow the scope of Sharia to some specific issues. The main difference between classical and modern Islamic scholars regarding the meaning and usage of the term "Sharia" is that classical scholars emphasize the

[70] Al-Ṭebarī (2000), p. 9.

[71] Al-Qurṭubī (1964), p. 4940.

[72] ʿUmar (2010), p. 287.

[73] Kamali (2008), pp. 4–5.

[74] Ibn Qayyim al-Jawziyya (2006), p. 3.

wide scope of Sharia. In contrast, most modern Islamic scholars not only limit the scope of Sharia but also emphasize the sources that Sharia principles are derived from.

These two different perspectives regarding the meaning and usage of Sharia in the present day have caused ambiguity and often misunderstanding in public debates. Speaking generally, Sharia covers all the divinely provided orders and religious affairs within the scope of Islam, which includes spiritual activities, family law, crimes and punishments, transactions, contracts, etc. This perspective is close to the classical description of Sharia.

Reviewing some definitions provided by modern scholars, it is clear that there are some factors that cause dissimilarity regarding the definition and usage of Sharia. Most likely, the difference has been derived from the variety of opinions and principles followed by Islamic scholars. Different schools of thought (madhabs) have used the term Sharia in different ways based on their schools' principles. Time and place are other factors that have affected this and led to the multiple explanations for and usages of this term.

Historically, Islamic jurisprudence has evolved through many periods, and each of them has its own characteristics. Islamic jurists continue to view the same issue from different angles, and their answers have differed, primarily, by geographical location. These differences continue to have an impact on modern Islamic scholars, how they define Sharia, and the range of issues they believe are addressed by Sharia.

As an example, Cherif Bassiouni, a contemporary Islamic scholar, believed that the concept of Sharia includes all Allah's orders in the Quran, which were sent down to Prophet Mohammad.[75] He believed that using the term Sharia refers to all Quranic orders and principles reflected in the verses of the Holy Quran. In his view, the term Sharia also includes general principles and guidance regarding what to do or what not to do.[76] In contrast, some modern academics, especially most non-Muslims in Europe and many Turkish European citizens, believe that Sharia refers only to some constricted and specific topics relating to family and inheritance law and personal status, which is called *(al-aḥwāl al-shakhṣiyya)*[77] This demonstrates that there is no consensus among contemporary Islamic scholars regarding the definition of the term Sharia, and they define Sharia in different ways:

a) *"Sharia means the revealed or canonical law of Islam; the whole body of rules governing the life of Muslims which are derived from the Holy Quran and Sunnah."*[78]
b) *"Sharia 'Islamic law' covers both civil and criminal justice as well as regulating individual conducts both personal and moral. The custom-based body of law based on the Quran and the religion of Islam."*[79]

---

[75] Bassiouni (2014), p. 39.

[76] Bassiouni (2014), p. 39.

[77] Rohe (2004), p. 325.

[78] Dictionary of Islamic Terms Arabic-English (Terms: Sharia).

[79] See Duhaime's Law Dictionary, Sharia Law Definition. Available at http://www.duhaime.org/LegalDictionary/S/ShariaLaw.aspx.

c) *"Sharia is generally defined as Allah's eternal and immutable will for humanity. This ideal Islamic law is expressed in the Quran and Mohammad's examples (Sunna) and developed by jurisprudence (fiqh)."*[80]
d) *"A shared opinion of the [Islamic] community, based on a literature that is extensive, but not necessarily coherent or authorized by any single body."*

Some other modern scholars believe that the term "Sharia" refers to the verses of the Holy Quran, sent down to Prophet Mohammad, and his sayings, acts, and deeds "hadith," which are considered as explanations complementary to the Quranic text and set as guidelines for practical performance, obligations, and prohibitions.[81] There are two major elements in the modern Islamic scholars' definitions regarding Sharia that differ from the classical scholars: first, the scope of Sharia is more specific and specifically includes legal issues; second, the main sources of Sharia are the Quran and Sunnah.[82] Generally, these two elements make Sharia very close to *fiqh*, Islamic law, which was a part of Sharia in the classical approach, not in the modern definition. Islamic scholars claim that the Quran is not only a religious book including only moral principles but also a legal document.[83] Additionally, there is not only a single source within Islamic jurisprudence to deal with legal issues; Islamic law has many sources that address legal issues and different schools of thought (madhabs) that deal with them in different ways.

1.5 The Meaning of Fiqh

Before exploring the use of Sharia and *fiqh* in the context of Afghanistan, it is necessary to define *fiqh* and its usage by classical and modern scholars. Many Islamic scholars believe that the literal meaning of *fiqh* is "absolute understanding," whether the issue is obvious or complicated.[84] They claim that the term *fiqh* carries the same meaning as knowledge.[85] They accept that the terms *faqīh*[86] or *ʿālim*[87] are

[80] Otto (2008), p. 7.

[81] Al-Zarqā' (1988), p. 153.

[82] Islamic scholar Said Mahmoudi claims that Sharia is divine law that is made up of two major parts: God's own words, as expressed in the verses of the Holy Quran, and the Sunnah, the traditions of the Prophet Mohammad. Please see Mahmoudi (2004), pp. 1–2.

[83] Hallaq (2004), p. 4.

[84] Al-Fayyūmī al-Ḥamawī (1987) Al-Misbāḥ al-Munīr fī Gharīb al-Sharḥ al-Kabīr [This is an explanatory book on *FatḤ al-ʿAzīz ʿalā Kitāb al-Wajīz*, another book written by ʿAbd al-Karīm ibn Mohammad Rāfiʿī, who wrote an explanatory book on famous Islamic scholar, Mohammad Al-Ghazālī's book by the name of *Al-Wajīz fī al-Furūʿ*.

[85] Al Ashqar (1982), p. 10.

[86] *Faqīh* (Arabic: فقيه) usually used to someone, who is expert in Islamic jurisdiction.

[87] *ʿĀlim* (Arabic: عالم) is a general term that refers to someone who has general knowledge about Islamic sciences; however, *faqīh* and *ʿālim* could be used interchangeably.

synonyms, and there is no difference in the meaning.[88] They rely on the usage of this term in some verses of the Holy Quran, such as "And remove the impediment from my speech. So, they understand what I say."[89] In this verse, the term *fiqh* has been used in the context of understanding what the prophet says. Another verse of the Holy Quran states, "*They said: O Shuʿayb! Much of what you say we do not understand,*"[90] while another verse says, "There is not a thing but celebrates His praise; and yet ye understand not how they declare his Glory."[91] In these verses, the word *fiqh* means absolute understanding. On the other hand, some scholars believe that it means a deep and accurate understanding of a concept.[92] They claim that the word *fiqh* in this verse of the Holy Quran has been used to mean a deep and accurate understanding of a concept, not just surface knowledge: "It is He Who hath produced you from a single person: here is a place of sojourn and a place of departure: We detail our signs for people who understand."[93] It.[94]

Examining the usage of the word *fiqh* in the Holy Quran and other Arabic texts, we see that this term has been used in deep understanding of verbal and ideological concepts rather than of objective issues. Al-Rāghib al-Iṣfahānī, a famous Islamic scholar, also believed that *fiqh* means a deep understanding of a concept.[95] Thus, it is different from absolute knowledge or common understanding. The term *fiqh* therefore, based on al-Rāghib's view, refers to a deep understanding, not a common understanding, of a concept.[96] In the holy Quran, the term "*Fiqh*" has been used to understand conceptual and theoretical topics that are limited only to verbal and textual issues; it is not used to understand physical or real things. For instance, in Arabic, it is correct to say *faqahtu kalāmaka* ففهت کلامک: "I understand what you said, but it is incorrect to say" or *faqahtu sayyāratuka* فقهت سیارتک : "I understand your car." Generally, the literal meaning of the term *fiqh* refers to understanding a verbal concept deeply and accurately, not a shallow level of understanding. In practice, there are many usages of the term *fiqh* among Islamic scholars. These differences come from different periods of time and various interpretations by scholars.

---

[88] Ibn Manẓūr (1994), term *fiqh*.

[89] The Holy Quran, Sura Ṭa-Ha (20: 27–28) (وَاحْلُلْ عُقْدَةً من لسَانِي يَفْقَهُوا قَوْلِي) (The Quran English translation by Abdullah Yusuf Ali, Available at www.islam101.com/quran/yusufAli/.

[90] Sura al-Hūd, Āya 91 ((قالوا يا شُعَيْبُ مَا نَفْقَهُ كَثِيرًا مما تَقُولُ The Quran English translation by Abdullah Yusuf Ali, Available at www.islam101.com/quran/yusufAli/.

[91] The Holy Quran, Sura al-Isrāʾ (17: 44) (وَإِن من شَيْءٍ إِلَّا يُسَبِحُ بِحَمْدَهِ وَلَكِن لَا تَفْقَهُونَ تَسْبِيحَهُمْ إِنَّهُ كَانَ حَلِيمًا غَفُورًا) The Quran English translation by Abdullah Yusuf Ali, Available at www.islam101.com/quran/yusufAli/.

[92] See Ministry of Awqāf and Islamic Affairs of Kuwait, p. 11.

[93] The Holy Quran, Sura al-Anʿām (06: 98) (وَهُوَ الَّذِيَ أَنشَأَكُم من نَفْسٍ وَاحِدَةٍ فَمُسْتَقَرٌ وَمُسْتَوْدَعٌ قَدْ فَصَّلْنَا الآيَاتِ لِقَوْمٍ يَفْقَهُونَ) English translation of The Quran by Ábdullah Yusuf Ali, Available at http://www.islam101.com/quran/yusufAli/.

[94] Ministry of Awqāf and Islamic Affairs of Kuwait, p. 12.

[95] Iṣfahānī (2008), term "*fiqh*".

[96] Shabli (1985), p. 32.

Differences can also depend on the scope of related topics discussed and the range of issues covered by this term.

Historically, before Islam, Arabs used the word *fiqh* for general knowledge. However, in the early era of Islam, the term *fiqh* was used for general knowledge regarding the religion of Islam.[97] After a while, Islamic scholars like Abū Ḥanīfa[98] also used this term to mean general knowledge regarding the Islamic religion. He defined *fiqh* as knowledge of a Muslim regarding his religious rights and duties: *ma'ifat al-nafs mā lahā wa mā 'alayhā*. According to his definition, *fiqh* included Islamic jurisprudence, theology, and moral issues. But when Islamic sciences developed, theology and moral issues were excluded from *fiqh*, and since that period of time this term only primarily refers to Islamic jurisprudence.

The definition of *fiqh* in *Majallat al-Aḥkām al-ʿAdliyya*[99] illustrates the incremental evolution of the concept of *fiqh* in Islamic society. After this evolution in 1876, it was defined differently and referred to knowledge about the practical orders (*aḥkām*) of Sharia and included their legal reasoning.[100] The term *aḥkām* refers to all the principles that Allah sent down to Prophet Mohammad, principles regulating social, moral, economic, and other aspects of Muslim life in light of Islam.[101] It specifies that knowledge about these orders should be in detail and supported by legal reasoning. The definition of fiqh in *Majallat al-Aḥkām* is more acceptable for current Afghan judges because this book is one of the accepted sources besides the Civil Code of Afghanistan. Commonly, Afghan judges have used it as a source of law and have made decisions in civil cases according to *Majalla*, along with the *Civil Code* of Afghanistan.

Modern Islamic scholars define *fiqh* more specifically as within the scope of jurisprudence. In his book *Introduction to Islamic General Jurisprudence*, Muṣṭafā AḤmad al-Zarqā' observes that the term *fiqh* is used to mean precise knowledge regarding the legal concepts of Islamic Sharia (*aḥkām*).[102] It means understanding a complete set of Islamic legal principles considered *fiqh*.[103] These Sharia orders are

[97] Al Ashqar (1982), p. 11.

[98] Imām Abū Ḥanīfa, al-Nuʿmān ibn Thābit, the founder of Ḥanafī school of thought, was born in 721.

[99] *Majallat al-Aḥkām al-ʿAdliyya* is one of the most valuable sources of the Ḥanafī school of thought. This book was written by a committee of seven Islamic scholars in 1869 in Turkey. This committee included AḤmad Jawdat Bāshā, Minister of Justice of the Ottoman emperor, who was appointed to write a civil code for the Ottoman emperor based on Ḥanafī jurisprudence and custom to respond to the needs of society. This committee accomplished its task after 7 years of hard work, and finally the code was published in 1876. This was the first time in Islamic history that an Islamic jurisprudence book existed (*Majalla* (Magazine)).

[100] Al-Atāsī (2002), Art 1.

[101] Al-Zarqā' (1988), p. 65.

[102] The term *ahkām* (Orders) refers to the recognition of all legal and illegal concepts, which have been regulated in the light of Islamic legal sources.

[103] Al-Zarqā' (1988), pp. 65–66.

based upon specific principles derived from the Holy Quran, Sunnah (Hadith), *ijmāʿ* (Muslim scholars' consensus), and Islamic scholars' opinions.

The *Uṣūl al-fiqh* (the Science of Principles of *fiqh*)[104] scholars claim that there are three major periods when the term *fiqh* has been used in the history of Islamic law. During the first period,[105] *fiqh* was synonymous with Sharia; it included almost all things Allah sent down to Prophet Mohammad. Thus, Imam Abū Ḥanīfa defined *fiqh* very broadly as the knowledge of a Muslim regarding his religious rights and duties *maʿrifat al-nafs mā lahā wa mā ʿalayhā*, which included theology, moral issues, and jurisprudence.[106]

In the second epoch, Islamic scholars added limitations on the usage of the term *fiqh*, which excluded theology from its scope, but moral issues were still part of it. In this era, the term *fiqh* referred to the field of knowledge that deals with detailed issues that are covered by the concept of Sharia. These detailed issues were derived from the primary sources of Islamic law, more particularly the Quran and Sunnah. In these sources, moral and ethical issues, which were titled later as Sufism (Arabic: *taṣawwuf*), were part of *fiqh*.[107] This approach, mixing jurisprudence with Sufism, was practiced in Khurasan and Transoxiana (currently Afghanistan and Central Asia) and was the main characteristic of the scope of Islamic jurisprudence in this region.[108] This method has also been continued by some Islamic madrasas, like *Dār al-ʿUlūm Diyūband*[109] in India, where students study and practice principles of Sufism, along with other Islamic sciences. These religious school scholars and graduates say that in conduct, they are Sufi[110] and follow the mystic path of the *Chishtiyya* sect of Sufism.[111] Historically, there have often been disagreements between Islamic jurists (*fuqahāʾ*) and Sufists in many predominantly Muslim countries, but most Sufism literature listed Islamic jurists, especially the founders of the four Sunni schools, as the leaders of Sufism (*taṣawwuf*).[112]

---

[104]Bassiouni (2014), p. 43.

[105]The first period refers to the first and second sanctuaries of the Islamic calendar.

[106]Ministry of Awqāf and Islamic Affairs of Kuwait, p. 12.

[107]Ministry of Awqāf and Islamic Affairs of Kuwait, p. 12.

[108]See The System of Education at Dār al-ʿUlūm Diyūband/India, available at http://darululoom-deoband.com/english/. Accessed 6 Nov 2020.

[109]*Dār al-ʿUlūm Diyūband* was established in the village of Deoband in the state of Uttar Pradesh, India, in 1867. In the late nineteenth and twentieth centuries, Deoband was considered the biggest Islamic science center in Asia, especially in the Ḥanafī school of thought. It is claimed that with the exception of al-Azhar University in Cairo, Egypt, there is no other institution in the Islamic world to have the same status as *Dār al-ʿUlūm Diyūband* has.

[110]See The Track (Maslak) of Dār al-ʿUlūm Diyūband, Available at http://darululoom-deoband.com/english/. Accessed 6 Nov 2020.

[111]*Chishtiyya* (Dari چشتیه) is one of the four sects of Sufism. Originally, it refers to *Chisht* (Dari: چشت), a district in Herat province in the west of Afghanistan. The founder of this sect is Khwajah Abdal Chishti, who died in 971. This sect prevents themselves from getting involved with politics and has a good internal management.

[112]Shay*kh Farīd al-Dīn Aṭṭār*, one of the very famous Sufis in the fourteenth century, in his book *Tadhkirat al-Awliyā*, introduced 96 famous Sufis as a leader of *taṣawwuf*. All founders of Islamic schools of thought, including Sunni and Shia jurists, are included in the list of big Sufis in that book.

In the third era, which continues up to the present, *fiqh* refers to those Sharia orders precisely related to those detailed practical issues derived from the Quran, Sunnah, and other sources. According to this definition, only the practical and jurisprudential parts of Sharia are included in the concept of *fiqh*. Moral issues are excluded from the field of *fiqh* and discussed under the scope of Sufism (*taṣawwuf*).[113] However, Sufism was not only excluded from the field of *fiqh* in most cases, but the practice of Sufism was considered to be against Sharia, and some famous Sufis were executed or considered not as Muslims under the verdict of the *fuqahā'* (the jurists).[114]

1.6 Sharia and Fiqh in the Context of Afghanistan

The terms Sharia and *fiqh* are also a controversial issue in Afghanistan. In general, there are two perspectives among Afghan legal experts regarding these two terms: (1) the terms Sharia and *fiqh* are the same and carry the same meaning, and (2) these two terms are not the same, and each of them refers to a different meaning. Most Afghans, and some Afghan legal experts, consider these two terms the same and claim that there is no considerable difference between Sharia and *fiqh*.[115] They believe there is no difference in meaning, whether it is stated that the decision has been made according to Sharia or according to *fiqh*, because they carry the same meaning. This interpretation means that both the terms Sharia and *fiqh* are synonyms and can be used interchangeably.

On the other hand, some Afghan legal scholars differentiate between these two terms and believe that each of them covers a separate scope of knowledge in the field of Islamic legal sciences.[116] They claim that the concept of Sharia is much broader than *fiqh*. Sharia, like a big circle, includes legal, moral, and even faith-related issues; on the other hand, *fiqh*, like a smaller circle within the Sharia circle, is limited to *aḥkām* (legal orders). In other words, *fiqh* can be described as a subcategory of Sharia. They believe that *fiqh* is those legal opinions that are inferred from Sharia sources, mainly Quran and Sunnah, and could be changeable from time to time and place to place. When these scholars talk about Sharia, it is not necessarily under the concept of *fiqh*, but when they discuss a concept regarding *fiqh*, it is considered to be under the general concept of Sharia. This perspective appears to be closer to other

[113] Ministry of Awqāf and Islamic Affairs of Kuwait, pp. 12–13.

[114] Ḥusayn ibn Manṣūr al-Hallāj, a famous Sufi in tenth Century was executed by *fuqahā'*, and Bā-Yazīd Busṭāmī 804–874 was another famous Sufi, who was prosecuted by *fuqahā'* and called non-Muslim.

[115] Interview with Judge Salam Qazizadah, former chief judge of the appellate court of Kabul, who made a decision regarding Parwīz Kāmbakhsh case at Kabul appellate court (August 9, 2015).

[116] Interview with Prof. Aziz, a member of the Supreme Court of Afghanistan and former dean of Kabul Sharia Faculty & also interview with some Kabul University Sharia faculty members (August 15, 2015).

Islamic scholars from outside Afghanistan, more precisely in the Arab nation countries. Thus, this perspective has roots in the Afghan academic environment, especially among Sharia faculties, where most professors have a background in Islamic studies from various Arab countries.

In conclusion, the terms Sharia and *fiqh* in the context of Afghanistan are generally considered the same; however, the second perspective is more widely held by scholars. In practice, most Afghans, including many judges and lawyers, favor the first point of view, and they do not differentiate between these two terms and commonly consider them to be the same. The majority of Afghan citizens follow the Ḥanafī school of thought, and Afghanistan's legal system is based on this school. Basically, plurality has been one of the main characteristics of Islamic law from the beginning because within the schools, including the Ḥanafī one, there is a variety of opinions (*ikhtilāf*) regarding particular legal issues, and this approach was very common among Islamic scholars, especially the early jurists. Therefore, I will use the terms Sharia and *fiqh* interchangeably, following the common usage of Sharia in Afghanistan and not distinguishing between both terms in this research.

References

Abdalhaq I (2006) Islamic law. An overview of its origin and elements. In: Ramadan H (ed) Understanding Islamic law: from classical to contemporary. Alta Mira Press, pp 1–42

Al Ashqar OS (1982) History of Islamic jurisprudence. Al Falah Publication, Kuwait

Al-Ālūsī, Shihāb al-Dīn Maḥmūd ibn ʿAbdallāh Al-Ḥusaynī, 1994. Tafsīr Ālūsī= Rūḥ al-Maʿānī, Verified by ʿAlī ʿAbd al-Bārī ʿAṭiyya, Beirut: Dār al-Kutub al-ʿIlmiyya

Al-Atāsī MK (2002) Sharah Majallat al-Ahkaam, Maktabah Rasheediya

Al-Dihlawī SWA (1995) Aqd al-Jayyid fī Aḥkām al-Ijtihād wa-l-Taqlīd, Dār al-FatḤ. Al Shareqah, Emirates

Al-Fayyūmī al-Ḥamawī A (1987) Al-Misbāḥ al-Munīr fī Gharīb al-Sharḥ al-Kabīr. Al-Maktaba al-ʿIlmiyya, Beirut

Al-Khāzin ʿAlāʾ al-Dīn ʿAlīibn Muḥammad ibn Ibrāhīm ibn ʿUmar (1994) Tafsīr al-Khāzin Beirut: Dār al-kutub al-ʿilmiyya

Al-Rāzī, Muḥammad ibn ʿUmar ibn Ḥasan (1999) Tafsīr al-Rāzī, Al-Tafsīr al-Kabīr, Beirut: Dār Ihyāʾ al-Turāth al-ʿArabī, Vol. 1

Al-Shawkānī, Muḥammad ibn ʿAlī ibn Muḥmmad ibn ʿAbdallāh (1994) Tafsīr Fatḥ al-Qadīr, Beirut: Dār ibn Kathīr

Al-Qurṭubī M (1964) Tafsīr al-Jāmiʿ li-Aḥkām al-Qurʾān = Tafsīr Qurṭubī. Dār al-Kutub al-Miṣriyya, Cairo

Al-Qurṭubī M (2003) Al-Jāmiʿ al-AḤkām Al-Qurʾān. Dār al-ʿIlm Publications, Riyadh

Al-Ṭebarī M (2000) Tafsīr al-Ṭebarī (Jāmiʿ al-Bayān fī Taʾwīl al-Qurʾān), Muʾassasa al-Risāla 22

Alukūzay AJ (1885) Asās al-Qużāt. Dār al-Salṭana Publication, Kabul

Al-Zarqāʾ MA (1988) Al-Madkhal al-Fiqhī al-ʿĀmm (Introduction to general Islamic jurisprudence). Dārul ʿIlm, Damascus

Barfield T (2003) Afghan customary law and its relationship to formal judicial institutions. Boston University

Bassiouni MC (2014) Introduction. In: Bassiouni (ed) The Sharia and Islamic criminal justice in time of war and peace. Cambridge University Press, pp 1–17. https://doi.org/10.1017/CBO9781139629249

Farhang MS (1992) Afghanistan during the last five centuries, vol 1. Qum. Ismāʿīliyya publications, Iran, pp 577–578
Ghani A (1983) Disputes in a Court of Sharia. Kunar Valley. Afghanistan. 1885-1890. Int J Middle East Stud 15(3):353–367
Ghubār GM (2015) Afghānistān Dar Masīr-i Tārīkh. Sarwar Sādāt Publications, Kabul, pp 1074–1075
Hallaq WB (2004) A history of Islamic legal theories. An introduction to Sunni Usul Al-fiqh. Cambridge University Press
Hunt J, Kahlmeyer A (2007) Islamic law: the Sharia from Mohammad's time to the present. McFarland & Co, Jefferson
Hussami HG (2009) History of judiciary in Afghanistan. Saeed Publications, Kabul
Ibn Manẓūr M (1994) Lisān al-ʿArab. Dār Ṣādir, Beirut
Ibn Qayyim al-Jawziyya M (2006) I'lam al-Muwaqqi'in 'an Rabb al-'Alamin. Dār al Kutub al ʿIlmiyyah, Beirut
Iṣfahānī R (2008) Al-Mufradāt al-Gharīb fī al-Qurʾān, Dar Ihya Al-Turath Al-Arabi Iran: Sadiq
Johnson C, Maley W, Thier A, Wardak A (2003) Afghanistan's political and constitutional development. Overseas Development Institute, London
Kamali MH (2008) Introduction. In: Id. (ed) Sharia law: an introduction. One World Publications, Oxford, Chapter 1, pp 1–13
Khan A (2003) The reopening of the Islamic code: the second era of Ijtihad. Univ ST. Thomas Law J 1.1
Layish A (2004) The transformation of the Sharia from Jurists' law to statutory in the contemporary Muslim world. Int J Study Mod Islam 44(1):85–113. https://doi.org/10.1163/157006004773712587
Mahmoudi S (2004) The Sharia in the new Afghan constitution: contradiction or compliment, Max-Planck foundation for peace and rule of law. ZaöRV 64:867–880
Ministry of Awqāf and Islamic Affairs of Kuwait, Al-Mawsūʿa al-Fiqhiyya al-Kuwaytiyya, (2008) vol 1
Murtazashvili J (2016) The political economy of village governance. In: Informal order and the state in Afghanistan, vol 4. Cambridge University Press, Cambridge, pp 111–152. https://doi.org/10.1017/CBO9781316286890.007
Otto JM (2008) Sharia and national law in Muslim countries: tensions and opportunities for Dutch and EU foreign policy. Amsterdam University Press
RaḤmānī AI (2006) The role of religious leaders in the provision of local services in Afghanistan. Open Society Institute. Central European University. Center for Policy Study, pp 8–9. Last visited: 10/04/2014
Rohe M (2004) Application of Sharia rules in Europe – scope and limits. Die Welt des Islams 44(3), Brill/Leiden
Rohe M (2014) Islamic law in the past and present. Themes in Islamic Studies 8. Brill. https://doi.org/10.1163/9789004281806
Shabli MM (1985) Introduction to definition of Islamic Fiqh, Beirut, Darul Arabia
Sirat AS (1969) Sharia and Islamic education in modern Afghanistan. Middle East J 23(2):217–219
ʿUmar A (2010) Dictionary of the Holy Qur'an. NOOR Foundation International Inc., Amsterdam
Vikør KS (2000) The Sharia and the nation state: who can codify the divine law. In: Utvik, Vikør (eds) The Middle East in a globalized world. Bergen/London, pp 220-250
Wakily Popalzaey A (1990) Dar al-Qaza in Afghanistan: from the beginning of Islam until republic era. Islamic Research Center, Kabul

Chapter 2
Legal Pluralism in Afghanistan

2.1 Introduction

As Baudouin Dupret observes, "law is as plural as social life itself";[1] the concept of law may differ from society to society. There are many standards acknowledged as law, such as international law, customary law, Islamic law, natural law, state law, canon law, and so on, which function as tools at both national and international levels to maintain social order and resolve disputes.[2] Additionally, law may appear in a society in different ways: it may be written in law books (codes), function as standards set by laypeople (custom), be implemented as religious or ethical values, or be exercised as norms to resolve disputes and keep communities harmonious.

As the authors of *Negotiating Justice Sector Reform in Afghanistan* claim, Isaiah Berlin's theory of *Value Pluralism* could be true in explaining the situation of legal pluralism in Afghanistan.[3] According to Berlin's theory, several values that may all be equally correct may nonetheless conflict with each other. He believed that there are some fundamental and common values that the majority of people in a region agree about and want to accept. He rejected the philosophy of monism, which holds that there is only one true answer for one genuine question and only one reliable way to find out the correct answer.[4] Although his theory is primarily a model of modern philosophical liberalism, it could also be accepted in the field of law. Different approaches could be practiced in various legal issues to reach the right answer; however, the answers might differ from each other.[5] Thus, the argument built by

[1] Dupret (2007), p. 2.

[2] Tamanaha (2008).

[3] Suhrke and Borchgrevink (2008), p. 2.

[4] Stanford Encyclopedia of Philosophy (2008). Isaiah Berlin. http://plato.stanford.edu/archives/spr2008/entries/berlin/. Accessed on 06, 07, 2021.

[5] Suhrke and Borchgrevink (2008), pp. 2–3.

L. Saeed, *Islam, Custom and Human Rights*, Interdisciplinary Studies in Human Rights 7, https://doi.org/10.1007/978-3-030-83086-1_2

Tamanaha that "legal pluralism is everywhere"[6] has been considered and has received approval from most legal experts, anthropologists, and legal sociologists.

In essence, legal pluralism in Afghanistan is derived from the country's multifaceted social structure and value systems, along with historical legal development and its having a multicultural society. In addition, its social structure has a variety of characteristics based on the varied ethnic groups and their positions in Afghan society. All these factors have paved the ground for different legal actors to play roles in the field. In Afghanistan, the distances between cities and villages can be very far and rural areas are often isolated and follow their own customs. The meaning of common concepts can differ from province to province and tribe to tribe. Societies have different values and symbolism that define the multilayered cultural structures and societal norms in Afghan society. These values present themselves as indicators and expressions of the major elements that are central to Afghanistan and can shape the legal landscape. Different legal sources are applicable to different legal issues, and different approaches may be practiced to resolve a problem. As a result, a variety of solutions have appeared that may be accepted by one party rather than another.

The concept of legal pluralism has different manifestations in the field of social sciences, particularly in legal sociology, and it may be defined in various ways. Some scholars maintain that legal pluralism means that law is not solely the product of state-based institutions. Others posit that it refers to a situation where a state recognizes, confirms, and supports multiple types of law for various groups in a society.[7] There is a broader definition provided by Hooker: "the term 'legal pluralism' refers to the situation in which two or more laws interact."[8] In fact, legal pluralism itself does not carry a negative meaning, despite some literature listing it as a challenge in the Afghan legal system, while it is considered as a value in developed countries.[9] However, legal pluralism could benefit from being regulated and having a clear line drawn between the scopes of different legal norms. Different forms of law, formal or informal, have advantages and disadvantages; by wisely regulating them, benefit can be had from the variety of sources, and the possible harm brought by a pluralistic legal system can be prevented.

It is a reality in Afghan society that different legal values can be used to address different legal problems, and the outcome could be acceptable to the parties, but other groups may prefer to follow different approaches. The Main Concern regarding legal pluralism in Afghanistan is the ambiguity of procedure and implementation, which means that in which circumstances which type of law is applicable. This vagueness typically has a negative outcome because different sources of applicable law require different approaches, which leads to dissimilar outcomes. Speaking generally, the three core sources of law in Afghanistan—state law, customary law,

[6]Tamanaha (2007), p. 375.

[7]Sherman (2006), pp. 158–159.

[8]Hooker (1975), p. 6; Bell (2006), p. 321.

[9]Suhrke and Borchgrevink (2008), pp. 211–230.

and Sharia—must be discussed because without recognition of these three elements, it would be difficult to understand how Afghan judges and other decision-makers have used these sources when they make a decision.

Legal pluralism is a distinguishing feature of the Afghan legal system. Afghan laws are mostly composed of three main parts: Islamic law (*Sharia*), laws passed by legislation (*qānūn*), and local tradition and custom (*ʿurf.*)[10] These laws have been applied to different legal matters in different parts of Afghanistan. Each of these three sources of law has been applied to a specific range of cases in Afghan society, and each one of them respects its own particular legal values and relies on exacting sources with specific procedures for implementation. The outcomes may differ from each other because different approaches lead to different consequences.

The plurality of legal sources could be considered a positive characteristic of a legal system if it has been wisely regulated. If it is not regulated, it may cause anarchy in the system, especially in court decisions if the choice is given to the judges to make decisions based on their own discretion. Authorizing judges to make decisions based on a variety of law sources without regulated principles can lead to a situation where judicial decision-making is so discretionary that it appears out of control.[11]

In the case of Afghanistan, legal pluralism provides room for Afghan judges to easily choose between sources and render different decisions on the same facts. The *Iftāʾ Department* of the Supreme Court is a section that is in charge of issuing legal opinions (fatwas) based on Sharia provisions. The "*Iftāʾ* Department"[12] of the Supreme Court sometimes also relies on custom (*ʿurf*) without any legal basis for their opinion, even when there may be state law or Sharia provisions that exist. For instance, in the case of transferring donkey skins,[13] the *Iftāʾ* and Research Department of the Supreme Court relied on Afghan custom (*ʿurf*) and stated in its opinion that since slaughtering a donkey and selling its skin is not common in Afghanistan, it is considered a crime and should be punished. This ruling goes against the Ḥanafī school provisions, wherein it is not a crime to sell donkey skins.[14]

This pluralistic system allows Afghan judges to make decisions in different ways regarding the same case with the same facts. This will have a significant impact on justice and rule of law in Afghanistan. Additionally, sometimes Afghan courts go beyond the law and the Ḥanafī school provisions and rely upon custom *(ʿurf)* to

---

[10] Yassari and Saboory (2010) and Barfield (2003).

[11] A good example is the looting/plundering cases, in which three judges in the same court, but in different court sessions, have made dissimilar decisions regarding cases with the same facts. In one case the judge sentenced the accused by 5 months in prison based on Article 130 of the Constitution, another judge sentenced the accused by 1 year and 6 months in prison based on Article 460 of the Penal Code. It will be discussed in more detail in the case study section.

[12] In many cases, if the state law is not clear, the Afghan courts send an inquiry to the *Iftāʾ* Department of the Supreme Court to issue a fatwa in the light of Sharia regarding the case.

[13] A driver of a truck was arrested and put on trial for transferring around 1000 donkey skins from Balkh province to Kunduz province in 2016. Will be discussed in the related chapter.

[14] See Chap. 7, Donkey Skin Case.

punish the accused harshly. For instance, in a case about selling dog meat, the court relied on custom (*ʿurf*) and not the law or the Ḥanafī school provisions to impose a harsher sentence.[15]

Furthermore, in some cases, the court has used the provisions of other schools of thought instead of the Ḥanafī school to convince common people that harsh punishment is justified. This issue arose from the blasphemy case of Parwīz Kāmbakhsh, in which the primary court based its decision on the Mālikī school of thought, going beyond the main doctrines of the Ḥanafī school and violating its core principles.[16] These cases will be explored in detail later in this work and will reveal the impact of legal pluralism on the court decision-making process.

The usage of different sources is not limited to some specific cases, but courts have applied different sources to make a decision. To unveil why the Afghan judges have used different sources when they make a decision, it is necessary to mention some provisions of the laws that allow judges to use a variety of sources in different circumstances. The Constitution says:

> In case under consideration, the court shall apply provisions of this Constitution as well as other laws. If there is no provision in the Constitution or other laws about a case, the courts shall, in pursuance of Hanafi jurisprudence, and within the limits set by this Constitution, rule in a way that attains justice in the best manner.[17]

Generally, the Constitution uses the phrase "case under consideration" without specifying the type of cases; therefore some Afghan legal experts claim that this pluralistic system can be applicable to all types of cases, including criminal cases.[18] However, the article clearly mentioned that the use of different sources should be within the limits set by this Constitution; one of the limits is the principle of legality declared in Article 27 of the Constitution.[19]

In addition, the penal code allows judges to use Sharia provisions in particular cases. The penal code stated:

> This Law regulates the "taʿzīrī" crime and penalties. Those committing crimes of "ḥudūd", "qiṣās" and "diya" shall be punished in accordance with the provisions of the Hanafi School of Thought.[20]

[15] See Chap. 6, Selling Dog Meat Case.

[16] See Chap. 5, Blasphemy Case of Parwīz Kāmbakhsh.

[17] The Constitution of Afghanistan (2004) Art. 130.

[18] Interview with Prof. Abdul Salaam Azimi (former Chief Justice of Afghanistan) Dated 29 September 2017. His view and others who agree and disagree with his opinion will be discussed in detail hereinafter.

[19] The Constitution of Afghanistan (2004) Art. 27: "No deed shall be considered a crime unless ruled by a law promulgated prior to commitment of the offense. No one shall be pursued, arrested, or detained without due process of law. No one shall be punished without the decision of an authoritative court taken in accordance with the provisions of the law, promulgated prior to commitment of the offense."

[20] Penal Code of Afghanistan (1976) Art. 1.

The penal code in the first article differentiated between different types of crime and allowed courts to use different laws in criminal cases. This classification of crimes allows the courts to apply not only different substantive laws, but even the procedure is not the same; for instance, in the case of murder or adultery, there are two substantive laws, Sharia and state law, that could be applied through different procedures and proof of standard.[21]

The usage of a variety of sources is not limited only to criminal cases; the Civil Code also declared that courts are allowed to use different sources of law in divergent situations. The Civil Code states:

> In case no provision of law exists, courts shall decide in according with general principles of Hanafi Jurisprudence of Islamic Sharia in order to secure justice in the best possible way.[22]

This article as a main principle allows the usage of Ḥanafī jurisprudence to fill the legal gap, but the second article of the Civil Code talks about the third source of law, which is custom (*ʿurf*). The Civil Code says:

> Where neither do provisions of law exist, nor any ruling is found among principle of Hanafi Jurisprudence of Islamic Sharia, courts shall decide according to common custom, provided that the custom does not contradict provisions of law no Principles of justice.[23]

This provision of law almost covers all players in the legal field to be used in different circumstances.

By directing the use of the Ḥanafī school of thought in the absence of state law, Article 130 of the Afghan Constitution demonstrates explicit acceptance of legal pluralism in Afghanistan. However, the text of Article 130 of the Constitution states that the scope of the article should be very limited, but in practice the Afghan courts have used widely this article and made decisions according to the provisions of the Ḥanafī doctrines or custom (*ʿurf*) instead of the law. The broad use of Article 130 is embodied in the saying, "Law is much more than state law."[24] This is a short quote, but it is considered a basic principle in legal sociology studies, and it is arguably true in most societies.

Therefore, there is no doubt that Afghanistan has a pluralistic legal system. The main players in this field are Sharia, customary law, and state law. Islamic Sharia, particularly the Ḥanafī school of thought, is considered the main player because directly or indirectly it has an impact on the other two sources of law. Customary law is a set of norms and standards that are established usually by laypeople in Afghan society. The third actor is state law (*qānūn*) and pretends to overcome the two other actors by increasing the number of laws and power of the state.

---

[21] Criminal law procedure based on state law and Islamic criminal procedure will be discussed in further detail in the future.

[22] Civil Code of Afghanistan (1976) Art. 2, clause 2.

[23] Civil Code of Afghanistan (1976) Art. 2.

[24] Dupret (2007), p. 1.

2.2 Sharia (Islamic Law)

Generally speaking, Sharia refers to what Prophet Mohammad declared during his duties as a messenger of Allah in Mecca and Medina. As mentioned before, Sharia in the context of Afghanistan almost has the same meaning as *fiqh* does; however, in a strict sense, Sharia has a broader meaning than *fiqh*. In other words, Sharia is like a big umbrella that covers the legal, moral, and religious tenets of Islam, while *fiqh* covers mostly the legal aspect and reveals what is prohibited and impermissible.

Since 99.7% of Afghan citizens are Muslim and only 0.3% others,[25] the Islam religion has a significant impact on every aspect of the life of the citizens and the social structure in Afghanistan. As Shaykh Nadawī observes, Afghanistan has been a well-known place for famous Islamic scholars, and Afghans have historically been faithful followers of the Islamic Sharia.[26] Those who live in Afghanistan, even for a short time, will understand the importance of Islam and the vital role of religious leaders in society. The religious leaders typically emphasize that implementing the provisions of Sharia will guarantee their happiness and a better life in this world and the life hereafter. Since the majority of Afghan citizens are Muslims and regularly attend prayers in mosques, it is a common belief of Afghan people that the implementation of the Sharia is the only way to have a successful life. Making decisions in accordance with the Islamic Sharia is thus more acceptable among Afghans than applying formal law, and it paves the way for the Sharia provisions to be implemented easily. Since the majority of citizens do not have independent knowledge regarding Islam and Sharia, religious leaders have a significant impact on the population.

Sharia, being a big umbrella, covers both customary law and statutory law in Afghanistan's legal system. As Kamali indicates, the importance of Islam is revealed in all constitutions of Afghanistan, except the 1980 Constitution. He further explained that reference to Islam has been reflected at least 17 times in various provisions of the 2004 Constitution.[27] For instance, the first article[28] of the Constitution named Afghanistan as an Islamic republic, the second article[29] declared Islam as a religion of the state of Afghanistan, and the third[30] says that laws must not contradict Islam. Basically, Sharia is considered the main source for the other two pillars of the legal system in Afghanistan. Thus, it is a common practice that in order

---

[25] Central Intelligence Agency (2019). The World Factbook. https://www.cia.gov/-library/publications/the-world-factbook/geos/af.html Accessed 1 June 2019.

[26] Nadawī (1974), p. 34.

[27] Kamali (2014).

[28] The Constitution of Afghanistan (2004) Art. 1, "Afghanistan shall be an Islamic Republic [. . .]."

[29] The Constitution of Afghanistan (2004) Art. 2, "The sacred religion of Islam is the religion of the Islamic Republic of Afghanistan[. . .]."

[30] The Constitution of Afghanistan (2004) Art. 3, "No law shall contradict the tenets and provisions of the holy religion of Islam in Afghanistan."

to give legitimacy to the decisions that have been made in the light of customary or state law, it is important to be supported by Sharia.

The meaning and scope of Sharia and the role it has played throughout legal history have been discussed previously, but here I will shed light on the pluralistic approach of Sharia by itself and then briefly discuss the sources of Sharia.

2.2.1 Legal Pluralism and Sharia (Islamic Law)

In fact, legal pluralism is the main feature of Islamic law (Sharia). Since there are different sources for Islamic law and Islamic jurists based on the circumstances have inferred laws from a variety of sources, it shows that sharia has approved the legal Pluralism by itself. There is a consensus among Islamic scholars that Islamic law has primary and secondary sources; the Quran and the Sunnah of Prophet Mohammad are both considered as primary sources, but there is no agreement among them, including Sunni and Shia, regarding *ijmāʿ* and *qiyās* as primary sources of Islamic law. Different schools referred to various sources of law to deal with a variety of legal issues.

These pluralistic views had been accepted by Prophet Mohammad and his successors from the beginning. Islamic scholars believe that all sources, whether explicit or implicit, must somehow be an interpretation of divine law and not be in contradiction to the primary sources.[31] So within Islamic law, the Quran and Sunnah are the primary basis, and in case there is no provision in these sources, then the case should be referred to other sources. This principle came from the Hadith, as narrated below:

> When Prophet Mohammad decided to send Muʿādh Ibn Jabal as a judge and his representative to Yemen, Prophet Mohammad asked him [before he left Medina for Yemen] which source will you use when you make a judgment? Muʿādh said he will make a judgment according to the Holy Quran. Prophet Mohammad said, [what] if [you] do not find [the answer] in the Quran? Muʿādh said, he will rely on the Sunnah, then Prophet Mohammad said [what] if you do not find it in the Sunnah? Muʿādh said, then he will do Ijtihad, (independent reasoning). Prophet Mohammad was happy with the answer. . . .[32]

This Hadith draws a concrete framework for Islamic scholars, especially the Ḥanafī school's followers, to obey the hierarchy of these sources and find a solution initially in the primary sources of Islamic law then refer the case to the secondary sources if needed. That conversation is the main basis and framework for the classification of the sources of Islamic law and how to make judgments accordingly.[33] Even though

[31] Ministry of Awqāf and Islamic Affairs of Kuwait (2008), Vol. 1, p. 21.

[32] Abū Dāwūd (2009), p. 489.

[33] This can be known, for instance, from the renowned *adhān* of the Muʿādh ibn Jabal: when the Prophet was sending Muʿādh to Yemen as a ruler and judge, he was asked three questions as to what he would refer to when making decisions in his capacity as a judge! Muʿādh mentioned firstly the Qur'an, then the Sunnah of the Prophet, and then his own considered judgment and *ijtihād*. There was no reference to Sharia in this *hadith* nor to *fiqh* as such. See Kamali (2008), p. 4.

this conversation is the foundation for the belief of most schools of thought to categorize the sources of Islamic law, there is no usage of the terms Sharia or *fiqh* in their dialogue.[34]

Moreover, there is another narration that reveals the methodology of Abū Bakr and ʿUmar, the first and second caliphs, regarding how they had dealt with legal issues. The narrator, Maymūn ibn IḤsān, says, "When any claim has been addressed to Abū Bakr, first he looked at the Quran, if he found the answer, he made decision accordingly. Otherwise, he refer the question to the Prophet Mohammad Sunnah, if he had not found the answer in the Sunnah, he asked people about the solution and consult with people and make a meeting with their leaders and discuss the issue with them in order to find the answer. When they agreed upon a solution, Abū Bakr made decision accordingly. This method was followed by the second caliph, ʿUmar ibn Khaṭṭāb, but besides seeking the answer from the Holy Quran and the Sunnah, he was also asking if there is any precedent had made by Abū Bakr, if there is no answer in the above sources, then he consult with people and made a decision."[35] The above texts show that in case of a legal lacuna in the Quran and Sunnah, it is acceptable to go beyond these two main sources and find a solution to a legal issue from secondary sources. This method has been widely practiced and accepted by the majority of Islamic scholars and jurists from the beginning. This method affirms that Sharia adopts a variety of sources to provide space for different players in the legal field in order to find a solution to a legal issue. To have a clear picture of different sources in the Sharia, it would be better to shed light on the sources of Sharia that Islamic scholars deduce legal provision from them.

2.2.2 The Sources of Sharia

A majority of Islamic scholars, especially Sunni jurists, recognize more than ten sources of Islamic law. There is a consensus among the Sunni schools' scholars that there are four main sources of divine law, namely the Holy Quran, the Sunnah,[36] a consensus of legal scholars (*ijmāʿ*), and legal analogy (*qiyās*). Furthermore, there are more sources that are accepted by one school of thought rather than others, or they accept these sources, but there is disagreement regarding the weakness and strength of these sources in their applicability to a case.

Among Muslims, the Holy Quran, without any doubt, is the main and highest source of Islamic Sharia. A famous Ḥanafī scholar, Taftāzānī (1322–1390), in his

[34] Kamali (2008), pp. 4–5.

[35] Rushdī (1977), p. 63.

[36] However, some Muslim scholars claim that the Prophet Mohammad's Sunnah is not considered as an independent source for Islamic Law and they believe that only Quran could be a source for Islamic Law. They called themselves *Al-Qurʾāniyyūn* (القرآنيون) See Ministry of Awqāf and Islamic Affairs of Kuwait (2008), Vol. 1, p. 41.

book *al-Talwīḥ ʿalā al-Tawḍīḥ* defined Quran as Allah's words sent down to Prophet Mohammad in the Arabic language;[37] the book asserts that no one can bring even a short chapter similar to Quran as it is written on pages and narrated frequently and its reading is prayer, which starts with Sura *al-Fātiḥa* and ends with Sura *al-Nās*.[38] It has more than 6230 verses, but around 500 verses are conceptually related to the legal orders *Āyāt al-AḤkām*, and laws have been derived from them. The rest of the verses mainly discuss the history of previous messengers and their religions, namely Christianity and Jewish; moral issues; and so on, which, in some cases, could be implicitly sources of some legal issues, but Islamic scholars directly interpret legal provisions based on around (500) Quranic verses.

The second source of Sharia is the Prophet Mohammad's *Sunnah*. Literally, it refers to a normative practice or method and established course of conduct.[39] However, the concept of Sunnah in jurisprudence includes the acts, sayings, and deeds of Prophet Mohammad that are related to legal issues.[40] The term *Sunnah* does not include some prophetic traditions and practices that do not convey the legal concept *Sunna ghayr tashrīʿiyya* and that are mainly considered as a human being's natural activities like the way he eats, sleeps, dresses, etc. So when we are talking about Sunnah, it should be related to legal issues. However, some schools draw a bigger scope for the Sunnah and do not limit its concept only to the Prophet's traditions and practices. For instance, the Mālikī school extended the concept of Sunnah to the practices of the Prophet's companions and the Muslims in the Medina community at that time.[41]

ijmāʿ is an Arabic term that means either to determine or to agree upon something. *ijmāʿ* refers to the consensus of Islamic jurists (*Mujtahidīn*) regarding any matter arising after Prophet Mohammad's death.[42] This system has been supported by the Quran and Prophet Mohammad's Hadith and practiced by the Prophet's successors right after his death.[43] It means when Prophet Mohammad was alive, there existed no *ijmāʿ*. Furthermore, *ijmāʿ* occurs only if jurists (Mujtahidūn), not laypeople, agree upon an issue. Also, it is not limited to a specific topic; it could be applicable to a

---

[37] From the above definition, it seems that the author of the mentioned book believes that Quran is considered both the meaning and the text together. However, it is a controversial issue among the Ḥanafī scholars whether Quran as direct words of Allah is only the meaning without text or considered the text and meaning together. In one narration, Imam Abū Ḥanīfa believed that only the meaning of the text of the Quran is considered as the direct words of Allah, not the text. Therefore, he allowed Muslims to perform prayers in their own language, rather than Arabic, if they can translate the verses of the Quran properly, but some Ḥanafī scholars said that Imam Abū Ḥanīfa changed his mind and said that both the meaning and text together considered Quran. See Abū Zuhra (n.d.), pp. 269–277.

[38] Taftāzānī (n.d.), p. 29.

[39] Taftāzānī (n.d.), p. 3; Kamali (2003), pp. 58–117; Id., pp. 66–73.

[40] Bassiouni (2014), pp. 49–50.

[41] Rohe (2014a), p. 66.

[42] Kamali (2003), pp. 229–230.

[43] Rohe (2014a), p. 74.

variety of matters related to legal issues, beliefs, customs, and even linguistic matters.[44] However, it is more common in juridical matters.[45]

Literally, *qiyās* means measuring the weight, length, and quality of two things and comparing them to see if they are equal or similar.[46] In the field of jurisprudence, arguably, it can be defined as a conclusion by analogy and other methods of deduction.[47] Kamali, in his book *Principle of Islamic Jurisprudence*, considered *qiyās* as an extension of Sharia value from an original case, which is already regulated by a text, to a new case, which is similar to the original case in term of effective cause.[48] In the field of Islamic law, an original case is called *aṣl.* There are several types of *qiyās* that are explained in the field of *fiqh* based on their usage, and the principles have been established by Islamic scholars.[49]

The abovementioned sources are accepted by most of the Sunni schools, especially the Ḥanafī school of thought, as the main sources of law,[50] but Shia disagree with Sunni schools and do not accept *ijmā* ʿas the third source of law, and they put intellectual reasoning (ʿ*aql*) in the third position. However, the first two sources (Quran and Sunnah) are not controversial among Islamic sects because both of them consider divine law (*waḤī*). The majority of Islamic scholars maintain that divine law, which is revealed by Allah, has two features: implied and direct inspiration from the Quran and manifest inspiration from the Hadith. In other words, the meaning of the Hadiths is considered revelation, but the words are not considered to have been sent down directly from Allah because the Holy Quran said: "Nor does he (Mohammad) speak out of desire. It is but a revelation revealed."[51] Thus, most classical Islamic scholars believe that the Quran and the Sunnah are the two uncontentious pure sources of Islamic law "Sharia."

Most Muslims agree that the Quran and Sunnah are the main sources to address any questions that may arise in the daily life of a Muslim. However, these sources do not provide all the details of Islamic law; they mostly provide general principles and a framework to be addressed for a variety of legal issues. There is consensus among the Sunni schools that the four mentioned sources are the primary sources of Sharia. If a clear answer to a legal question cannot be found in the primary sources of Sharia, there are additional sources that could be consulted to find answers to legal issues.

There is no consensus among Muslim scholars regarding the number of secondary sources of Islamic law. According to most Sunni schools, besides primary sources, there are other sources from which jurists could deduce laws based on a specific principle and circumstances. These other sources include *istiḥsān*

---

[44] Kamali (2003), p. 230.

[45] Kamali (2003), pp. 227–260; Rohe (2014a), pp. 74–79.

[46] Al-Sarakhsī (n.d.), p. 143.

[47] Rohe (2014a), p. 79.

[48] Kamali (2003), p. 264.

[49] Kamali (2003), pp. 265–301; Rohe (2014a), pp. 79–83.

[50] Al-Shāshī (n.d.), p. 13.

[51] The holy Quran, Sura al-Najm, (53: 3–4).

(considering something to be better), *istiṣḥāb al-Ḥāl* (presumption of continuity), *ʿurf* (custom and usage), *maṣāliḤ mursala* (consideration of public interests), *qawl al-ṣaḤābī* (opinions of the (individual) companions of Prophet Mohammad),[52] *sadd al-dharāʾiʿ* (blocking the means),[53] and *sharʿ man qablanā* (laws of the previous prophets who are mentioned in the Holy Quran).[54] Ḥanafī scholars have not accepted *istiṣḥāb al-Ḥāl*,[55] *sadd al-dharāʾiʿ*, and *maṣāliḤ mursala* as sources of Islamic law,[56] but they accepted the rest of the sources and have used them in different ways.

Among the secondary sources, *istiḥsān* is a significant part of *ijtihād* and plays a vital role in responding to the needs of society in different circumstances.[57] In accordance with the Ḥanafī doctrine, the term *istiḥsān* means "considering something to be better";[58] thus, in some cases, the jurists even preferred *istiḥsān* rather than *qiyās*. As Kamali mentioned, *istiḥsān* is an approach of choosing an easy and preferable option from among many.[59] The famous Ḥanafī scholar *al-Sarakhsī* maintained that *istiḥsān* is an approach of choosing a more convincing option for the people, and it has a deep root in the Islamic main sources, Quran and Sunnah, which refer to preventing hardships and seeking ease.

The Quran says: "God intends facility for you, and He does not want to put you in hardship."[60] Also, there is a hadith of the Prophet Mohammad that says: "The best of your religion is that which brings ease to the people."[61] Furthermore, it is a well-known narration that Prophet Mohammad had advised ʿAlī and Muʿādh when he was sending them as a judge to Yemen to gladden people and not scare them, make things easy for them and not make it difficult.[62] It means that if there are several options, according to the above texts, the best choice is the easy and more convenient one.

Overall, the Islamic legal system originally accepted legal pluralism, and from the beginning, there were multiplayer actors in the field of law. Since the Afghan legal system is deeply affected by Islamic law, obviously the Afghan legal system has the same feature as its main source.

---

[52]Rohe (2014a), p. 86.

[53]Rohe (2014a), p. 91.

[54]Kamali (2003); Rohe (2014a), pp. 82–92.

[55]Al-Sarakhsī (n.d.), p. 223.

[56]ZuḤaylī (2006), pp. 255–280.

[57]Kamali (2003), p. 324.

[58]Rohe (2014b), p. 28.

[59]Kamali (2003), p. 325.

[60]The Holy Quran, al-Baqarah (2185).

[61]Abū Dāwūd (1999), Hadith No: 1392.

[62]Al-Sarakhsī (n.d.), p. 145.

2.3 Customary Law[63]

Custom, *ʿurf*[64] has several meanings, but the common meaning refers to those acts that seem good for the majority of people in a society.[65] But in the context of Afghanistan, *customary law* refers to the rules by which local communities resolve disputes outside state-based institutions and use their common cultural and ethical norms to produce binding rules on their members.[66] The main source of customary law in Afghanistan is the standards set by laypeople, which are followed as rules by the majority of local citizens. Since Afghanistan is a multiethnic country, the customs vary from one ethnic group to another and from one region to another. Due to the scope of this research, the focus will be on the customs of the majority and regional customs.

The extant literature tends to suggest that the standards set by laypeople in Afghanistan do not affect the judiciary and are primarily used outside the courts; however, in reality, they have a significant impact on court decisions and are broadly used by the courts, even if there are provisions of the law and Sharia available. For instance, as explained in greater detail in Sect. 2, in the Donkey Skin Case, the Supreme Court relied only on the Afghan customary law and criminalized the act of selling donkey skins even though this act is not criminalized under the law and is even considered as permissible in accordance with the Ḥanafī school of thought.[67]

There are many other examples of noncriminal cases where courts have based decisions on customs and standards set by laypeople. In some cases, courts have even legalized these standards and then used them as a sort of precedent.[68] Since this

[63] Although customary law plays a significant role in the Afghan legal system, it is out of the scope of this research. However, this research will point out the impact of the customs in the court decisions, in which Sharia provisions have been applied, the focus will be more on the application of Sharia not custom.

[64] Originally "*ʿurf*" is an Arabic term, but like most other legal terms, it is very common in Afghanistan. In fact, with the exception of few terms, all legal terminology in Afghanistan is in Arabic.

[65] Ibn ʿĀbidīn (2019) Majmūʿa al-Rasāʾil ibn ʿĀbidīn: Risāla fī Nashr al-ʿUrf fī Bināʾ baʿzul AḤkām ʿalā al-ʿUrf. http://waqfeya.com/book.php?bid=793. Accessed 6 March 2019.

[66] Barfield (2003), p. 2.

[67] A famous Ḥanafī scholar and the author of the Al-MuḤīṭ al-Burhānī book say that if someone slaughters his donkey and sell its meat, it is legal, but it is prohibited to consume it as food. Please see Al-Bukhārī (2004), p. 349.

[68] For example, the exchange rate of the Afghan currency "Afghānī or Afs" has been significantly changed because of the broken economy and political crises. For instance, the exchange rate for one USD was between 40 and 50 Afs in the late 1960s, but after a few years the exchange rate for one USD was about 100,000 Afs; following the collapse of the Taliban regime, the exchange rate for Afs again improved and one USD was valued at approximately 45 Afs. So, if someone borrowed 50,000 Afs in the late 1960s, its value was around $1000, but the same amount of Afs, after a few years, was less than $1. If a court found that a party owed 50,000 Afs, but the exchange rate had changed significantly, the courts have referred the case to the main market of money exchange in Kabul city (Sarai Shahzāda) and asked them how they would deal with such a case. The custom of

research focuses only on criminal cases, it will not touch upon these civil cases and will emphasize the impact of Afghan customs on criminal matters and how this has worked in practice. This work will also shed light on the institutions dealing with customary law in Afghanistan and the language and terms that have been used in the procedures of customary law.

Customary law in Afghanistan is based on the common practices and specific values of Afghan society that have been exercised through community-based institutions, called *Jirgas*[69]and *shūrās*.[70] The term *Jirga* is used mostly among Pashtun tribes, while the term *shūrā* is more common among other ethnic groups in Afghanistan. *Jirga*[71] refers to a collection of praiseworthy morals of a true Pashtun. Historically, Jirga goes back to the era of ancient Aryans and has been practiced for several centuries in Afghanistan.[72] The concept of custom carries different connotations in different parts of Afghanistan. For example, customs in the south and east parts of the country are different from those in the north and west. Typically, customary law is practiced more frequently in the remote regions of Afghanistan, where governmental institutions do not exist or have no power to impose state law on local people; however, in some specific cases, regardless of where the parties are located, the application of customary law is usually preferred.

Although there is a lot of literature regarding customary law in Afghanistan, it is hard to precisely understand reality based on these writings. Due to the complexity of social structures in Afghanistan and their unique characteristics, many foreign researchers have not explained the situation accurately. The main characteristics of

---

businessmen was to check the exchange rate for the USD at the exact time he borrowed the money, then they asked for that much in USD, or Afghan currency currently equivalent to that amount, to match the value of the money he borrowed at that time.

[69]According to the Pashto Descriptive Dictionary (1978: 1272), *Jirga* is an original Pashto word, which in its common usage refers to the gathering of a few or a large number of people; it also means consultation according to this source. The word *jirga* is also used in Persian/Dari: according to *Ghayāth al-Lughat* (1871:119), it is derived from *jirga*, which means a "wrestling ring," or "circle," but is commonly used to refer to a gathering of people. See Wardak (2004).

[70]The term *shūrā* is an Arabic word that literally means "council." The term *shūrā* is used by non-Pashtun villages to indicate the village council. *Jirga* is a Pashto term that also means "council," although it translates literally to "circle," which reflects the seating arrangements participants take in the countryside. There are several varieties of *shūrā* or *jirga* at the village level. Because *shūrā* exists to deal with issues as they arise, they are flexible in membership as well as in scope. The *shūrā* that is indicated here is at the smallest level. See Brick (2008), p. 7.

Jirga or *shūrā* is a group of individuals which meets only in response to a specific need in order to decide how to meet the need. In most cases, this need is to resolve a conflict between individuals, families, groups of families, or whole tribes.' This description would seem to indicate that *shūrā* and *jirga* are fundamentally very similar Afghan informal (non-state) mechanisms of conflict resolution that operate in varying social and tribal contexts. See Wardak (2004).

[71]There are some other usages of the term Jirga and *shūrā* in Afghanistan that could be mentioned. The term Milli Shūrā (National Assembly) in Article 82 of the Afghan Constitution refers to the legislative body and consists of two houses: House of People and House of Elders. The first one is called Wolesi Jirga, and the second one is called Meshrano Jirga.

[72]The International Legal Foundation (2004).

customary law in Afghanistan are rooted in the unique structure of Afghan society and its values.

To draw a clear picture of customary law in Afghanistan, a deep understanding of the social values and particular concepts in the context of Afghan society is required. Furthermore, there are some acts that may not be considered as serious crimes in other cultures but according to Afghan custom are considered as such. For example, in some remote Pashtun areas, it is considered an offense for a strange (unrelated) man to remove the headscarf of a woman publicly by force; sometimes, people will even react seriously to it because they consider it like rape. In this circumstance, the woman's family is allowed to kill the wrongdoer or react strongly according to the doctrine of *ghayrat*[73] and to avoid *peghur*.[74] Afghan society is highly conservative.

It is necessary to consider the following key points to understand the functionality of customary law in Afghanistan.

2.3.1 The Unique Social Structure[75]

A distinct social structure of Afghan society makes Afghans think and behave differently from other societies. Most Afghans consider society as a judge and believe that they must have society's approval concerning their personal and social lives. They usually think that they must have the acceptance of the community in terms of their behavior and daily activities, even when it comes to their personal issues, such as their style of clothes; whether to have a beard and, if so, in which style; their public and private relationships; their methods of communication with others; their praying habits; etc. It would be very difficult to go against the norms that society has established for its members in Afghanistan. This strong connection between individuals and society and the strong effect of public perception on personal lives push most Afghan citizens to have a kind of double personality, which causes them to deal differently with the same issue publicly and privately.[76] Speaking generally, Afghans will answer the same question differently depending on whether they have been asked publicly or privately. People in other societies may also do the same, but in the case of Afghanistan, there is very strong pressure. It would be very challenging for a researcher to find the truth by talking to Afghans publicly.

Since Afghanistan does not have a strong state welfare system to provide support for its citizens, people strongly rely on the support of society and feel compelled to stay on the path that is paved by the norms of the community. The duty to demonstrate good social support pushes people to accept the customary and ethical

[73]The term *ghayra* is an Arabic term and it means zealotry in English.

[74]The term *peghur* is a Pashto word and it means sarcasm in English.

[75]This section is mostly based on my personal experiences and observations as an Afghan.

[76]It is my personal experience as an Afghan.

norms set by society. These norms are often represented by the decisions made by *Jirga* or *shūrā* members, who are most-respected leaders of society. If Afghan individuals do not accept the decisions made by the Jirga or *shūrā*, they will lose the support of the community. This makes life very difficult, in fact almost impossible, for the individuals within the society.

2.3.2 Customary Law Terminology

The conceptual analysis of the terminology that has been used in the customary law approach is considerable, especially when it deals with criminal matters. Without understanding the accurate meaning and power of these terms in the context of Afghanistan, it would be impossible to understand the reality of customary law and its function in Afghanistan. Terms such as *Pashtunwali,*[77] *ghayra,*[78] *tasali,*[79] *peghur,*[80] *nenawāti,*[81] *peshaimāni,*[82] *bakhshish,*[83] *sharmendah,*[84] *shram,*[85] and so on represent particular values and carry specific meanings in the context of Afghanistan that may or may not be found in other cultures. Although these terms may

[77] *Pashtunwali*: A collection of admirable behaviors of a true Pashtun that are accepted by most Pashtuns. A true Pashtun is not only to speak Pashto, but he has to behave according to those norms that are accepted as the main characteristics for a Pashtun. Pashtun must practice Pashto according to the ethical principles and its code of conduct.

[78] *Ghayra*: it is usually translated as zeal, but the concept of ghayra in the context of Afghanistan has a much deeper meaning and covers a much wider concept. It refers to any kind of sensitivities to those values that are accepted in society. This feeling may not be rational or according to Islamic principles, but people's reaction is very strong. For instance, an outsider knowing the names of female family members is not against Islam because the names of Prophet Mohammad's wives and daughters are widely known and Islam has no prohibition on disclosing Muslim family members' name. However, if an Afghan female's name is disclosed publicly, it can cause a big problem in society, especially in rural areas of Afghanistan.

[79] *Tasali*: in English, it may refer to consolation, but in Afghanistan it means making the victim and his family calm and convincing the victim or losing party to forgive or ignore the offenders.

[80] The term *peghur* in English may be translated to irony, scoff, taunt, jeer, etc. But it has a strong effect; an Afghan is made to feel *peghur* because of something that happened. To avoid *peghur*, most Afghans, especially Pashtuns, act very strongly and sometimes put themselves at high risk to be not subject to *peghur*.

[81] *Nenawati*: This is a Pashtun custom where a group of elders, including the criminal's family, go to the victim's family and ask for forgiveness. More often, female relatives of the criminal (mother, sister, and wife) play a significant role in this process by going to the victim's family to express their apologies to help make the victim's family ready for forgiveness.

[82] In English, it may refer to regret or being sorry.

[83] The proper translation of this term in English would be Forgiveness.

[84] Ashamed: This term carries a stronger meaning in the context of Afghanistan than its translation in English.

[85] In English, the term shame could be a better translation for this term.

appear simple, the impact and shared societal meanings of these terms are much stronger than any translation can convey.

For instance, in a serious criminal case, the wrongdoer's close family members, along with religious leaders (*mullā imām*) and respected members of the community, go to the victim's family and ask for *bakhshish* (forgiveness). If the wrongdoer publicly announces that he is really *sharmendah* (shamefully remorseful) because of the crime he committed, the victim's party will be convinced to forgive the criminal and there will be no revenge or punishment, like prison or execution, even in a murder case. This approach repairs the reputation of the victim's family and proves that although they have the power to take revenge or punish the wrongdoer, they forgive him and respect the religious and community leaders to keep harmony in the society. This act (forgiveness) will reward the victim's family with more prestige and respect. Consequently, asking for forgiveness publicly makes the victim's family at peace; they will not think about revenge, and the problem will be solved between the two parties, which benefits the entire community.

2.3.3 Decision-Makers

Customary law decision-makers usually consist of elders, religious, and tribal leaders who have a strong spiritual and moral influence on society, so others obey their decisions. The members usually make decisions based on the standards and norms accepted by the majority of the community members. It is very difficult for community members to go against the elders' and religious leaders' decisions, even though sometimes the decisions may include some violations of Sharia or state law. The elders and religious leaders have earned this power and position through their life experience and the trust they have gained over the years through their public service and hard work in resolving community problems. The decision-making process for them is not easy; they have to build trust and meet people's expectations in terms of justice when they resolve a dispute. Not all elders have the capability to be a part of the decision-making in a *Jirga* or *shūrā*, and they must prove that they are fair, impartial, and benevolent in their decisions. Indeed, the author has personally witnessed one of these decision-makers declining to attend a dinner party because it was held by an individual who had a dispute with one of his colleagues. He declined to attend the dinner party because his colleague would not trust him if they asked him to resolve their dispute. So these characteristics of the decision-makers build trust among people and convince them that the decision will be made fairly and impartially to the benefit of the parties and society.

Mediation and arbitration are the main methods of solving disputes under customary law in Afghanistan, generally implemented by experienced religious leaders *ʿulamāʾ* elders *Reesh Safedān* and, recently, powerful people of the community (or *warlords*). Although customary law may permit violations of some principle of human rights, especially women's rights, Islamic law, and state law, but the time and cost effectiveness, accessibility, inclusion of indigenous values in the decisions, along with the perception of less corrupt procedures than formal procedure system, make the majority (more than 80%)[86] of Afghan citizens utilize customary law when they have a legal issue.[87] The Supreme Court of Afghanistan, however, disagrees with the above statistics released by the Ministry of Justice and national and international organizations and claims that a smaller number of cases are resolved through the customary law approach and, instead, most cases are resolved by official courts.[88]

2.3.4 Legal Issues as Social Problems

Jirga members usually deal with the issue as a social problem, not as a legal case. Most of the elders of a community feel responsible to try to resolve the dispute and bring harmony back to society. Usually, they deal with the problem in the light of common customs to guarantee that the decision would be acceptable for the parties. Thus, in most cases, including serious criminal cases, there is no punishment involved. Instead, they use a restorative justice approach. The Jirga members' goal is to convince and appease the parties and bring synchronization back to the community. In many cases, they order compensation from the offender, and they avoid calling it punishment. To guarantee the implementation of the decision of the Jirga, they mostly use financial punishments against the parties who violate Jirga decisions.[89]

In Afghanistan, in accordance with customary law principles, it is reasonable to compensate or pay the victim rather than punish the offender because most families have only one source of financial support: the man who works on the land or does business; the rest of the family members rely on his income, and even if a woman has wealth, it would be difficult for her to buy things or do business alone without a man from her family. Therefore, for example, in a murder case, putting the wrongdoer in prison for a long time will not help the offended party with their needs. In contrast, paying compensation in the form of cash or a piece of land by the wrongdoer will be a reasonable solution to help the offended party in terms of having support for their family's future.

---

[86]The United States Institute of Peace (2014), p. 42.

[87]Hashimi SM (2015) Advisory Workshop Regarding Field Assessment Report. Ministry of Justice of Afghanistan. http://moj.gov.af/fa/news/38308 Accessed 12 Dec 2015.

[88]Interview with Dr. Abdul Malik Kamawi (Member of the Supreme Court of Afghanistan). May, 17, 2017.

[89]The International Legal Foundation (2004) The Customary Law of Afghanistan. http://theilf.org/news/publications/ Accessed 24 Aug 2017.

The rate of literacy is very low in remote areas of the country; it is very close to 0% among Afghan female villagers.[90] The men usually work outside, and the women are in charge of indoor activities. Speaking generally, it is customary in villages that women cannot go outside without a male family member companion. It is not an exaggeration to say that most, if not all, women in remote parts of Afghanistan would not be able to find their house if they traveled alone 10 km away from their residential area. In such a culture, if we assume that a man with a wife and four children injured or killed another man of the same family size, there are two choices: first, go to the police and prosecute the offender and send him to jail; second, the elders would step in and solve the problem according to customary law.

With the first choice, if the offender is put in jail, the problem will be solved temporarily and the victim's family will still take revenge when he is released from jail. In such a case, in fact, both women and their children are punished more than the wrongdoer. The wrongdoer will have food, shelter, and a safe place in jail, but the two families will suffer more and be in a much worse situation with no food and safe place because they will not have anyone to support them, and it would be difficult for them to go out for work. In contrast, the second choice will make the offender apologize and convince the victim's family to forgive him, and then he must pay enough money or a piece of land or a couple of animals to the victim's family so that they could have financial help. Aside from that, he must work hard and support his family as well.

In a country like Afghanistan with a high level of corruption, especially in the judicial sector, people do not trust the legal system to bring justice; it is hard for the victim to accept the court's decision, remain calm, and not think about revenge. Moreover, there is no welfare system to support the families and provide food, shelter, or care for the families of either the victims or wrongdoers. There are additional reasons, including expenses, lost time, lack of guaranteed justice, and lack of access to courts and law enforcement institutions, for many Afghans to rely on customary law instead of formal law. It is beyond the scope of this work to touch upon all the factors that make people want to resolve their legal issues and seek justice through customary law systems, but these examples shed some light on why this is a complicated issue in Afghanistan.

Otto states that from the point of anthropology, studies prove that at a community level, people do not differentiate between religious principles and local and tribal customs. In an Islamic traditional society, most community members, even religious leaders, neglect the clear border between Sharia and customs, and they practice them jointly without any contradiction.[91] This is exactly what happens in cases in Afghanistan.

---

[90] UNESCO (2016) Enhancement of Literacy in Afghanistan. https://uil.unesco.org/case-study/effective-practices-database-litbase-0/enhancement-literacy-afghanistan-afghanistan Accessed 20 Aug 2017.

[91] Otto (2008), p. 30.

Most Afghans, especially in remote areas, think that there is no conflict between their customs and Sharia; however, sometimes there is a conflict between customary law norms and practice and the Sharia principles.[92] For example, sometimes Afghans practice *bad*[93] to resolve disputes, especially in serious criminal cases. There is no doubt that this practice violates the Quran[94] and state law,[95] as well as international human rights principles, because the principle of personal criminal responsibility has been authorized by the Quran and national and international laws, but the decision-makers in the customary law system do not think there is any conflict between these two approaches. For example, women's issues are very sensitive and highly serious in the Afghan community. In accordance with the customs of most Afghans, the name of female family members is treated as a secret matter and should not be publicized, but there is not a single source in Sharia that prohibits naming a Muslim female publicly. In fact, people know the names of the female family members—mothers, sisters, wives, and daughters—of Prophet Mohammad and his successors and companions, and they could be shared publicly. Nevertheless, according to the customs of most Afghans, others should not know their female family members' names, and they must not share them with others.

On the other hand, there are some simple issues that are not considered a violation of Islamic law but people take seriously and react strongly against based on customs. The most concrete example is divorce in the context of Afghanistan. Divorce is legal in Islam, but based on the custom of most Afghans, it is considered a big shame on the wife's family and they are not happy if their daughter is divorced. Even in cases of domestic violence, the wife usually is advised to be patient and tolerate the situation rather than ask for a divorce. Most Afghans are very sensitive about divorce; in the majority of the country, the wife's family would prefer their daughter to be killed rather than divorced. Divorce brings shame on the husband and his family as well. If an Afghan man divorces his wife, people will blame him based on *ghayra* (zeal) and consider him not a zealous man because an integral part of being a zealous man in Afghanistan is to have total control over the female members of his family, especially his wife. If he divorces his wife, it means that he cannot control his

---

[92] Center for Strategic & International Studies (2015) Why Are customary Pashtun Laws and Ethics Causes for Concern? https://www.csis.org/blog/why-are-customary-pashtun-laws-and-ethics-causes-concern. Accessed 23 Oct 2015.

[93] In *bad,* instead of punishing the criminal, one or more women of the blamed party must be given to the victim's family as a servant or bride to compensate for the crime.

[94] The Quran in five different places says (لَا تَزِرُ وَازِرَةٌ وِزْرَ أُخْرَىٰ) Sura al- Anʿām (6: 164), Sura al-Isrāʾ (17: 15), Sura Fāṭir (35: 18), Sura al-Zumar (39: 7), Sura al-Najm (53: 38)/ The Constitution of Afghanistan (2004) Art. 27/ The Penal Code of Afghanistan (1976) Art. 3.

[95] The Constitution of Afghanistan (2004) Art. 26: "Crime is a personal act. Investigation, arrest and detention of an accused as well as penalty execution shall not incriminate another person." Also, the Penal Code of Afghanistan says: "No one can be punished, but in accordance with the provisions of the law, which has been enforced before commitment of the act under reference," Penal Code of Afghanistan (1976) Art. 3.

wife and he will be considered *beghayra*[96] or even *dayyūth*,[97] an act of not being zealous.

Under Afghan customary norms, a woman having a sexual relationship without a marriage contract could be enough reason for her to be killed. If a woman talks or spends time even privately with an unrelated man, it is considered a serious crime and can warrant severe punishment. It is worth noting that usually in the countryside, and sometimes even in big cities, if a woman is walking alone outside her house, she will be accused of not being a good woman because she should not go out without the company of a male family member. If there is no man available to go out with her, she may go out with a child. These cultural norms provide justification for Afghan courts to punish women who have contact with strangers or run away with them. Even though in accordance with Sharia, particularly the Ḥanafī school of thought, young women have the right to choose their husbands, it is not acceptable in Afghan society for a woman to implement this Sharia provision in her life. Afghan customary norms therefore easily accept the punishment of women who violate these cultural standards even if their actions do not violate formal law or Sharia.[98]

2.4 State Law (*Qānūn*)

In Afghanistan, *qānūn* refers to laws that have been passed by both houses of the National Assembly and endorsed by the President.[99] Historically, the application of state law was started by Amir ʿAbd al-RaḤmān's government (1880–1901) when judges were put on the state payroll.[100] During his government, judges started to work full time in offices just like other governmental staff; previously, according to Islamic jurisprudence, they had been allowed to hold court sessions in their houses or in mosques.[101] This was the first step to regulate judges' activities and limit their place and free working time, like other state employees. In 1885, for the first time, a manual for Afghan judges, called *Asās al-Qużāt*, was enacted.[102] This manual had 136 articles based on Ḥanafī school provisions and was intended as guidance for judges in making their judgments. Amir ʿAbd al-RaḤmān also established a madrasa (religious school) and hired famous Islamic scholars (*ʿulamāʾ*) to train students in Islamic sciences and prepare them to serve in courts. Additionally, these scholars

[96]*Be ghayra* refers to a person, who is not zealous about his reputation or his family members.

[97]*Dayyūth* is an Arabic term and it means cuckold. This term is more insulting than the first one.

[98]The Independent Commission of Human Rights of Afghanistan, A Special Report, available at http://www.aihrc.org.af/fa/research-reports/1570/qatle-namosi-kholasa-gozarish.html accessed Oct, 5, 2017.

[99]The Constitution of Afghanistan (2004) Art. 94.

[100]Barfield (2003), p. 1.

[101]Alukūzay (1885), p. 26.

[102]Ghubār (2015), p. 840; Farhang (1992), p. 431.

started to write a book of fatwas under the title *Żiyā' al-Aḥkām*, but Amir ʿAbd al-RaḤmān Khān died before its completion.[103] This is considered to be the primary phase of judicial reform in Afghanistan.

After Amir ʿAbd al-RaḤmān Khān, his son, Amir Ḥabībāllāh Khān, came into power from 1901 to 1919 and continued his father's judicial reform. In his era, Sharia, more specifically the Ḥanafī school of thought, continued to be the main source of law and religious scholars served as judges; courts continued to use Ḥanafī jurisprudence as a legal source for their decisions. Part of his legal reform was to change the classical modes of punishment to imprisonment. He issued a legislative decree for police officers (*Kutwāly*) and prison guards, stating that they should follow the new method of punishment rather than the old one. The decree said: *After this time, November 9, 1912, blinding and cutting of ears or hands is prohibited. Instead of blinding, the convict should be punished by 12 years imprisonment, instead of cutting of an ear, the convict should be punished by 6 years imprisonment and instead of amputation of a hand, the convict should be punished with 10-year imprisonment.*[104] At that time, it was common to punish convicted people differently based on their personality and the will of the ruler or prison officers. This decree is considered the first action toward regulating the form of punishment for convicts, which imposed imprisonment in place of physical punishments.

Amir Ḥabībāllāh Khān also established a research center for Islamic sciences, called *Bayt al-ʿulūm mubāraka Ḥabībiyya* (the Ḥabībiyya Holy House of Sciences), where Islamic scholars could research Islamic legal issues. Additionally, he completed the fatwa book, which had been started by his father, Amir ʿAbd al-RaḤmān Khān, and renamed it *Sarāj al-Aḥkām fī Māmelāt al-Islām*. This fatwa book was published in four volumes. The first volume contained a code of conduct for judges, *Ādāb al-Qāḍī*. The second volume is about witnesses; the third is about the legal profession, *Wakāla*; and the last volume, *Daʿwa*, concerns civil claims and lawsuits.[105]

During this period, there was also a council of *ʿulamā'*, composed of 50 persons working under ten famous Islamic scholars. They were in charge of testing candidates to be hired as judges and *Muftis*[106] in courts. They were also in charge of reviewing laws (*Niẓām Nāma*)[107] and lower court decisions in serious cases and of

---

[103] Hussami (2009), p. 38.

[104] Ghubār (2015), p. 915.

[105] Wakily Popalzaey (1990), p. 399.

[106] Mufti is an Arabic term that refers to a scholar who issues fatwas (nonbinding legal opinions) for people regarding their legal questions. The difference between a judge and Mufti is that a judge's decision is binding and Mufti's opinion is not. In accordance with the Islamic law principles, the Mufti must have a certain level of knowledge of the primary and secondary sources of Islamic law and shall be aware of the principles that make them capable to formulate legal opinions from the sources.

[107] *Niẓām Nāma* was a term that was used at a time in state laws. Because of the use of Sharia principles as law and the sensitivity of people when it comes to the term Qānūn (law), they used the

carrying out research on legal issues according to the Ḥanafī school of jurisprudence. In addition, for the first time, an explanatory book, listing 99 legal maxims for the use of judges, was published, written by a famous scholar, Mawlānā Abdul Razāq.[108] These sources were an important part of the judicial reform and had a significant impact on the judges at that time.

Amir Amānallāh Khān, the son of Amir Ḥabīballāh Khān, continued the legal reforms of his father and grandfather and adopted more than 50 laws and regulations, also called *Niẓām Nāma*.[109] During his reign, Afghanistan's first Constitution, called *Niẓām Nāma Asāsī Dawlat Aleyah Afghānistān*, consisting of 73 articles, was passed in 1923. That Constitution announced Islam as the official religion of the state and the Ḥanafī school of thought as the main source of law.[110] Amir Amānallāh Khān's time is considered the era of the modernization of the legal system and the codification of Sharia, and his approach to legal reform in Afghanistan has been continued until now.

Many scholars maintain that the previous governments used the term *Niẓām Nāma* instead of law *Qānūn* because of the sensitivity of the latter among the Afghan people.[111] Mahmood Tarzee, in his article *Qawanīn wa Niẓamāt* ("Laws and Regulations") claims that all the terms that have been used in legal documents, such as *Qānūn*, *Niẓām*, *Ḥudūd*, *Sharʿ*, *Dastūr* al-*ʿAmal*, and so on, are almost the same. Both *Qānūn* and *Niẓām Nāma* were created to regulate the relationship between the state and its citizens, as well as their life. Thus, it was necessary to explain the term *Qānūn* along with other common legal terms.[112]

In Afghanistan, state law, especially procedural law, is influenced by western laws. On the other hand, substantive state law is primarily rooted in Sharia, particularly in the Ḥanafī school of thought. For example, the current Civil Code is almost an exact translation of some Ḥanafī classical books.[113] However, in particular cases, some provisions of laws are based on other schools of thought, rather than the Hanafi School, because they have been considered as a preferable solution to the situation.

---

term *Niẓām Nāma*. At that time, people were thinking that canon (law) is an imported term from the western countries and does not have roots in Islam, so the government used a different terminology.

[108] Hussami (2009), pp. 41–42.

[109] Farhang (1992), p. 545. These Niẓām Nāmas are available at http://www.moj.gov.af/content/files/egov/Nezamnama.htm also at Afghanistan Digital Library available at http://afghanistandl.nyu.edu/index.html.

[110] Niẓām Nāma Asāsī Dawlat Aleyah Afghānistān (1923) Art. 2.

[111] In Afghanistan, most people do not like the term "Qānūn" and believe that it is something against Sharia and came from western countries where people follow other religions (Christianity or Judaism). Therefore, the rulers did not use the term Qānūn; instead, they used the term Niẓām Nāma to avoid any misunderstanding and to decrease the level of sensitivity of the people to this term.

[112] Tarzee (1919).

[113] Interview with Judge Abdul Aziz (retired member of the Supreme Court). Dated 15 August 2015.

One example of reliance on a different school of thought is Article 327 of Afghanistan's 1977 Civil Code, which addresses the issue of what happens when a wife's husband is lost (*mafqūd*) and there is no evidence to prove whether he is alive or dead. Article 327, is borrowed from the Mālikī school of thought, provides that a wife should wait four years for her lost husband, but after four years, she can remarry.[114] Had Afghanistan relied on the Ḥanafī school of thought, the wife should be waiting for 90 years or 120 years (the length of time it would take for all villagers of his same age to die a natural death) for her husband to be considered deceased, to be permitted to remarry, and for her husband's inheritance to be distributed among his inheritors.[115]

Article 2182 of Afghanistan's Civil Code provides another example when a child's father had died but the grandfather is still alive. According to the Ḥanafī school, the child cannot receive an inheritance from his grandfather because a grandchild cannot receive inheritance directly from his grandparent. Instead, the Civil Code accepted *Ibn Ḥazm al-Ẓāhirī's* idea of inheritance. Article 2182 of the Civil Code says:

> If the deceased does not make a will for descendant of his son who died when the deceased was alive or had died, really or legally, simultaneously with the deceased, on an amount equal to the share to which the mentioned son would have been entitled had he been alive at the time of his death, a will for the mentioned descendant, proportionate to the mentioned amount of entitlement, within the limits of one third of the inheritance, shall be obligatory, provided that the descendant is not and heir and that the deceased, when alive, did not gratuitously give him a property by another action that was proportionate to the obligatory portion. If he gave him the property but it is less than the obligatory share, he shall be entitled, through obligatory will, to an amount that will complete the mentioned share.[116]

In these situations, Afghan courts apply the state laws, which were written according to *Ibn Ḥazm's* opinion, not the Ḥanafī doctrine.

In Afghanistan today, state law is applied in the official courts, where the central government has authority and power. The central government wants to control all areas of the legal system and to exclude other legal actors from playing a role. According to the 2004 Afghan Constitution, the authority of the judiciary covers all cases filed by natural or legal persons, including the state, whether as plaintiffs or defendants, before the courts in accordance with the provisions of law.[117] The Constitution draws a clear red line as regards the court's jurisdiction and limits the power of other organs to remove any case from the judiciary:

> No law shall, under any circumstances, exclude any case or area from the jurisdiction of the judicial organ as defined in this chapter and submit it to another authority. . .[118]

[114]The Civil Code of Afghanistan (1976) Art. 327.

[115]ʿAlāʾ al-Dīn (1986), p. 59.

[116]The Civil Code of Afghanistan (1976) Art. 2182.

[117]The Constitution of Afghanistan (2004) Art.120/ Law on Organization and Jurisdiction of the Judiciary Branch of Islamic Republic of Afghanistan (2013) Art. 8.

[118]The Constitution of Afghanistan (2004) Art. 122/ Law on Organization and Jurisdiction of the Judiciary Branch of Islamic Republic of Afghanistan (2013) Art. 8.

Afghan courts must apply the provisions of the Constitution and other laws to all cases under consideration.[119] In addition, courts must specify the reasons for their judgment when they make a decision. The Constitution says:

> In issuing decision, the court is obligated to state the reason for its verdict. . . .[120]

Since the late nineteenth and early twentieth centuries, Afghan rulers have tried to codify Islamic jurisprudence, especially the provisions of the Ḥanafī school of thought, and apply it through state-trained judges.[121] However, there are some signs of recklessness against the dominating role of Sharia in the legal system of Afghanistan during the reign of Amir Amānallāh Khān[122] (1918–1929) and the Communist party regime (1978–1991). Thus, during the drafting of the 2004 Constitution, the state leaders faced a strong reaction from the nation, which insisted that all laws must be in compline with Islam. Therefore, the principle of conformity and compatibility of all state laws with Islamic principles was accepted in the Afghan legal system.[123]

Although some provisions of the 2004 Afghan Constitution may appear paradoxical[124] and demonstrate an embodiment of legal pluralism, historically state law has always tried to play a dominating role over other sources of law in Afghanistan. Generally, to design a state law, there are three major models in Islamic countries to reconcile between the Sharia principles and state law, and it could provide an answer to the potential paradox in the 2004 Constitution of Afghanistan.[125] In the case of Afghanistan, particularly the 2004 Constitution, the first model is practical and closer to reality on the ground.

---

[119] Law on Organization and Jurisdiction of the Judiciary Branch of Islamic Republic of Afghanistan (2013) Art. 13.

[120] The Constitution of Afghanistan (2004) Art. 129/ Law on Organization and Jurisdiction of the Judiciary Branch of Islamic Republic of Afghanistan (2013) Art. 12.

[121] Barfield (2003), p. 2.

[122] King Amānallāh Khān wanted to quickly modernize and started reforming the legal system of the country by adopting the first Constitution. He also expanded womens' rights and gave women more opportunities to enhance their capability to be more active in society. The religious leaders stood against him, which finally collapsed his regime.

[123] The Constitution of Afghanistan (2004) Art. 3.

[124] For example, Article 3 of the Constitution states: "No law shall contravene the tenets and provisions of the holy religion of Islam in Afghanistan." In contrast, Article 7 of the Constitution says: "The state shall observe the United Nations Charter, inter-state agreements, as well as international treaties to which Afghanistan has joined, and the Universal Declaration of Human Rights. The state shall prevent all kinds of terrorist activities, cultivation and smuggling of narcotics, and production and use of intoxicants." Obviously, there are some provisions in these international documents that contradict Islamic principles. For instance, Articles 16 and 18 of the Universal Declaration of Human Rights provide the right to have freedom of marriage and the right to free choice of religion, respectively; however, both of these rights face some issues in Islam.

[125] Layish (2004), p. 98.

2.4.1 Judicial System in Afghanistan

The Afghan Constitution guarantees judicial independence and indicates the composition and hierarchy of courts. The Constitution states as follows:

> The Judiciary shall be an independent organ of the state of the Islamic Republic of Afghanistan. The Judiciary shall be comprised of one Supreme Court, Courts of Appeal as well as Primary Courts whose organization and authority shall be regulated by law. The Supreme Court shall be the highest judicial organ, heading the judicial power of the Islamic Republic of Afghanistan.[126]

In accordance with the above article, there are three types of courts in Afghanistan: primary courts, appellate courts, and a supreme court. The Supreme Court is the highest judicial authority and an independent organ of the state. Initially, all legal cases are adjudicated in the primary courts; cases can be appealed and reviewed by the appellate courts or Supreme Court. The Supreme Court is based in Kabul city, the appellate courts are located in the center of the provinces, and the primary courts are located in the center of cities and districts.[127]

Based on Article 117 of the Constitution, the Supreme Court is composed of nine members who are appointed by the President with the endorsement of the House of People. The Supreme Court justices are appointed for a period of 10 years and cannot be dismissed till the end of their term,[128] with the exception of conditions stated in Article 127 of the Constitution.[129]

The Supreme Court justices shall not be less than 40 years of age; shall not have been convicted by a court of any crime against humanity, a felony, or deprivation of civil rights; and shall not be a member of any political party during his term of duty. Furthermore, the justices must be a citizen of Afghanistan, have higher education in legal studies or Islamic jurisprudence; and have adequate experience in the judicial

---

[126]The Constitution of Afghanistan (2004) Art. 116.

[127]Law on Organization and Jurisdiction of the Judiciary Branch (2013) Art. 5.

[128]The Constitution of Afghanistan (2004) Art. 117: "The Supreme Court shall be comprised of nine members, appointed by the President and with the endorsement of the House of People, and in observance of the provisions of clause three of Article Fifty as well as Article One Hundred Eighteen of this Constitution, shall be initially appointed in the following manner: Three members for a period of four years, three members for seven years, and three members for ten years. Later appointments shall be for a period of ten years. Appointment of members for a second term shall not be permitted. The President shall appoint one of its members as Chief Justice of the Supreme Court. Members of the Supreme Court, except under circumstances stated in Article One Hundred Twenty Seven of this Constitution, shall not be dismissed till the end of their term."

[129]The Constitution of Afghanistan (2004) Art. 127: "If more than one third of the members of the House of People demand the trial of the Chief Justice of the Supreme Court or any of its members accused of a crime related to job performance or committing a crime, and, the House of People approves this demand by two thirds majority of all members, the accused shall be dismissed and the issue referred to a special court. The formation of the court and procedure of the trial shall be regulated by law."

system of Afghanistan.[130] The Supreme Court justices must take an oath in front of the President before they take office.[131]

The Supreme Court has the power to adjudicate all cases involving natural or legal persons. The Constitution provides: "The authority of the judicial organ shall include consideration of all cases filed by real or incorporeal persons, including the state, as plaintiffs or defendants, before the court in accordance with the provisions of the law."[132] The Constitution gives power to the judiciary to hear all cases that are brought to the courts. Principally, the Supreme Court has the authority to review decisions of the lower courts, resolve issues concerning the jurisdiction of courts, and transfer a case from one court to another upon the request of the Attorney General's Office or one of the parties based on justifiable reasons. In addition, the Supreme Court has the authority to have careful scrutiny on the lower courts' inquiries to provide further explanation and interpretation of the law to have a unified process of the cases and the lower courts. Putting judges on trial in case of commission of crimes related to their duties and the enactment of regulations, bills, and guidance are also under the power of the Supreme Court.[133] The Supreme Court High Council is composed of Supreme Court justices and is considered the highest body in the judiciary in the country.[134] The Supreme Court has five divisions, namely public criminal division, public security division, public law and civil division, commercial law division, and military crime division. For each division, the Supreme Court High Council appoints one of the justices to act as chairperson.[135]

Also, the Supreme Court has the power to check the constitutionality of laws, legislative decrees, and international laws based on the request of the government and lower courts. The Constitution indicates:

> At the request of the Government or courts, the Supreme Court shall review the laws, legislative decrees, international treaties as well as international covenants for their compliance with the Constitution and their interpretation in accordance with the law.[136]

Although the above article guarantees the power of judicial review by the Supreme Court, the history of the Constitutional Drafting Committee (CDC) shows an intention to establish a constitutional court with a judicial review power; however, that chapter was eliminated from the final draft, and Article 121 was inserted in the chapter on the judiciary.[137] The text of the article allows the lower courts to request

[130] The Constitution of Afghanistan (2004) Art. 118.

[131] The Constitution of Afghanistan (2004) Art. 119: "In the name of God, the Most Gracious, Most Merciful, I swear in the name of God Almighty to attain justice and righteousness in accordance with tenets of the Holy religion of Islam, provisions of this Constitution as well as other laws of Afghanistan, and to execute the judicial duty with utmost honesty, righteousness and impartiality."

[132] The Constitution of Afghanistan (2004) Art. 120.

[133] Law on Organization and Jurisdiction of the Judiciary Branch (2013) Art. 31.

[134] Law on Organization and Jurisdiction of the Judiciary Branch (2013) Art. 24.

[135] Law on Organization and Jurisdiction of the Judiciary Branch (2013) Art. 42.

[136] The Constitution of Afghanistan (2004) Art. 121.

[137] Haress (2017), p. 10.

for the constitutionality of the legislation, applying to a case under consideration. Furthermore, the executive branch can also ask the Supreme Court for the constitutionality of the laws, presidential decrees, etc. Thus, based on the above article, the Supreme Court of Afghanistan has the power of both "concrete" and "abstract" review of laws and other national and international legal documents.[138]

The wording of Article 121 shows that Afghanistan has a strong type of judicial review and the Supreme Court has the final word on the constitutionality of legislation, but in practice, it represents a weak type of judicial review. A good example is the law of the Independent Commission for Overseeing the Implementation of the Constitution (ICOIC) that president Karzai based on Article 94 of the constitution sent to the Supreme Court to check the constitutionality of that law.[139] Article 94 of the Constitution says if the House of People passed law by the two-third of votes, the president has the power to send it to the Supreme Court to check its constitutionality. The Supreme Court issued an opinion regarding the ICOIC law stating that some provisions of the ICOIC law are unconstitutional, however, the parliament has not accepted the court opinion, and even the president office by itself has not respected the Supreme Court decision and sent some inquiries to ICOIC to check the constitutionality of the laws.

In Afghanistan, court sessions are held publicly and every individual has the right to attend, but courts may hold secret trials if it is expressed by law or the court considers it necessary.[140] However, in practice, only a few cases had been held publicly, and they were those that were attractive to the media and civil society. Because of security threats against judges and the participants of court sessions, the majority of cases in Afghanistan have been held semi-publicly or in private.

Every province has one appellate court, which is composed of a chief judge and heads and members of divisions.[141] Each appellate court has five divisions: public criminal law division, public security division, civil law and personal status law (*al-aḥwāl al-shakhṣiyya*) division, public law division, and commercial law division. The members of each division shall not exceed six judges.[142] However, in practice, in some cases there can be 12 judges in one division, depending on the workload. These extra judges work based on temporary employment, and especially those who

---

138 Haress (2017), p. 12.

139 The Constitution of Afghanistan (2004) Art. 94: "Law shall be what both houses of the National Assembly approve and the President endorses, unless this Constitution states otherwise. In case the President rejects what the National Assembly has approved, the President shall send it back, within fifteen days from the date it was presented to the House of People mentioning the reasons for rejection, and, with expiration of the period of fi the House of People re-approves it with two thirds of all the votes, the draft shall be considered endorsed and enforceable."

140 The Constitution of Afghanistan (2004) Art. 128.

141 Law on Organization and Jurisdiction of the Judiciary Branch (2013) Art. 52.

142 Law on Organization and Jurisdiction of the Judiciary Branch (2013) Art. 53.

are unable to go to some insecure districts, they are appointed to work in those divisions that have heavy loads of work.[143] The appellate courts have the authority to review primary courts' decisions and opinions, and based on law, they can correct, overrule, affirm, or modify said decisions.[144]

The primary courts are located in the center of each province and in each district as well. In the center of all provinces, there is a primary court called the city primary court. The city primary court has several divisions, like the public criminal law division, civil division, public law division, public security division, and traffic law division. Each division is composed of one judge as head of the division and at least two judges as members of the bench, but a division cannot have more than five judges, including the head of the division.[145] However, military cases shall be heard in special military courts that are established in each province.[146]

In addition, there are some departments of the Supreme Court that provide services such as registration of legal documents like deeds, guaranty agreements, etc. The head and professional staff of these departments are judges. In some provinces or districts where such a department has not been established, the primary courts are authorized to issue such legal documents.[147]

Generally, the court system in Afghanistan has three levels: primary, appellate, and supreme. Commonly, cases are submitted to the primary courts for adjudication and reviewed by the appellate courts and the Supreme Court. Besides this, there are some special courts regulated by separate laws that deal with crimes committed by ministers or justices of the Supreme Court, including the chief justice.[148] In case of accusations against the President, a separate procedure shall be held involving the House of Representatives and the justices of the Supreme Court, as stated in Article 69 of the Constitution.[149]

[143] Interview with Judge Nasremenallah (chief judge of the second judicial zone of Kabul). Dated 12 November 2018.

[144] Law on Organization and Jurisdiction of the Judiciary Branch (2013) Art. 54.

[145] Law on Organization and Jurisdiction of the Judiciary Branch (2013) Art. 62.

[146] Law on Organization and Jurisdiction of the Judiciary Branch (2013) Art. 77.

[147] Law on Organization and Jurisdiction of the Judiciary Branch (2013) Art. 74.

[148] Law on Structure and Jurisdiction of Special Courts (April 2014) Art. 3.

[149] The Constitution of Afghanistan (2004) Art. 69: "The President shall be responsible to the nation as well as the House of People in accordance with the provisions of this Article. Accusations of crimes against humanity, national treason as well as a crime against the President shall be demanded by one third of all members of the House of People. If this demand is approved by two thirds of the House of People, the House of People shall convene the Loya Jirga within one month. If the Loya Jirga, by two-thirds majority, approves the accusation, the President shall be released from duty and the issue shall be referred to a special court, which shall be comprised of the President of the House of Elders, three members of the House of People, and three members of the Supreme Court appointed by the Loya Jirga. The case shall be presented by the individual appointed by the Loya Jirga. In such a situation the provisions of Article Sixty-Seven of this Constitution shall be applied."

2.4.2 Legal Education in Afghanistan

Afghanistan is unique in terms of its legal education. In almost all public universities, there are two institutions that train lawyers for the justice sector. One is the Law and Political Science faculty, and the other is the Sharia faculty. However, the Supreme Court allows graduates of madrasas to get admission to the Supreme Court Stage Course.[150] It is also worthy to note that most students of the Sharia faculty are graduates of madrasas, while graduates of public schools get admission to law schools. It means that the majority of students at Sharia faculties are familiar with Sharia principles and have a background in Islamic law.

Generally, the Sharia faculty curriculum is a combination of Islamic classical texts in the Arabic language, along with some modern law courses. This structure of the curriculum has roots in the philosophy of the establishment of the faculty and the educational background of professors. The reason behind the establishment of the Sharia faculty was to provide an advanced modern study of Islamic law and positive law and train qualified Islamic scholars. Thus, most of the Sharia professors are being sent to Arabic-language-speaking countries, especially Egypt, for further studies in the field of Islamic sciences, particularly Islamic law. For instance, most of the Kabul Sharia professors in the 1960s and 1970s graduated from al-Azhar University in Cairo/Egypt, and some Egyptian professors had been teaching at the Kabul Sharia faculty prior to the Soviet Union occupation. The curriculum of the Sharia faculty echoes those of al-Azhar University *Sharia and Qānūn and Islamic Studies* faculties.[151] This kind of partnership provides an opportunity for the graduates of madrasas to continue and increase their knowledge of Islamic sciences in the Sharia faculties. Overall, the Sharia faculties in Afghanistan have somehow followed a hybrid approach of Islamic studies through a combination of contemporary Islamic thought with traditional interpretations of Islam, especially in the field of Islamic jurisprudence and studies of modern laws, which have roots in western jurisdictions. The law courses are taught by Law faculty members in local languages, but most courses in Islamic sciences are taught in Arabic languages by Sharia faculty members.

On the other hand, in the Law and Political Science faculty, the focus is mostly on positive laws that are written in local languages. Law professors mostly have backgrounds in western-style education and have graduated from American and European universities, and at the time of the communist regime of the Soviet Union. In the curriculum of the Law faculty, there are some Islamic law courses, like inheritance law, principles of Islamic jurisprudence, Islamic legal maxims, Islamic criminal law, and so on, that are being taught by Sharia faculty members in local languages.

---

[150] The Supreme Court has a special judiciary training program called (Judiciary Training Stage Course). The Sharia, Law, and the madrasa graduates attend a competitive entrance exam and only 100 people get admission to that program.

[151] Sirat (1969), p. 218.

Based on a recent study by the Asia Foundation organization,[152] most of the Sharia graduates are weak in the field of positive law and most of the law graduates have low knowledge in the field of Islamic law. Recently, the Ministry of Higher Education developed a new curriculum for Law faculties that include some new courses regarding Islamic jurisprudence to fill the gap and strengthen the weak point of the law graduates regarding Islamic law knowledge.[153]Also, the Sharia curriculum is under review, and the members of the review committee tend to add more law courses to the Sharia curriculum to respond to the needs of the justice sector in this regard.[154]

2.4.3 Who Becomes a Judge in Afghanistan?

In the judiciary of Afghanistan, there are two categories of judges: the first category includes members of the High Council of the Supreme Court, and the second category includes judges of the primary and appellate courts and the different chambers of the Supreme Court. The requirement of the first-category judges has been discussed previously, but with regard to the second-category judges, the Constitution gives power to the Supreme Court to propose the appointment of judges, which shall be approved by the President. The Constitution provides:

> Judges are appointed at the proposal of the Supreme Court and approval of the President.
>
> Appointment, transfer, promotion, punishment and proposals for retirement of judges, carried out according to provisions of the laws, shall be within the authority of the Supreme Court. To better regulate judicial as well as judicial administrative matters and attain necessary reforms, the Supreme Court shall establish the Office of General Administration of the Judiciary.[155]

The appointment of all judges, except the Supreme Court High Council members, shall be proposed by the Supreme Court to the President, and they shall become judges after the President's approval. However, there are other processes and administrative activities that are under the authority of the Supreme Court, which is regulated by the Law on Organization and Jurisdiction of Judiciary.

[152]Interview with Dr. Taqi Munaqebi (legal advisor for Asia Foundation in Kabul) and Dr. Munir Ahmad Azizi (the focal point of Asia Foundation for Ministry of Higher Education) regarding Law and Sharia faculties' curriculum development program, December 2019.

[153]The new law faculties' curriculum has been reviewed and developed in several meetings of law faculties' members from most law faculties at public and private universities and submitted the final draft of a unified curriculum for approval of MoHE on 6 Feb 2019.

[154]I am a member of both, law and Sharia faculties' curriculum reviewing committee and most of the Sharia faculty members are in favor of adding more law courses in the Sharia faculty curriculum to cover the weakness of Sharia graduates in terms of positive laws.

[155]The Constitution of Afghanistan (2004) Art. 132.

With respect to the qualifications of judges and the requirements for being a judge, the Constitution refers them to the specific law. The Constitution says:

> With respect to the provisions of this Constitution, statutes related to the formation, authority, as well as proceedings of courts and matters related to judges, shall be regulated by law.[156]

It is to be noted that drafting a law must be made by the executive or legislative, but exceptionally, the Supreme Court is authorized to draft a law related to the regulation of the judiciary. The Constitution says that "[t]he proposal for drafting laws shall be made by the Government or members of the Notional Assembly or, in the domain of regulating the judiciary, by the Supreme Court, through the Government. . . ."[157]

The Constitution authorizes the Supreme Court to draft a law that regulates the judiciary's activities. This provision of the Constitution guarantees the independence of the judiciary in terms of self-regulation, its jurisdiction, and other internal activities.

First, the Law on Organization and Jurisdiction of Judiciary defines a judge as a person who carries a certificate of judgment (*Insilāk*)[158] and adjudicates cases and makes judgments in accordance with law.[159] Furthermore, the requirements and qualifications for obtaining the judgment certificate are listed in Article 81 of the Law on Organization and Jurisdiction of Judiciary. The conditions have been listed below:

1. Having at least 10 year of citizenship of Afghanistan while gaining the certificate.
2. Not being convicted of felony or intentional misdemeanor by an authorized court.
3. Having a BA or higher degree from Sharia or Law faculties or a certificate from public religious secondary schools (madrasas) or equivalent institutions.
4. Not being infected with any contagious diseases or a kind of disability that prevents him/her from normal work.
5. Completion of the age of 23 at maximum.
6. Successfully completion of the Judicial Stage Course.
7. When the number of qualified applicants exceeds the number of vacancies available, the Supreme Court may add more conditions for its admission. Those who already got the Judgment certificate before this law became in acted; they are exempt from the No 6 clause.[160]

The text of Article 81 in most Laws on Organization and Jurisdiction of the Judiciary enacted in different periods looks almost the same, but if one looks deeper to the text of the current law, there are some changes that should be taken under consideration. For example, the third clause of the above article indicates the legal

[156] The Constitution of Afghanistan (2004) Art. 123.

[157] The Constitution of Afghanistan (2004) Art. 92.

[158] *Insilāk* is a certificate, which is signed by the President and officially authorizes judges to adjudicate cases in the court.

[159] Law on Organization and Jurisdiction of the Judiciary (2013) Art.4, clause 16.

[160] Law on Organization and Jurisdiction of the Judiciary (2013) Official Gazette No 1109, Art. 81.

background of the judges as a requirement and gives priority to Sharia graduates, while previous Laws on Organization and Jurisdiction of Judiciary put Law faculty graduates first.[161] For example, Laws on Organization and Jurisdiction of Judiciary enacted in 1965, 1967, 1981, 1989, 1991, and 2005 prioritize law graduates Sharia graduates. Furthermore, the Law on Organization and Jurisdiction of Judiciary enacted in 1981 indicates that besides the graduates of three institutions (law faculty, Sharia faculty, and madrasa) law and Sharia faculty members, clerks of the courts, professional staff of Attorney General Office, and professional staff of law department at Ministry of justice, are qualified to become a judge if they have worked consecutively for 10 years in the mentioned organizations.[162] That provision relied upon the 10-year work experience of laypeople without a legal background. Those staff members could be high school graduates without any law degree, or they might not even have graduated from high school at all because at that time, some graduates of secondary schools were appointed as members of staff in governmental institutions.

Also, graduates of madrasas[163] are considered equivalent to Sharia and law school graduates in terms of getting admission to the Supreme Court Judiciary Training Program (Stage Course). Historically, madrasas have played a significant role in the legal education of Afghanistan.[164] According to Abdul Satar Sirat,[165] for many decades, Islamic education doctrines have been considered the foundation of official education in Afghanistan. *Dār al-ʿUlūm ʿArabī* was the first official madrasa that was established in Kabul during King Ẓāhir Shāh, and later many other madrasas were established in different parts of the country.[166] Furthermore, Sirat indicates that religious traditions and customs were the foundation of the Afghan legal system some decades ago. Religious men received training in regional Islamic centers in India, including the current Pakistan and central Asia, such as Bukhara, Samarqand, Tashkent, etc. Most of these graduates from madrasas have been working as judges (*Qāḍī*) in courts.[167]

Currently, in Afghanistan, there are two types of madrasas: one is run by the government and operating under the Ministry of Education of Afghanistan, and the second type is the private madrasas that get support from the community. The Ministry of Education (MoE) has a separate department for religious education

[161] All Laws on Organization and Jurisdiction of the Judiciary enacted in 1965, 1967, 1981, 1989, 1991, and 2005 gave priority to law graduates rather than Sharia graduates.

[162] Law on Organization and Jurisdiction of the Judiciary (1981) Official Gazette No 479, Art. 105, clause 3.

[163] Madrasa is a religious high school with a more focused curriculum on classical Islamic sources.

[164] Williams (1981–1982), p. 249.

[165] Prof. Abdul Satar Sirat, dean of the Sharia faculty at Kabul University (1960–1969) and a former Minister of Justice, chief justice, and special advisor to the Prime Minister of Afghanistan (1969–1973).

[166] Sirat (1969), p. 217.

[167] Sirat (1968), p. 569.

and provides financial and logistical support for around 1200 madrasas; also, around 200 private madrasas are covered by the support.[168] This department provides curriculum and books for these madrasas, which are supported by the government like other public schools. The curriculum of these madrasas is a combination of classical Islamic sources and some modern subjects, like chemistry, physics, biology, literature, etc.

The private madrasas get support from the community and do not follow the exact curriculum of the Ministry of Education (MoE). In these private madrasas, religious leaders like mullahs[169] and *mawlawī*,[170] who are usually prayer leaders (imams) in mosques of communities, teach students (Ṭālibān). The focus of these types of madrasas is mostly on religious classical books and no modern science subjects. According to Mawlawī Saiqali, there are more than 5000 private madrasas in the country.[171] This illustrates that the madrasas have played a significant role in the legal system of Afghanistan, specifically in the judicial branch.

Besides madrasas, two separate institutions (Sharia and Law faculties) also train judges and lawyers. This parallel system of legal education causes ambiguity in the path of legal training and sometimes causes competition between these two faculties and their graduates in getting sources from the government and other institutions. Statistics show that most of the Sharia graduates serve in the judiciary, and the majority of Law faculty graduates become prosecutors and get jobs at the General Attorney Office. To have a clear picture of the role of Sharia in the judiciary of Afghanistan, it would be worthy to look at the Supreme Court members' short biography and judges' educational backgrounds to find out the legal knowledge base of the professional staff of the judiciary.

2.4.4 Short Biography of the Supreme Court Justices in Post-Taliban Judiciary

The Supreme Court of Afghanistan has had nine members[172] since its establishment based on the 2004 Constitution; most of the members of the Supreme Court are Sharia graduates or experts in Islamic law. For instance, the members of the High Council of the Supreme Court of Afghanistan post-Taliban were chaired by **Mawlawī Fazal Hadi Shinwari** (1927–2011). He served as chief justice of

[168] Interview with Mawlawī Mohammad Shuayb Saiqali (head of Religious Studies Department at MoH). Dated 8 Feb 2019.

[169] Mullah is a general term used for those who have knowledge of Islamic sciences.

[170] *Mawlawī* is a term that usually refers to religious people who have a higher level of knowledge and are capable of teaching students (Ṭālibān) in madrasas.

[171] Interview with Mawlawī Mohammad Shuayb Saiqali (head of Religious Studies Department at MoH). Dated 8 Feb 2019.

[172] The Constitution of Afghanistan (2004) Art. 117.

Afghanistan from 2001 until 2006. He studied Islamic Sciences in Afghanistan and Pakistan, and his major was Hadith, the Prophet's narration. He died on February 11, 2011; then after him, **Prof. Abdulsalām Azimi** became the chief justice of the Supreme Court. Justice Azimi graduated from the Kabul Sharia faculty[173] and got his master's degree from al-Azhar University and had taught at the Sharia faculty of Kabul University for several years. He served as the chief justice of the Supreme Court from 2006 to 2015.

Justice Baha-u-din Baha was appointed as a member of the Supreme Court in 2006. Justice Baha was a graduate of the Arabic Studies Center in Kabul in 1960, which was considered an equivalent to a bachelor's degree by al-Azhar University. Mr. Baha, after receiving a specialization in Islamic law in 1964, later continued his education at the master's level at Belford University of USA.[174]

Justice Muhammad Qasim carries a bachelor's degree from the Kabul Sharia faculty (graduated in 1961).[175] He was appointed as a member of the Supreme Court in 2006.[176]

Justice Ghulam Nabi Nawayee became a member of the Supreme Court in 2006.[177] He graduated from the Kabul Sharia faculty in 1980.[178]

Justice Muhammad Alim Nasimi graduated from the Kabul University Sharia faculty in (1967).[179] He was appointed as a member of the Supreme Court in 2006 and served for a period of 10 years.[180]

Justice Muhammad Omar Babrakzai became a member of the Supreme Court in 2006 and served for 7 years. He graduated from the Law and Political Science faculty at Kabul University. Justice Babrakzai also received a diploma in the judicial field from the Public Administration Institute of France.[181]

Justice Abdul Rashid Rashed graduated from the Sharia faculty of Kabul University in (1963).[182] He was a member of the Supreme Court for 10 years.[183]

---

[173] Asadullah Jahedi, Editor in Chief (2013), p. 207.

[174] Pajhwok Afghan News (2019) Pajhwok Afghan News (2019) Biography of the Supreme Court Members. http://elections.pajhwok.com/en/content/biography-supreme-court-members. Accessed 29 Jan 2019.

[175] Asadullah Jahedi, Editor in Chief (2013), p. 209.

[176] Pajhwok Afghan News (2019) Pajhwok Afghan News (2019) Biography of the Supreme Court Members. http://elections.pajhwok.com/en/content/biography-supreme-court-members. Accessed 29 Jan 2019.

[177] Ibid.

[178] Asadullah Jahedi, Editor in Chief (2014), p. 141.

[179] Asadullah Jahedi, Editor in Chief (2016), p. 230.

[180] Pajhwok Afghan News (2019) Pajhwok Afghan News (2019) Biography of the Supreme Court Members. http://elections.pajhwok.com/en/content/biography-supreme-court-members. Accessed 29 Jan 2019.

[181] Ibid.

[182] Asadullah Jahedi, Editor in Chief (2013), p. 210.

[183] Pajhwok Afghan News (2019) Pajhwok Afghan News (2019) Biography of the Supreme Court Members. http://elections.pajhwok.com/en/content/biography-supreme-court-members. Accessed 29 Jan 2019.

Justice Abdul Aziz Aziz studied his secondary education at Abū Ḥanīfa Madrasa and continued his education at the Sharia faculty at Kabul University. After he graduated from the Kabul Sharia faculty in 1960,[184] he got his master's degree in Islamic Jurisprudence (Personal Status) from Azhar University in 1967. Upon his return from Egypt, he started teaching at the Kabul University Sharia faculty and then served as the dean of the faculty till his appointment as a member of the Supreme Court in 2007, which lasted for 7 years.[185]

Justice Zamen Ali Behsodi graduated from the Sharia faculty Kabul University in 1959[186] and got a higher degree in Islamic Jurisprudence from al-Azhar University in Egypt in 1974. He has some experience teaching at the Kabul Sharia faculty as well.[187]

Justice Dr. Abdul Mālik Kamawi studied at Abū Ḥanīfa Madrasa and got his bachelor's degree from the Sharia faculty at Daʿwa-wa-Jihad University in Peshawar/Pakistan. For further studies, he went to Egypt and got his master's and Ph.D. degrees in Law and Islamic Jurisprudence from al-Azhar University. He was appointed as a member of the Supreme Court in 2012, which lasted for a period of 10 years.[188]

Justice Barat Ali Matin was appointed as a member of the Supreme Court in 2013. After the completion of his secondary studies at Dār al-ʿUlūm RūḤānī Baba Madras in Gardez city, the center of Paktia province in the south of Afghanistan, he continued his further study at the Sharia faculty of Kabul University.[189] He graduated from the Kabul Sharia faculty in 1984.[190]

Justice Deen Mohammad Gran was appointed as a member of the Supreme Court in early 2014. He got his BA from the Sharia faculty Kabul University in 1964[191] and his master's degree in Comparative Islamic Jurisprudence from al-Azhar University in Egypt. Prior to his appointment as a member of the Supreme Court, he was teaching at the Kabul Sharia faculty and then became the dean of the faculty.

Justice Abdul Qader Adalatkhwa completed his secondary school at Takharistan Madrasa in Kunduz province and then continued at the Kabul Sharia faculty. He got his master's degree in Family Law from Uzbekistan. Upon his return

---

[184] Asadullah Jahedi, Editor in Chief (2013), p. 208.

[185] Pajhwok Afghan News (2019) Biography of the Supreme Court Members. http://elections.pajhwok.com/en/content/biography-supreme-court-members. Accessed 29 Jan 2019.

[186] Asadullah Jahedi, Editor in Chief (2013), p. 207.

[187] Pajhwok Afghan News (2019) Pajhwok Afghan News (2019) Biography of the Supreme Court Members. http://elections.pajhwok.com/en/content/biography-supreme-court-members. Accessed 29 Jan 2019.

[188] Supreme Court of the Afghanistan, http://supremecourt.gov.af/en/page/ff614/619/44457 Accessed 7 Feb 2019.

[189] http://supremecourt.gov.af/fa/page/ff614/619/44458 Accessed 7 Feb 2019.

[190] Asadullah Jahedi, Editor in Chief (2016), p. 131.

[191] Asadullah Jahedi, Editor in Chief (2014), p. 137.

from Uzbekistan, he started teaching at the Law and Political Science faculty of Kabul University.[192]

Chief Justice Said Yusuf Halim became a member of the Supreme Court in 2015. After his appointment, President Mohammad Ashraf Ghani assigned him as the chief justice of the Supreme Court of Afghanistan. He got his BA from the Law and Political Science faculty of Kabul University and got his master's degree in General Politics from the Islamic Azad University of Iran.[193]

Justice Abdul Hasib Ahadi graduated from Abū Ḥanīfa Madrasa and got his BA from the Sharia faculty of Kabul University in 1990.[194] He was appointed as a member of the Supreme Court in early 2016.[195]

Justice Mohammad Zamam Sangari was appointed as a member of the Supreme Court in 2016.[196] He graduated from Najm al-Madāris Madrasa[197] in Jalalabad city. He continued his study at the Sharia faculty of Kabul University and graduated in 1976.[198]

Looking at the above information on the educational background of the members of the Supreme Court of Afghanistan, it indicates that since 2004, most Supreme Court justices have had an Islamic background, except Chief Justice Halim and Justice Babrakzai, who have a law background. It reveals the important role of Sharia in Supreme Court decisions and sheds light on the question of how they interpret the laws and make decisions accordingly.

2.4.5 *Judicial Training in Afghanistan*

With the exception of the Supreme Court justices, all judges in Afghanistan must fulfill the requirements mentioned in the law. Besides other requirements, the main requirement is to have a degree from Sharia or Law faculties or from a madrasa. Another requirement is to successfully complete the Supreme Court Judiciary Training Program (Stage Course). The Supreme Court established the Judiciary Training Program (Stage Course) in 1968 to provide training for Sharia, law, and madrasa graduates. Since the establishment of the Stage Course, the majority of judges have had Sharia and Islamic law backgrounds, whether they have graduated

---

[192] Supreme Court of Afghanistan http://supremecourt.gov.af/fa/page/ff614/619/44459 Accessed 7 Feb 2019.

[193] Supreme Court of Afghanistan http://supremecourt.gov.af/page/ff614 Accessed 7 April 2019.

[194] Asadullah Jahedi, Editor in Chief (2017), p. 173.

[195] Supreme Court of Afghanistan http://supremecourt.gov.af/fa/page/ff614/619/44460 Accessed 7 April 2019.

[196] Supreme Court of Afghanistan http://supremecourt.gov.af/fa/page/ff614/619/44461 Accessed 7 April 2019.

[197] Najm al-Madāris Madrasa is one of the ten oldest madrasas in Afghanistan, which is located in Jalalabad city of Nangarhar province is located in the east of Afghanistan.

[198] Asadullah Jahedi, Editor in Chief (2017), p. 169.

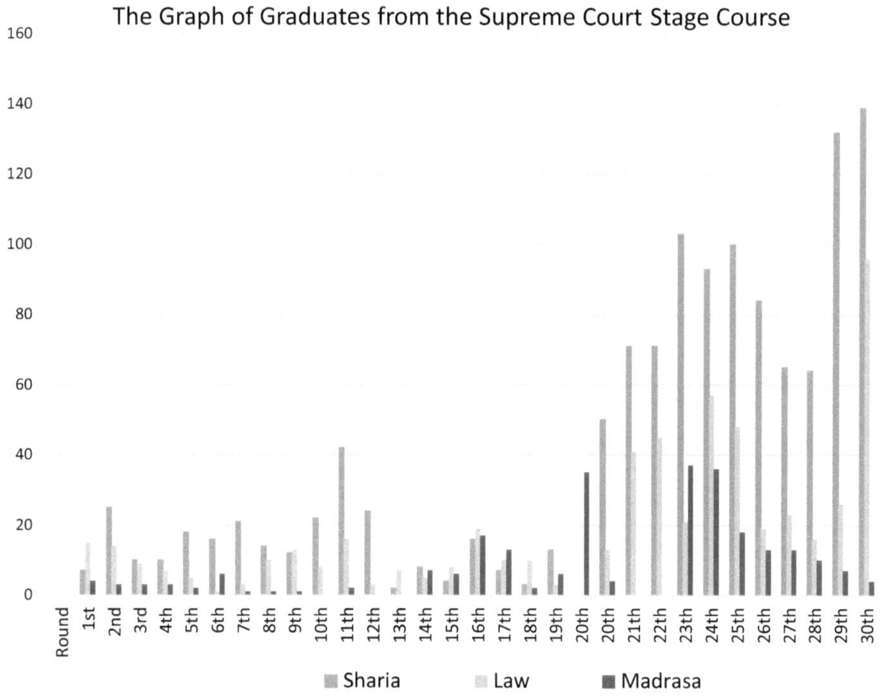

Fig. 2.1 This graph is created by the author based on the primary data included in Table 2.1

from Sharia faculties or madrasas (religious schools). Statistics show huge differences among the Sharia, law, and madrasa graduates in terms of getting admission to the Supreme Court Stage Course (Fig. 2.1, Tables 2.1 and 2.2).

The above diagram shows that there is an increase and decrease in the number of graduates from different institutions who got admitted to the Supreme Court stage-training course. It shows that at the beginning, more law graduates got admitted, but gradually they were outnumbered by graduates from the Shariah faculties, and this continued over time. In addition, the chart shows that in some cases, like in the 10th, 12th, 13th, 21st, and 22nd rounds, there were no graduates from madrasas at all. Meanwhile, in the first 20 rounds, only madrasa graduates, not law and Shariah graduates, were accepted into the program because it happened in 1998, when the Taliban ruled most parts of the country, including Kabul. Overall, the Sharia faculty and madrasa graduates constituted a qualified majority in the judiciary of Afghanistan.

Table 2.1 This is a scanned copy of the records of the Supreme Court's Judicial Training Department of the graduates of the judicial stage program from the first to 30th rounds

ریاست تعلیمات قضائی ستره محکمه جمهوری اسلامی افغانستان
لست فارغین ستاژ قضائی از دور اول الی دور 30

تاریخ		تعداد مجموعه	رشته						دوره	شماره
			مدارس		حقوق		شرعیات			
تاریخ فراغت	تاریخ آغاز		اناث	ذکور	اناث	ذکور	ناث	ذکور		
1348	1347	31	0	4	5	15	0	7	اول	1
1349	1348	42	0	3	0	14	0	25	دوم	2
1350	1349	22	0	3	0	9	0	10	سوم	3
1351	1350	21	0	3	1	7	0	10	چهارم	4
1352	1351	25	0	2	0	5	0	18	پنجم	5
1353	1352	25	0	6	1	1	1	16	ششم	6
1354	1353	25	0	1	0	3	0	21	هفتم	7
1355	1354	25	0	1	0	10	0	14	هشتم	8
1356	1355	29	0	1	3	13	0	12	نهم	9
1357	1356	30	0	0	0	8	0	22	دهم	10
1358	1357	71	0	2	1	16	10	42	یازدهم	11
1358	1357	36	0	0	0	3	9	24	دوازدهم	12
1359	1358	21	0	0	0	7	12	2	سیزدهم	13
1360	1359	36	0	7	12	5	4	8	چهاردهم	14
1362	1361	27	0	6	4	8	5	4	پانزدهم	15
1364		72	0	17	13	19	7	16	شانزدهم	16
1367		66	0	13	26	10	10	7	هفدهم	17
1367		30	0	2	13	10	2	3	هجدهم	18
1374		32	0	6	3	3	7	13	نوزدهم	19
1377		35	0	35	0	0	0	0	بیستم	20
1383		75	0	4	5	13	3	50	بیستم	21
1383		125	0	0	9	41	4	71	بیست و یکم	22
1384		131	0	0	6	45	9	71	بیست و دوم	23
1384		174	1	37	6	21	6	103	بیست و سوم	24
1386		203	0	36	6	57	11	93	بیست و چهارم	25
1387		195	0	18	13	48	16	100	بیست و پنجم	26
1390		141	0	13	2	19	23	84	بیست و ششم	27
1391	1389	123	0	13	5	23	17	65	بیست و هفتم	28
1392	1390	115	0	10	5	16	20	64	بیست و هشتم	29
1393	1392	207	0	7	10	26	32	132	بیست نهم	30
1396	1394	297	1	4	28	96	29	139	سی ام	31
		2487	2	254	177	571	237	1246	مجموعه	
			256		748		1483			

This table is not publicly available, and I got it through an official letter signed by the Chief Justice, Said Yusuf Halim

Table 2.2 This is the translation by the author of Table 2.1 regarding the graduates of the Supreme Court's judicial stage program from the first to the 30th rounds

Department of Judicial Training of the Supreme Court Number of graduates of the Supreme Court Stage Course since its establishment in 1968									
	Sharia		Law		Madrasa				
Round	Male	Female	Male	Female	Male	Female	Score	Start Date	End Date
1st	7	0	15	5	4	0	31	1347	1348
2nd	25	0	14	0	3	0	42	1348	1349
3rd	10	0	9	0	3	0	22	1349	1350
4th	10	0	7	1	3	0	21	1350	1351
5th	18	0	5	0	2	0	25	1351	1352
6th	16	1	1	1	6	0	25	1352	1353
7th	21	0	3	0	1	0	25	1353	1354
8th	14	0	10	0	1	0	25	1354	1355
9th	12	0	13	3	1	0	29	1355	1356
10th	22	0	8	0	0	0	30	1356	1357
11th	42	10	16	1	2	0	71	1357	1358
12th	24	9	3	0	0	0	36	1357	1358
13th	2	12	7	0	0	0	21	1358	1359
14th	8	4	5	12	7	0	36	1359	1360
15th	4	5	8	4	6	0	27	1361	1362
16th	16	7	19	13	17	0	72	–	1364
17th	7	10	10	26	13	0	66	–	1367
18th	3	2	10	13	2	0	30	–	1367
19th	13	7	3	3	6	0	32	–	1374
20th	0	0	0	0	35	0	35	–	1377
20th	50	3	13	5	4	0	75	–	1383
21st	71	4	41	9	0	0	125	–	1383
22nd	71	9	45	6	0	0	131	–	1384
23rd	103	6	21	6	37	1	174	–	1384
24th	93	11	57	6	36	0	203	–	1386
25th	100	16	48	13	18	0	195	–	1387
26th	84	23	19	2	13	0	141	1389	1390
27th	65	17	23	5	13	0	123	1390	1391
28th	64	20	16	5	10	0	115	1392	1392
29th	132	32	26	10	7	0	207	1394	1393
30th	139	29	96	28	4	1	297	–	1396
Total	Sharia 1483		Law 748		Madrasa 256		Overall total 2487		

2.5 Conclusion

Afghanistan has a Supreme Court, which is located in Kabul, and one appellate court in each province. Furthermore, there is a primary court in the center of each province and at the district level as well. The Supreme Court has the power to review and check the compatibility of appellate decisions with applicable laws. The Supreme Court has the power to affirm or overrule the appellate courts' decisions. Also, the Supreme Court can review laws, legislative decrees, international treaties, and international covenants in terms of their compliance with the Constitution. On the other hand, the appellate courts have the authority to review the primary courts' decisions and have the power to affirm or reject the lower courts' decisions. Finally, the primary courts shall hear all cases that are brought to the courts and make decisions in accordance with law. All courts mentioned above have several divisions, like, civil, criminal, commercial, traffic, public security, family, and personal status divisions, that deal with respective cases.

As it is mentioned before, generally in Afghanistan, there is a hybrid system of legal education. Mainly, graduates of three institutions, the Sharia faculty, Law faculty, and madrasas, are being hired as members of the professional staff in the justice sector, especially the judiciary. The Sharia faculties' curriculum is mostly composed of classical Islamic sources with a combination of positive law courses. The Sharia curriculum is echoed by some foreign Islamic universities, namely al-Azhar University in Egypt. The Law faculties follow the western-style legal education with a few Islamic law courses. Most law professors have a western-style study background and are mostly trained in non-Islamic countries, especially in the US and Europe. The madrasas follow the traditional teaching approach and mostly use the old classical textbooks of the Ḥanafī school.

The short biography of the justices of the Supreme Court and the statistics on the Supreme Court Stage Course graduates show that the majority of judges and professional staff members of the judiciary of Afghanistan have been trained under the sphere of Islamic law. Most of the judges, including the justices of the Supreme Court, graduated from Sharia faculties. Furthermore, the third category of applicants who got admitted in the Stage Course consists of madrasa graduates who traditionally studied the Ḥanafī school's doctrines through classical textbooks. Overall, this majority of judges in the judiciary has a dominating role in the decision-making process and has a significant impact on the interpretation of laws based on Sharia principles.

References

Abū al-Maʿālī Burhān al-Dīn MaḤmūd ibn AḤmad ibn ʿAbd al-ʿAzīz ibn ʿUmar ibn Māza al-Bukhārī (2004) Al-Muhīṭ al-Burhānī fī al-fiqh al-Nuʿmānī, verified by ʿAbd al-Karīm Sāmī al-Jundī, vol. 6. Dār al-kutub al-ʿilmiyya, Beirut

Abū Dāwūd S (1999) Musnad Abī Dāwūd, verified by MuḤammad ibn ʿAbd al-Shukūr al-Turkī. Dār Hejir, Egypt
Abū Dāwūd S (2009) Sunan Abī Dāwūd, verified by Shuʿayb Arnūt and MuḤammad Kāmil Qara blalī. Dār al-Risāla al-ʿĀlamiyya, vol 9
Abū Zuhra M (n.d.) Abū Ḥanīfa, Ḥayātuhu wa ʿAṣruhu, wa Ārāʾuhu wa Fiqhuhū. Dār al-Fikr al-ʿArabī, Beirut
ʿAlāʾ al-Dīn, Abū Bakr ibn Masʿūd ibn AḤmad al-Kāsānī, (1986) Badāʾiʿ al-ṣanāʾiʿ fī tartīb al-sharāʾiʿ, Beirut: Dār al-Kutub al-ʿIlmiyya, vol. 14
Al-Sarakhsī M (n.d.) Uṣūl al-Sarakhsī. Dār al-Maʿrifa, Beirut, vol. 2
Al-Shāshī N (n.d.) Uṣūl al-Shāshī. Dār al-Kitāb al-ʿArabiyya, Beirut, p 13
Alukūzay A (1885) Asās al-Qużāt. Dār al-Salṭana Publication, Kabul
Asadullah Jahedi, Editor in Cheif (2013) Sharaiat. J Kabul Sharia Faculty vols. 7 and 8
Asadullah Jahedi, Editor in Chief (2014) Sharaiat. J Kabul Sharia Faculty 11:141
Asadullah Jahedi, Editor in Chief (2016) Sharaiat. J f Kabul Sharia Faculty 16–17:230
Asadullah Jahedi, Editor in Chief (2017) Sharaiat. J Kabul Sharia Faculty 20:173
Barfield T (2003) Afghan customary law and its relationship to formal judicial institutions. Boston University
Bassiouni MC (2014) The Sharīca, Islamic law (Fiqh), and legal methods (cIlm Uṣūlal-Fiqh). In: Id. (ed) The Sharia and islamic criminal justice in time of war and peace. Cambridge University Press, Cambridge, pp 18–87
Bell G (2006) Multiculturalism in law is legal pluralism – lessons from Indonesia, Singapore and Canada. Singapore J Legal Stud pp 315–330
Brick J (2008) The political economy of customary village organizations in rural Afghanistan. Department of Political Science. University of Wisconsin, Madison, pp 1–49
Center for Strategic & International Studies (2015) Why Are customary Pashtun Laws and Ethics Causes for Concern?. http://csis.org/blog/why-are-customary-pashtun-laws-and-ethics-causes-concern. Accessed 23 Oct 2015
Civil Code of Afghanistan (1976) Ministry of Justice, official Gazzete No: 353
Dupret B (2007) Legal pluralism, plurality of law, and legal practices. Eur J Leg Stud 1(1)
Farhang M (1992) Afghanistan during the last five centuries. Ismāʿīliyya publications, Qum, 1
Ghubār GM (2015) Afghānistān Dar Masīr-i Tārīkh (History of Afghanistan). Sarwar Sādāt Publications, Kabul
Haress G (2017) Judicial review in Afghanistan: a flawed practice. Afghanistan Research and Evaluation Unit
Hooker M (1975) Legal pluralism. Introduction to colonial and neo-colonial law. Clarendon Press 36(1):185–186. https://doi.org/10.1017/S0008197300014471
Hussami HG (2009) History of judiciary in Afghanistan Kabul. Saeed Publications, Kabul
Kamali MH (2003) The Sunnah. In: Id. (ed) Principles of Islamic Jurisprudence. The Islamic Texts Society, Cambridge, Chapter 3, pp 58–116
Kamali MH (2008) Introduction. In: Id. (ed) Sharia Law. An introduction. One World Publications, Oxford, Chapter 1, pp 1-–13
Kamali MH (2014) Afghanistan's constitution ten years on: what are the issues?. Afghanistan Research and Evaluation Unit
Law on Organization and Jurisdiction of the Judiciary Branch of Islamic Republic of Afghanistan (2013) Ministry of Justice, official Gazette No: 1109
Layish A (2004) The transformation of the Sharia from jurists' law to statutory in the contemporary Muslim world. Int J Study Mod Islam 44(1):85–113. https://doi.org/10.1163/157006004773712587
Ministry of Awqāf and Islamic Affairs of Kuwait (2008) Al-Mawsūʿa al-Fiqhiyya al-Kuwaytiyya, vol. 1
Nadawī A (1974) Min Nahr al-Kabul ilā Nahr al-Yarmūk (from Kabul River to Yarmouk River). Dar al-Ḥalāl, Ankara
Niẓām Nāma Asāsī Dawlat Aleyah Afghānistān (1923) (The First Constitution of Afghanistan)

Otto JM (2008) Sharia and national law in Muslim countries: tensions and opportunities for Dutch and EU foreign policy. Amsterdam University Press. https://doi.org/10.26530/OAPEN_595098
Rohe M (2014a) The development of the dogmatics of Islamic law. In: Id. (ed) Islamic law in past and present. Brill, Leiden, Chapter 2, pp 54–93
Rohe M (2014b) The origins of the Islamic state and its legal system. In: Id. (ed) Islamic law in past and present. Brill, Leiden, Chapter 1, pp 25–53
Rushdī A (1977) Al-Ijmāʿ fī al-Sharīʿa al-Islāmiyya, Al-Jāmiʿa al-Islāmiyya. Madinah, Saudi Arabia
Sherman J (2006) Legal pluralism between Islam and the nation-state: romantic medievalism or pragmatic modernity?. Fordham Int Law J 30(1)
Sirat AS (1968) The modern legal system of Afghanistan. Am J Comp Law 16(4)
Sirat AS (1969) Sharia and Islamic education in modern Afghanistan. Middle East J 23(2)
Suhrke A, Borchgrevink K (2008) Negotiating justice sector reform in Afghanistan. Crime Law Soc Chasnge 51(2). https://doi.org/10.1007/s10611-008-9154-0
Taftāzānī S (n.d.) Sharḥ al-Talwīḥ ʿalā al-Tawḍīḥ. Maktaba Ṣabīh, Egypt, vol. 1
Tamanaha B (2007) Understanding legal pluralism: past to present, local to global. Sydney Law Rev 30. St. John's Legal Studies Research Paper Nr.07-0080
Tamanaha B (2008) Law. Oxford International Encyclopedia of Legal History. St. John's Legal Studies Research Paper Nr. 08-0095
Tarzee M (1919) Sarajul Akhbar Newspaper, 3rd year, 1st valium, September 4, 1919
The Civil Code of Afghanistan (1976) Ministry of Justice, official gazette No 353
The Constitution of Afghanistan (2004) Ministry of Justice, official gazette No 818
The Independent Commission of Human Rights of Afghanistan. http://www.aihrc.org.af/fa/research-reports/1570/qatle-namosi-kholasa-gozarish.html Accessed 5 October 2017)
The International Legal Foundation (2004) The customary laws of Afghanistan. United States Institute of Peace
The Penal Code of Afghanistan (1976) Ministry of Justice, Official Gazette No: 347
The Quran, Sura: al-Najm, (53: 3-4)
The Supreme Court of Afghanistan. http://supremecourt.gov.af/en/page/ff614/619/44457. Accessed 7 April 2019
The United States Institute of Peace (2014) A Guild to Tradition of Dispute Resolution in Paktia
Wakily Popalzaey A (1990) Darul Qaza in Afghanistan: from the beginning of Islam till republic era. Islamic Research Center, Kabul
Wardak A (2004) Jirga- a traditional mechanism of conflict resolution in Afghanistan. Center of Criminology, University of Glamorgan, United Kingdom
Williams RF (1981–1982) Legal education in Afghanistan prior to the soviet occupation. Suffolk Transnatl Law J 6(2)
Yassari N, Saboory MH (2010) Sharia and national law in Afghanistan. Available at https://www.juragentium.org/topics/islam/en/yassari.htm. Accessed 29 Dec 2018
ZuḤaylī MM (2006) Al-Wajīz fī Uṣūl al-Fiqh al-Islāmī, Dār al-Khayr. Damascus 1:255–280

Chapter 3
Analysis of Article 130 of the Afghan Constitution

3.1 The Language and Meaning of Article 130

Article 130 of the Afghan Constitution of 2004 states the following:

> In cases under consideration, the courts shall apply provisions of this Constitution as well as other laws. If there is no provision in the Constitution or other laws about a case, the courts shall, in pursuance of Hanafi jurisprudence, and, within the limits set by this Constitution, rule in a way that attains justice in the best manner.[1]

The article is composed of a variety of concepts that authorize the Afghan courts to fill the legal lacuna by using Ḥanafī school provisions. At first glance, the text of the article includes some conditions that must be taken into consideration. Without a deep understanding of the text of the article, it would be difficult to comprehend the circumstances that authorize Afghan courts to make decisions in accordance with Article 130 of the Afghan Constitution. An analytical look at the text of the article will pave the ground for understanding how and under which conditions the courts should apply Article 130 to a case under consideration.

The article begins with "In cases under consideration," which means the court is only authorized to make a decision regarding a case when it is under its consideration. In the *Law on the Structure and Jurisdiction of Courts of Afghanistan*, the term *case* is defined as follows:

> [A]n event related to the criminal, civil, public rights, personal status, and commercial matters that has been brought to a court by the parties to be adjudicated.[2]

This law reveals that whenever parties officially submit a case to a court by entering it in the registry book of the courts, it becomes subject to the court's jurisdiction to adjudicate the case. It also means that if a case is not officially registered in the court, there is no authority for the court to deal with that case. In

[1]The Constitution of Afghanistan (2004) Art. 130.

[2]Law on Organization and Jurisdiction of the Judiciary Branch (2013) Art. 4, clause 15.

L. Saeed, *Islam, Custom and Human Rights*, Interdisciplinary Studies in Human Rights 7, https://doi.org/10.1007/978-3-030-83086-1_3

Afghanistan, there are separate procedures for how criminal and noncriminal cases are processed and officially submitted as cases to the courts. Criminal cases are filed by the police then go to the prosecutor's office, and after the necessary investigation, the prosecutor submits the case to the court.[3] However, noncriminal cases are brought directly to the court by the parties or are initiated in the Law Department of the Ministry of Justice.

The second major point in the article is the obligation of the courts with regard to the applicable law. The courts have to respect the superiority of state law first and must apply the provisions of the Constitution and other laws when making a decision. Indeed, the courts are required to state the legal reasons for their judgments and refer to the precise provisions of the law in their decisions. The Constitution states:

> In issuing a decision, the court is obligated to state the reason for its verdict. . . .[4]

In addition, the *Law on the Structure and Competencies of Courts* also requires the courts to provide reasons for their judgments:

> The courts shall be duty bound to rely on the reasons, grounds and legal provisions for issuing a decision.[5]

So it is the duty of the judges to make decisions in accordance with the law and point to a specific provision of the related law to which the case is subject. If a judge has not applied the law accurately, the appellate court will overrule the lower court's decision and send it back to the lower court for correction.[6]

Article 130 also gives priority to the law to be applied to all cases by stating that "If there is no provision in the Constitution or other laws about the case..." Principally, the courts must first confront the provisions of the Constitution and other laws to make a decision regarding a case. If there is a provision in the law that is applicable to the case, the court must apply that provision and should not go beyond the law and refer to another source in the case. If this happens, the decision of the court would be unconstitutional and should not be implemented. Only if the Constitution and state laws are silent regarding a case can a court make a decision in accordance with the doctrines of the Ḥanafī school of thought.

Article 130 also imposes another condition: courts shall consider the limits set by the Constitution. There are many limitations that the Constitution provides for applying the Ḥanafī school of thought to a case, but Article 27 of the Constitution is one of the concrete examples that must be taken into consideration. Article 27 of the Afghan Constitution accepts the principle of the legality of crime and punishment and states:

---

[3]This issue will be discussed in more detail below in the section titled Criminal Procedure in Accordance with Law.

[4]The Constitution of Afghanistan (2004) Art. 129.

[5]Law on the Structure and Competencies of Courts of Afghanistan (2013) Art. 12.

[6]Law on Organization and Jurisdiction of the Judiciary Branch (2013) Art. 27.

> No deed shall be considered a crime unless ruled by a law promulgated prior to commitment of the offense. No one shall be pursued, arrested, or detained without due process of law. No one shall be punished without the decision of an authoritative court taken in accordance with the provisions of the law, promulgated prior to commitment of the offense.[7]

This article clearly accepts the principle of legality, which is widely recognized among most legal systems around the world. The requirements for the applicability of Article 130 of the Afghan Constitution should therefore effectively limit the use of Article 130 in criminal cases because it offends the principle of legality, which is guaranteed in the Constitution. Although Article 27 of the Constitution clearly accepts the principle of legality, the Afghan courts have not considered this limitation in practice and have used Article 130 in a wide range of criminal cases. In fact, judges must consider the principle of legality as a provisional tool when they use Article 130 of the Constitution for their decisions. Kamali, in his book *The Right to Personal Safety*, claims: "The judge may not punish anyone on the basis of his own wishes, without lawful evidence and proof. Even then, the legal text that is applied must have been in existence at the time the offence was committed."[8]

The final stipulation in Article 130 is the insistence on the application of the Ḥanafī school of thought when there is a legal gap. The article indicates that in the case of a legal lacuna, the Ḥanafī school of thought should be used as the legal basis for the court's decision. Indeed, the article allows Afghan judges to use Ḥanafī doctrines regarding a case if the law is silent; however, they still have to follow the order of the law and provide legal reasons for their judgment.[9] Using the doctrine of the Ḥanafī school as a legal basis for court decisions requires following the Ḥanafī principles, such as the principle of preference, and applying the hierarchy of opinions and sources within the Ḥanafī school to guarantee the legitimacy of the decision. These principles will be discussed in detail later in this chapter.

Finally, Article 130 also authorizes the court to make a decision in a way that achieves justice in the best possible way if there is no applicable provision in the Constitution or other laws. There is no evidence to prove that justice is guaranteed only by applying the Ḥanafī school because Imam Abū Ḥanīfa, the founder of the school, and other Ḥanafī scholars have never claimed that all that they said is true and justice is covered only by their opinions. Imam Abū Ḥanīfa says: "We are human beings, we may issue an opinion today, but reject it tomorrow. Also, he instructed his student Abū Yūsuf, 'Don't write all what you hear from me; I say something today, and reject it tomorrow, and say something tomorrow, and leave it the day after tomorrow.'"[10] This means Abū Ḥanīfa believed that addressing a legal issue requires matching the concept of truth and the reality that exists in each society because in the legal field, the knowledge of human beings is always evolving; legal

---

[7] The Constitution of Afghanistan (2004) Art. 27.

[8] Kamali (2000).

[9] The Constitution of Afghanistan (2004) Art. 129.

[10] Al-Dihlawī (1995), pp. 6–7.

opinions should match the reality existing at that time, understanding that they may not work in the future.

There is an important point that must be taken into consideration when discussing how judges can secure justice in the best possible way by applying the Ḥanafī provisions to a case when there is no provision of law. Article 130 of the 2004 Afghan Constitution uses the same sentence that was in the 1964 Afghan Constitution that provided flexibility to judges to make decisions in accordance with the Ḥanafī school provisions.[11] Dr. Kamali considers the last point, raised in Article 130 of the Afghan Constitution, important and observes that because of the inclusiveness and flexibility of the Ḥanafī sources, the Afghan judges may be willing to rely more on the Ḥanafī sources in the case of constitutional ambiguity.[12]

The former Afghan chief justice, Abdul Hakim Zeyaey, indicated that the last part of Article 102 of the 1964 Constitution allowed the Afghan judges to do *Judicial ijtihād*. In the case of a legal lacuna, Afghan judges are allowed to make a decision regarding a case based on their own discretion.[13]

Dr. Mālik Kamawi,[14] one of the justices of the Supreme Court of Afghanistan, also believes that Article 130 of the Constitution indirectly states that judges are allowed to do *ijtihād* in the case of a legal lacuna. He explained that if there is a new issue that is not regulated by law, like organ transplants or cybercrime, and there is no provision in the classical Ḥanafī texts, this article allows the Afghan judges to make a decision based on their own *ijtihād*. So, in his opinion, the implementation of this article has its own complexities and should be applied very carefully to avoid any malpractice.[15]

The parallel provisions Article 102 of the 1964 Afghan Constitution and Article 130 of the 2004 Afghan Constitution are a perfect example of the theory of *Constitutional Stickiness*,[16] a principle of constitutional law that has been developed by Ozan O. Barol. The drafters of the 2004 Constitution copied the text of Article 102 of the 1964 Constitution, with some minor changes. In Article 130, the omission of the phrase "in their [Judges] opinion" provides more room for the Afghan judges to conduct judicial *ijtihād*.

[11] The Constitution of Afghanistan (1964) Art. 102: "In cases under consideration, the courts shall apply provisions of this Constitution and state laws. If there is no provision in the Constitution or other laws about a case, the courts shall, in pursuance of Ḥanafī jurisprudence of Islamic Sharia, and within the limits set by this Constitution, rule in a way that attains justice in the best manner."

[12] Kamali (2014), p. 5.

[13] Kamali (1985a), p. 232.

[14] Dr. Abdul Malik Kamawi studied at Abū Ḥanīfa Madrasa and got his bachelor's degree from the Sharia faculty at Daʿwa-wa-Jihad University in Peshawar/Pakistan. For further studies, he went to Egypt and got his master's degree and PhD in Law and Islamic Jurisprudence from *al-Azhar University*. He was appointed as a member of the Supreme Court in 2012 and served as such for a period of 10 years.

[15] Interview with Dr. Malik Kamawi (justice at the Supreme Court of Afghanistan). Dated 15 August 2017.

[16] Varol (2015).

Kamali posits, however, that the elimination of some phrases from the text of Article 102 of the 1964 Constitution has not significantly changed the meaning of Article 130 of the 2004 Constitution. The omission of the phrase *Islamic Sharia* from the 1964 Constitution, which is mentioned right after *Hanafi Jurisprudence*, reveals that Afghan judges cannot go directly to the primary sources of the Sharia, namely the Quran and Sunnah, to make a decision, and there is no room for the provisions of other Islamic schools to be used by judges.[17]

Thus, the text of Article 130 of the 2004 Afghan Constitution has some significant limiting conditions that Afghan courts must respect when relying on this article as a legal basis for their decision in criminal cases. If courts fail to bear in mind these conditions, the legitimacy of the court decision will be challenged and the decision will be considered unconstitutional.

3.2 Historical View on Article 130 of the Afghan Constitution

As mentioned above, Islamic law "Sharia" has been used as the main source of law for several centuries in Afghanistan. Most Afghans, for many decades, consider Sharia, chiefly the Ḥanafī school of thought, the superior law of the state. Islamic scholars have addressed all legal issues according to the Sharia and provide solutions in the light of the Sharia by issuing new fatwas (scholarly legal opinions). Thus, the question of creating and using state laws instead of Sharia had never been raised in the legal history of Afghanistan before the mid-twentieth century.[18] After the colonial era in the mid-nineteenth century, one of the impacts of western rule on colonial countries, especially Great Britain and France on South Asia, the Middle East, and North Africa, was the initiation of the idea of the codification of Sharia and adoption of constitutions. Many Muslim countries subsequently have adopted constitutions and codified their laws.[19] Originally, the idea of using Islamic law to fill gaps in state law of Afghanistan has been imported from other Muslim majority states through development in political and scholarly exchanges relationships between Afghanistan and other Islamic countries. These relationships paved the way for Afghan scholars to adopt the legal system of other countries and integrate other scholars' ideas to modify Afghanistan's legal system.

[17] Kamali and Mohammad Hashim (2004) Islam and its Sharia in the Afghan Constitution, also see, Yassary (2005), pp. 30–31.

[18] Farhang (1992), p. 735.

[19] Lombardi (2013), p. 743.

3.3 The Sources of Article 130 of the Afghan Constitution

The concept of the applicability of Islamic jurisprudence in the absence of state law was first codified by ʿAbd al-Razzāq as-Sanhūrī, the author of the Egyptian Civil Code, in 1949.[20] The first article of the Civil Code of Egypt says:

> Provisions of laws govern all matters to which these provisions apply in letter or spirit. In the absence of a provision of a law that is applicable, the Judge will decide according to custom and in the absence of custom in accordance with the principles of Muslim Law. In the absence of such principles, the Judge will apply the principles of natural justice and the rules of equity.[21]

Sanhūrī's idea of giving authority to the judges, where there is a lack of provisions in the state laws, to make decisions according to several sources such as customs, Islamic law, natural justice, and the rule of equity, was a new page in the history of Islamic jurisprudence. His idea of making Islamic jurisprudence a backup source for Egyptian judges when making decisions in the absence of state law was warmly welcomed in most Muslim countries.[22]

Making decisions freely and choosing one source among many was not a common way to find a solution for a legal issue in the context of Islamic jurisprudence because it is against the principle of preference without reason (*tarjīḥ bilā murajjaḥ*).[23] Muslim scholars after the late thirteenth century have been prevented from dealing with new issues and doing *ijtihād*[24] by issuing new fatwas. Because of factors like dictatorship, a lack of qualified scholars, the fear of doing *ijtihād* incorrectly, and misinterpretation of Islamic sources, Islamic scholars gave fatwas that doing *ijtihād* is not allowed. They maintain that Muslims should revert to the classical way of thinking, where they are not allowed to bring new ideas outside of their school of thought (madhab).[25] The first article of the Sanhūrī Code implicitly allowed the judges and the system to be more flexible and allowed Egyptian judges to rely on different sources of law and ensure that justice is obtained through their decisions.

The 1949 Egyptian Civil Code encouraged other Muslim scholars, initially in the Arab world and then in non-Arab Muslim countries, to adopt such a provision in their laws. Although the terms used in Article 1 might have a different meaning and interpretation in other Arab or Muslim societies, the impact of the message sent

[20] Id., p. 742.

[21] The Civil Code of the Arab Republic of Egypt (1949) Art. 1.

[22] Lombardi (2013), p. 4.

[23] Tarjīḥ bilā murajjaḥ is a common principle among the Islamic jurists that if there is more than one opinion regarding a specific issue, there shall be a reason to prefer one idea rather than others. It is not accepted if we prefer one idea over the others without a reason.

[24] Literally, Ijtihād means diligence and hard work, but it is used for Islamic Scholars' great diligence to obtain a legal order from the legal texts. Mohammad ibn ʿAlī ibn Qāḍī Mohammad Ḥāmid Kashshāf (1996) Tafsīr Kashshāf.

[25] Zaydān (n.d.) also see, Ministry of Awqāf and Islamic Affairs of Kuwait (2008), p. 42.

through this article has been significant. For instance, the term *custom* in Egyptian legal culture refers to *fiqh* (Islamic jurisprudence),[26] but *custom* in Afghanistan does not mean the same thing. The term custom in Afghanistan refers to the "common culture, which is an ethical code that generates binding rules on its members." Thus, in Afghanistan, *customary law* is the means by which local communities resolve disputes outside state-based institutions and use their common cultural and ethical norms, which produce binding rules on its members.[27] The concept of custom may even be different within the same country. For example, the term custom in the south and east parts of Afghanistan is different from that in the north and west. In the south and east, the term refers to a collection of praiseworthy morals of a true Pashtun.[28]

In the postcolonial era, when Arab nations achieved freedom, Islamic scholars (*fuqahāʾ*) continuously pushed states to reform the laws that were inconsistent with the Islamic political thought *Siyāsa Sharʿiyya*.[29] The Sanhūrī Code was the most important factor in that movement. In addition, other Arab scholars, including Shaikh Rashīd Riḍā, had a significant impact on Muslim thinkers and political parties, namely the Muslim Brotherhood, which had pushed states to include Islamic principles in their new constitutions.[30]

Although other religious minorities that were present in the Arab region made some resistance against the Islamization of laws, the process of Islamization moved forward. For example, in Syria, there are many religious minorities, including Christians, Jews, and some non-Sunni school followers, that were against the Islamization of laws.[31] In 2012, the Syrian government added a provision in its Constitution for the first time stating that "... Islamic jurisprudence shall be a major source of legislation..."[32] The Syrian 1950 Constitution did not say that all state laws must be consistent with Islamic legal principles or *fiqh*; however, Article 3 says that "Islamic *fiqh* shall be the major source of legislation," which means that other laws could exist even if they are not consistent with Islamic law.[33] Article 3 of the Syrian Constitution opened the door for other Muslim countries to include this concept in their constitutions. After a political disorder, Syria and Egypt formed a political union, the United Arab Republic (UAR), in late 1950, and this Constitution was suspended.[34] The UAR adopted a new constitution in 1959, which was

---

[26] Lombardi (2013), p. 19.

[27] Barfield (2003), p. 2.

[28] The International Legal Foundation (2004), p. 7.

[29] Lombardi (2013), p. 753.

[30] Id. p. 740.

[31] Ziadeh (2008) p. 5.

[32] Syrian Constitution/Al-Dustūr Al-Sūrī (2012) Art. 3.

[33] Lombardi (2013), p. 4.

[34] Ibid. p. 5.

approved by 99.9% of voters.[35] The new Constitution did not say that Islamic law is a source for other laws.[36]

Following Egypt and Syria, the idea of considering Islamic law as the main source of other laws spread out to other Islamic countries, and over time the following Muslim countries adopted this clause in their constitutions: Kuwait,[37] Sudan,[38] the Yemen Arab Republic,[39] the Arab Republic of Egypt,[40] the United Arab Emirates,[41] the Arab State of Qatar,[42] the Kingdom of Bahrain,[43] the Republic of Iraq,[44] and the Islamic Republic of Iran.[45] All of these countries have a provision proclaiming Sharia as the main source or only source of their legislation.

3.4 When Did It Appear in the Afghan Constitution?

As history shows, the Ḥanafī school of thought has been applied to all legal issues and used as the main source of law since Islam came to Afghanistan.[46] Historically, *ʿulamāʾ* have played a significant role in the legal history of Afghanistan. Since Sharia (Ḥanafī school of thought) was applied as a main source of law in the Afghan

[35] Lang (2013), p. 10.

[36] QazmaKhūry Yūsūf, Constitutions in Arabic world "Texts and amendments", available at http://www.righttononviolence.org/mecf/wp-content/uploads/2012/03/1958Egypt.pdf.

[37] The Constitution of Kuwait (1962) Art. 2: "The religion of the State is Islam, and the Islamic Sharia shall be a main source of legislation."

[38] The Constitution of Sudan (1973) Art. 9: "The Islamic Law and custom shall be a main source of Legislation." available at http://www.righttononviolence.org/mecf/wp-content/uploads/2012/01/Constitution-Sudan-1973-+-amendment-1975.pdf.

[39] The Constitution of Yemen Arab Republic (2001) Art. 3: "Islamic Shariah is the source of all legislation." available at http://www.refworld.org/pdfid/3fc4c1e94.pdf.

[40] The Constitution of the Arab Republic of Egypt (1949) Art. 2: "Islam is the religion of the State and Arabic is its official language. The principles of Islamic Sharia are the main source of legislation." Available at http://www.sis.gov.eg/Newvr/Dustor-en001.pdf.

[41] The Constitution of the United Arab Emirates (1996) Art. 7: "The Islamic Shariah shall be a main source of legislation in the Union." Available at http://www.refworld.org/pdfid/48eca8132.pdf.

[42] The Constitution of Arab State of Qatar (2004) Art. 1 "Qatar is an independent sovereign Arab State. Its religion is Islam and Shari'a law shall be the principle source of its legislations." http://www.ilo.org/wcmsp5/groups/public/%2D%2D-ed_protect/%2D%2D-protrav/%2D%2D-ilo aids/documents/legaldocument/wcms_125870.pdf.

[43] The Constitution of Kingdom of Bahrain (2002) Art. 2: "The religion of the state is Islam. The Islamic Sharia is a principal source for legislation." http://www.bahrain-embassy.or.jp/en/constitution.pdf.

[44] The Constitution of Republic of Iraq (2005) Art. 2: "Islam is the official religion of the State and is a foundation source of Legislation" http://www.wipo.int/wipolex/en/text.jsp?file_id=230000.

[45] The Constitution of the Islamic Republic of Iran (1989) Art. 4: "All civil, penal financial, economic, administrative, cultural, military, political, and other laws and regulations must be based on Islamic criteria." https://faculty.unlv.edu/pwerth/Const-Iran(abridge).pdf.

[46] Wakily Popalzaey (1990), p. 47.

courts, there was no codified law on which judges could base their decisions. For the first time, in 1923, King Amānallāh started a legal reform by adopting a new constitution.

After Amānallāh Khān was appointed as King in 1919, Afghanistan's first Constitution, *Niẓām Nāma Asāsī*, was approved by the Luya Jirga (*Nationwide council*) on March 02, 1923. It declared that Islam is the state's official religion and the Ḥanafī school of thought is the official school of jurisprudence of the state of Afghanistan.[47] According to the 1923 Constitution, Sharia, and particularly the Ḥanafī school of thought, is officially the main source of law in Afghanistan. That Constitution gave more power to the King and declared that the King is a venerable and responsible person.[48] In contrast, it limited the power of tribal and religious leaders. There was no separation of powers, and the King held all the legislative power. However, all judges were chosen from among the *ʿulamāʾ* and made decisions according to the Ḥanafī school of thought.[49] The Constitution allowed only the state courts to hear a case; it prohibited any other institutions like religious courts or any informal judicial body from making a decision regarding a case.[50]

After the book of *Asās al-Qużāt*, adopted by King ʿAbd al-RaḤmān, the second legal book in Dari language that codified the Ḥanafī school's provisions was *Tamassuk al-Qużāt al-Amāniyya*, enacted by Amānallāh Khān in 1921.[51] The book clearly stated that since the sources of the Ḥanafī school of jurisprudence are mostly in Arabic, it is adopted in Dari language to unify the sources and make it easier for the judges to make a decision accordingly and avoid using other sources for their verdict.[52] The book is like a set of opinions collected from different sources of the Ḥanafī school. Even though the book cited sources for most of the provisions, it generally discussed those crimes that are recognized as religious crimes (*ḥudūd*).

The concept of Article 130 of the current Constitution is derived in some ways from that book. It stated that if there is no provision in that book that is applicable to a case, the case should be suspended and sent to the Ministry of Justice, and the Ministry of Justice should immediately inform the King about the case. The *ʿulamāʾ* Council should discuss the case in the light of the Ḥanafī school's principles, and the decision had to be signed by the King and included in the book.[53] This approach

---

[47] The Constitution of Afghanistan (1923) Art. 2.

[48] The Constitution of Afghanistan (1923) Art. 6.

[49] ʿAbd al-Wāsiʿ et al. (1921), p. 1.

[50] The Constitution of Afghanistan (1923) Art. 55.

[51] Tamassuk al-Qużāt al-Amāniyya was the first criminal code, written by a famous scholar, Mawlawī ʿAbd al-Wāsiʿ and reviewed by the chief justice, along with a group of famous judges, including appellate court and primary court judges. This book was adopted and published during King Amānallāh's government in 1921. In contrast to other Ḥanafī school's sources, the language of this book is in Dari and is composed of 14 chapters and 1113 articles. In this book, each article has been referred to a Ḥanafī school book, and there is not even one source from other schools of jurisprudence named in the book.

[52] ʿAbd al-Wāsiʿ et al. (1921), p. 2.

[53] ʿAbd al-Wāsiʿ et al. (1921), p. 3.

shows that the Ḥanafī school doctrines were gradually codified and used as the main source of law.

After King Amānallāh, King Nādir Shāh continued the reform and adopted the second Constitution on October 31, 1931, called *Uṣūl Asāsī Dawlat Aleyah Afghānistān*. The Turkish, Iranian, and French constitutions had a strong impact on the 1931 Constitution of Afghanistan. The 1931 Constitution imposed an additional condition for the King. According to it, besides being a Muslim, the King must be a follower of the Ḥanafī school of thought.[54] Also, official courts were the only place to initiate a legal case, and the Ḥanafī school was to be applied to all cases.[55] The Constitution declared that no one would be arrested or punished except according to Sharia and the laws (*Uṣūl Nāma*).[56] Supremacy was given to the Ḥanafī doctrine, and it was introduced as the main source of law and made applicable to all types of cases.[57]

The idea of the superiority of state law over Sharia was raised for the first time during the grand council (Luya Jirga) of 1964. Remarkably, a revolutionary change happened when the Jirga members protested for a new Afghan constitution. Article 69 of the 1964 Constitution indicates:

> Law is a resolution passed by both houses, and endorsed by the king. In the area where no such law exists, the provisions of the Ḥanafī Jurisprudence of Sharia of Islam shall be considered as law.[58]

In this Constitution, for the first time state law became the primary source applicable to all cases; Sharia provisions were announced as a backup source to be used if there were gaps in the state laws. According to Louis Dupree, Article 102 of the 1964 Constitution was the most important provision because there is a sign of shifting toward secularism.[59] On the other hand, Article 1 indicates that the establishment of the state was based on the sovereignty of the people, not Islam,[60] but the official religion of the state is Islam.[61] The 1964 Constitution brought a remarkable change in the Afghan legal system because, for the first time, the supremacy of state law over Sharia was accepted constitutionally. Article 102 of the 1964 Constitution said:

> The courts in the cases under their consideration shall apply the provisions of this Constitution and the laws of the state. Whenever no provision exists in this Constitution or the laws for a case under consideration, the courts shall, by following the basic principles of the Hanafi jurisprudence of the Sharia of Islam and within the limitations set forth in this Constitution, render a decision that in their opinion secures justice in the best possible way.[62]

---

[54]The Constitution of Afghanistan (1931) Art. 1.

[55]Id., Art. 87.

[56]Id., Art. 11.

[57]Id., Art. 88.

[58]The Constitution of Afghanistan (1964) Art. 69.

[59]Dupree (2014), p. 582. /Art. 102 of The Constitution of Afghanistan (1964) is discussed below.

[60]The Constitution of Afghanistan (1964) Art. 1.

[61]The Constitution of Afghanistan (1964) Art. 2.

[62]The Constitution of Afghanistan (1964) Art. 102/for translation see Dupree (2014), p. 583.

There was a hot debate between conservative religious leaders and open-minded, new scholars who graduated from the West. The conservative party was represented by Mawlawī Ghulam Nabi Kamawi, a famous religious leader, and the opposite party was represented by his son, Dr. Mohammad Moosa Shafiq, who earned his Ph. D. in the United States. The conservative party claimed that Sharia and the Ḥanafī doctrine should remain the primary sources of law. The opposing party, however, cited Article 64, which stated: "... *No law shall be repugnant to the basic principle of the sacred religion of Islam....*"[63] This conformity clause ensured that there will not be any law that stands against Islamic Sharia. Furthermore, there is a considerable minority who follow other schools of thought and religions, so the government should take care of them as well.[64] Finally, the draft article was approved unanimously, and it was the first time that laws passed as legislation became the primary source of law, and the Ḥanafī school of jurisprudence was to be considered as a backup that would fill the gap if there was no provision of law regarding a specific case.

Afghanistan's 1976 Constitution retained Article 102 of the 1964 Constitution, but after the 1978 coup and collapse of President Dāwūd's government, the process of secularization was accelerated, which reduced the role of Sharia and Islamic concepts in the field of law. In the early days after the coup, the leaders of the communist regime under the leadership of Nūr Mohammad Tarakī formed a revolutionary council, which replaced the former government. Under the communist regime, the role of Sharia was decreased and there was no legislative body; instead, it was governed by decrees rather than laws.

Following the invasion of the Soviet Union and the assassination of President Ḥafīẓallāh Amīn, the new president, Babrak Kārmal, came to power. In 1978, he issued the Fundamental Principles of the Democratic Republic of Afghanistan, which is called the fifth Constitution of the country. This Constitution gave authority to the Revolutionary Council as the highest institution of the state. The Constitution did not make any reference to Marxism; it declared that in the Democratic Republic of Afghanistan, only official courts (the Supreme Court, provincial courts, district courts, and military courts) could adjudicate cases.[65]

Article 56 of the 1978 Constitution applied a concept very similar to Article 130 of the current Constitution:

> The court has the power to do judicial proceeding and process all civil cases and giving the verdict by the court shall be according to the principle of equality of the citizens in front of the law and the court. During proceeding process, the courts shall apply the laws of Democratic Republic of Afghanistan. If law does not have clarity regarding a case, the courts can make decision according to the sharia orders, democratic principles, and justice.[66]

[63]The Constitution of Afghanistan (1964) Art. 64.

[64]Farhang (1992), p. 545.

[65]The Fundamental Principles of the Democratic Republic of Afghanistan (1978) Art. 54.

[66]The Fundamental Principles of the Democratic Republic of Afghanistan (1978) Art. 56.

There were considerable changes in the text of the article in that it excluded the Ḥanafī school of thought and referred cases generally to *Sharia* and *democratic principles* and *justice*. This shift was not well received by Afghans, and following the Soviet Union invasion, most Afghans started fighting against the communist regime. President Babrak Kārmal was replaced by Dr. Najīballāh, another leader of the Communist party. He changed the policy of his government and enacted a new constitution through a Luya Jirga in 1987. The 1987 Constitution declared the independence of the judiciary and accepted that judges could decide independently during judicial proceedings and decision-making.[67]

In cases of a legal lacuna, the 1987 Constitution brought some changes in the provisions of the 1978 *Fundamental Principles of the Democratic Republic of Afghanistan* by removing the phrase *democratic principles* and retaining the Sharia order, and it gave some power to the judges to make decisions in accordance with Sharia principles in the way they think is just. The 1987 Constitution provided as follows:

> Judges shall apply provisions of this constitution and the laws of republic of Afghanistan to cases under the consideration. In case of lack of specificity in the law, the court makes a decision according to the provisions of Islamic Sharia, in the way that obtains justice in best manner.[68]

The 1987 Constitution also excluded the Ḥanafī school of thought; instead, it drew a bigger circle for judges, allowing them to apply Sharia provisions in the event of a legal lacuna in the law to be applied to a case under consideration. However, although judges were allowed to use Sharia provisions, there is no evidence that under the communist regime, the courts made a decision in accordance with Sharia for a single criminal case.

In the case of Afghanistan, Kamali claims that "except for the 1980 Constitution, which was introduced under the communist party, all the previous constitutions of Afghanistan upheld the Ḥanafī School of thought as a main source of the law in Afghanistan and exclude all the other Schools 'madhabs' existed in the country. However, they do not proclaim that all laws must be according to Ḥanafī School of Thought."[69]

After the 1987 Constitution came the current Constitution, which was enacted in 2004 and which modified Article 112 of the 1987 Constitution as follows:

> In cases under consideration, the courts shall apply provisions of this Constitution as well as other laws. If there is no provision in the Constitution or other laws about a case, the courts shall, in pursuance of Hanafi jurisprudence, and within the limits set by this Constitution, rule in a way that attains justice in the best manner.[70]

[67] The Constitution of Afghanistan (1987) Art. 111.

[68] The Constitution of Afghanistan (1987) Art. 112.

[69] Kamali (1985b), p 175.

[70] The Constitution of Afghanistan (2004) Art. 130.

This version of the article still has some ambiguity, which can lead to different interpretations by legal experts and judges. This ambiguity provides room for different practices, and consequently Afghan courts have felt free to apply the above article to all kinds of cases, including in criminal matters; however, there are some norms and standards that may contradict the implementation of the article in criminal matters.

References

ʿAbd al-Wāsiʿ et al (1921) Tamassuk al-Qużāt al-Amāniyya. Maṭbaʿa Sangī Māshinkhāna, Kabul, vol. 2

Al-Dihlawī S (1995) ʿAqd al-Jayyid fī Aḥkām al-Ijtihād wa-l-Taqlīd. Dār al-FatḤ, Emirates: Al Shareqah

Barfield T (2003) Afghan Customary law and its relationship to formal judicial institutions. Boston University

Dupree L (2014) The constitutional period begins: 1963-?. In: Id. (ed) Afghanistan. Princeton University Press, Princeton, Chapter 24, pp 559–658

Farhang M (1992) Afghanistan during the last five centuries. Ismāʿīliyya publications, Qum, vol. 1

Kamali, Mohammad Hashim Islam and its Sharia in the Afghan Constitution (2004). Available at https://hashimkamali.com/index.php/component/k2/item/171-islam-and-its-shariah-in-the-afghan-constitution-2004-with-special-reference-to-personal-law

Kamali MH (1985a) The Judiciary. In: Id. (ed) Law in Afghanistan: a study of the constitution, matrimonial law, and the judiciary. Brill, Leiden, pp 203–251

Kamali MH (1985b) Matrimonial law. In: Id. (ed) Law in Afghanistan: a study of the constitution, matrimonial law, and the judiciary. Brill, Leiden, pp 81–202

Kamali MH (2000) The right to personal safety and the principle of legality in the Sharī'ah. Islamic Stud 39(2):249–289

Kamali MH (2014) Afghanistan's constitution ten years on: what are the issues?. Afghanistan Research and Evaluation Unit

Lang AF (2013) From revolutions to constitutions: the case of Egypt. Int Aff 89(2):345–363. https://doi.org/10.1111/1468-2346.12021

Law on Organization and Jurisdiction of the Judiciary Branch (2013) Ministry of Justice, official gazette No: 1109

Lombardi CB (2013) Constitutional provisions making Sharia 'A' or 'The' Chief source of legislation: where did they come from? What do they mean? Do they matter? Am Univ Int Law Rev 28(3):733–774

Ministry of Awqāf and Islamic Affairs of Kuwait (2008) Al-Mawsūʿa al-Fiqhiyya al-Kuwaytiyya, vol. 1

MuḤammad ibn ʿAlī ibn Qāḍī MuḤammad Ḥāmid Kashshāf (1996) Iṣṭilāḥāt al-Funūn wa-l-ʿUlūm, verified by ʿAlī Daḥrūj. Maktaba Lubnān Nāshirūn, Beirut

Qazma Khūry Yūsūf (1989) Constitutions in Arabic world "Texts and amendments". Available at http://www.righttononviolence.org/mecf/wp-content/uploads/2012/03/1958Egypt.pdf

Syrian Constitution/Al-Dustūr Al-Sūrī (2012). Available at https://www.google.com/search?q=syrian+constitution+2012+pdf&sxsrf=ALeKk02BT3WDpe85vTnD-CIlfY-OAhMucA%3A1622986900318&ei=lNC8YIzoEtSE9u8P1buEgAY&oq=syrian+constitution+1950+pdf&

gs_lcp=Cgdnd3Mtd2l6EAEYADIHCAAQRxCwAzIHCAAQRxCwAzIHCAAQRxCwAzIHCAAQRxCwAzIHCAAQRxCwAzIHCAAQRxCwAzIHCAAQRxCwAzIHCAAQRxCwA1AAWABg05oFaAFwAngAgAFYiAFYkgEBMZgBAKoBB2d3cy13aXrIAQjAAQE&sclient=gws-wiz
The Civil Code of the Arab Republic of Egypt (1949). Available at http://www.sis.gov.eg/Newvr/Dustor-en001.pdf. Accessed 6 May 2021
The Constitution of Afghanistan (1923) The First Constitution of Afghanistan
The Constitution of Afghanistan (1931) The second Constitution of Afghanistan
The Constitution of Afghanistan (1964) The Third Constitution of Afghanistan
The Constitution of Afghanistan (1987) The Fourth Constitution of Afghanistan
The Constitution of Afghanistan (2004) Ministry of Justice, Official Gazette No: 818
The Constitution of Arab State of Qatar (2004). http://www.ilo.org/wcmsp5/groups/public/%2D%2D-ed_protect/%2D%2D-protrav/%2D%2D-ilo aids/documents/legaldocument/wcms_125870.pdf
The Constitution of Kingdom of Bahrain (2002). Available at http://www.bahrain-embassy.or.jp/en/constitution.pdf
The Constitution of Kuwait (1962). Available at https://www.google.com/search?q=Constitutioin+of+Kuwait+pdf&oq=Constitutioin+of+Kuwait+pdf&aqs=chrome..69i57j0i13i30.17223j1j15&sourceid=chrome&ie=UTF-8
The Constitution of Republic of Iraq (2005). Available at http://www.wipo.int/wipolex/en/text.jsp?file_id=230000
The Constitution of Sudan (1973). http://www.righttononviolence.org/mecf/wp-content/uploads/2012/01/Constitution-Sudan-1973-+-amendment-1975.pdf
The Constitution of the Islamic Republic of Iran (1989). https://faculty.unlv.edu/pwerth/Const-Iran(abridge).pdf
The Constitution of the United Arab Emirates (1996). http://www.refworld.org/pdfid/48eca8132.pdf
The Constitution of Yemen Arab Republic (2001). http://www.refworld.org/pdfid/3fc4c1e94.pdf
The Fundamental Principles of the Democratic Republic of Afghanistan (1978) the Fifth Constitution of Afghanistan
The International Legal Foundation (2004) The customary laws of Afghanistan. United States Institute of Peace
Varol O (2015) Constitutional stickiness. U.C. Davis Law Rev 49:899. Lewis & Clark Law School Legal Studies Research Paper No. 2015-6
Wakily Popalzaey A (1990) Dar al-Qaza in Afghanistan: from the beginning of Islam until Republic Era. Islamic Research Center, Kabul
Yassary N (2005) Personal law. In: Yassary N (ed) The Sharia in the constitutions of Afghanistan, Iran and Egypt - implications for private law. Max-Planck-Institute for Peace and Rule of Law. Mohr Siebek, Tübingen, pp 30–31
Zaydān ʿA (n.d.) Al-Wajīz fī Uṣūl al-Fiqh. Muʾassasa Qurṭuba Ṭibāʿa, Nashr, Tawzīʿ
Ziadeh R (2008) The Muslim brotherhood in Syria and the concept of "Democracy" CSID's 9th Annual Conference, Washington, DC

Chapter 4
Implementing Article 130 in Practice: Norms and Standards

4.1 Introduction

This chapter begins by explaining some norms and standards that are embedded in the legal system of Afghanistan, and from there it moves to an analysis of Article 130 of the Afghan Constitution. One of these is the principle of legality of crime and punishment, which guarantees freedoms of the citizens and prevents law enforcement institutions, especially judges, from limiting these freedoms or punishing the citizens solely according to judges' wishes. The principle of legality means that both the crime and the punishment must be recognized by law. Adversely, it means that if an act is not criminalized, the actor shall not be punished. This principle is accepted as one of the main principles of contemporary world legal systems and included in the laws of almost all civilized countries.[1]

Generally, there are two outcomes for this principle: the first one is a rejection of the retrospective application of law in criminal cases, and the second one is a narrow interpretation of the law. However, although this concept is recognized as a product of the modern western legal systems, many Islamic sources demonstrate that this principle is also accepted as a main principle in Islamic law. Furthermore, this principle is accepted in the legal system of Afghanistan, and it will be discussed briefly in light of Sharia and the law of Afghanistan to have a clear view of the implementation of Article 130 of the Afghan Constitution by the Afghan courts.

[1] The Universal Declaration of Human Rights (1948) Art. 9 and Art. 11. https://www.un.org/en/universal-declaration-human-rights/ Accessed 06,06, 2021.

L. Saeed, *Islam, Custom and Human Rights*, Interdisciplinary Studies in Human Rights 7, https://doi.org/10.1007/978-3-030-83086-1_4

4.2 The Principle of Legality in Sharia

The Holy Quran says: "[N]or do we ever punish until we have sent a messenger."[2] This verse means that individuals will not be punished because of an act that is not criminalized before the commission of that act. The Prophet never did apply the provision of Sharia to those who violated Quranic prohibitions before their acceptance of Islam.[3] Thus, one of the main principles in Islamic criminal procedure is that law is not applied retroactively.

The famous Islamic scholar al-Ṭebarī believed that this verse clearly says there should be no punishment before a messenger is sent to tell people what to do and what not to do and there should be no punishment unless a crime (sin) has been committed. Al-Ṭebarī believed that Allah never punishes anyone unless he commits a sin (crime) that is already defined prior to its perpetration.[4] Another Islamic scholar, Ibn Kathīr, in explaining this verse, said that Allah never punishes people unless He has already given an ultimatum by sending a messenger to tell them what is prohibited and what is allowed.[5] Imām al-Rāzī, another famous Islamic scholar, believed that justice means punishing wrongdoers after the messengers had already told them what is legal and what is illegal.[6] Because the messenger has already informed them about the rules, they will be punished if they violated the rules.

There are also other Quranic verses that welcome the principle of legality and accept it as a foundational rule. The Quran says: "Messengers delivering good news, and bringing warnings; so that people may have no excuse before Allah after the coming of the messengers."[7] This means that the messengers told people what is allowed and what is prohibited and Allah has given all the reasons, and He will punish someone if he commits a prohibited act. Furthermore, another Quranic verse states: "Had we destroyed them with a punishment before him (Messenger), they would have said, 'Our Lord, if only you had sent us a messenger, we would have followed your revelations before we were humiliated and disgraced."[8] Thus, the Quran predicts that if we punish people because of their illegal actions, they will complain that a messenger has not been sent to them to make them understand what is legal and what is illegal.

The Holy Quran also says: "There is no community but a warner has passed through it."[9] Moreover, it states: "Your Lord never destroys cities without first sending a messenger in their midst, reciting to them our revelations. And we never

[2]The Holy Quran, Sura Al-Isrā', (17: 15).

[3]Lippman (1989), p. 47.

[4]Al-Ṭebarī (2000), p. 402.

[5]Ibn Kathīr (1999a), p. 353.

[6]Al-Rāzī (1999), p. 207.

[7]The Holy Quran, Sura Al-Nisā' (4: 165) (رّسُلاً مّبَشّرِينَ وَمُنذِرِينَ لِئَلَا يَكُونَ لِلنَاسِ عَلَى الله حُجّةٌ بَعْدَ الرسل).

[8]The Holy Quran, Sura Ṭā-Hā (20: 134) (وَلَوْ أَنَآ أَهْلَكْنَٰهُم بِعَذَاب من قَبْلِهِۦ لَقَالُواْ رَبَنَا لَوْلَآ أَرْسَلْتَ إِلَيْنَا رَسُولاً فَنَتَبِعَ ءَايَٰتِك
مِن قَبْلِ أَن نَذِل وَنَخْزَىٰ).

[9]The Holy Quran, Sura FāṬir (35: 24) (وَإِن منْ أُمَةٍ إِلَا خلاَ فِيهَا نَذِيرٌ).

destroy the cities, unless their people are wrongdoers."[10] These are some of the Quranic verses that clearly demonstrate the principle of legality in Islamic law and reject punishing people because of an act that is not considered a crime prior to its commission.

Furthermore, understanding the law creation process in Islam took several years to achieve at the time Prophet Mohammad was alive. Obviously, not all Sharia laws were enacted at once. The verses of the Holy Quran were based on the need of society, in response to a problem, or aimed at addressing a question that arose from the community. Sometimes it took several days to receive a response from Prophet Mohammad regarding an issue. There are many acts that were practiced by Prophet Mohammad's followers that were permissible during their time but later on declared to be illegal. When a new order prohibited an act, it did not include those actors that had done it in the past.

Islamic Sharia not only accepts the principle of legality, but it also supports the main result of it: that there should be no retrospective application of law in criminal cases. With some exceptions in criminal matters, the law does not operate retrospectively.[11] Thus, when the new verses of the Holy Quran disclosed a new law, it did not apply to previous cases. For instance, the Quran says: "Do not Marry women your fathers married, except what is already past. That is improper, indecent, and a bad custom."[12] Those who married their stepmothers before this rule were not subject to this new law, and there was not any punishment for them. So before Prophet Mohammad received this order, it was a common custom among some Arabs, especially Medina citizens, to marry their stepmothers after the death of their father. In fact, they inherited their stepmothers,' along with their fathers,' property.[13]

Furthermore, there are some principles that are widely accepted by the majority of Islamic scholars that support the conclusion that the principle of legality is included within the framework of Sharia. One of these principles is as follows: *Lā Ebrata le Afa�alel Uqalā-i Qabla Worūd al Naṣ-i* ("There is no validity for the people's acts, prior the existence of the text of Sharia").[14] It means there is no penalty for an act if there is no text in the Sharia to specify the status of that act within the Sharia framework. Thus, there should be no punishment if there is no text that recognized the act as a crime.

In the Shia Jaʿfarī school of thought, there is a legal maxim that says *indecency of punishment without expression* (*qubḥ al-ʿiqāb bilā bayān*). The concept of this maxim was discussed for the first time by a famous Shia scholar, Shaykh Ṭūsī, in his famous book *Al-Tibyān fī Tafsīr*, where he explained the above verse of the Holy

[10]The Holy Quran, Sura al Qaṣaṣ (28: 59) (وَمَا كَانَ رَبُّكَ مُهْلِكَ الْقُرَى حَتَّى يَبْعَثَ فِي أُمِّهَا رَسُولاً يَتْلُو عَلَيْهِمْ آيَاتِنَا وَمَا كُنَّا مُهْلِكِي الْقُرَى إِلَّا وَأَهْلُهَا ظَالِمُونَ).

[11]Munir (2018), p. 9.

[12]The Holy Quran, Sura Al-Nisāʾ (04:22) (وَلَا تَنكِحُواْ مَا نَكَحَ ءَابَآؤُكُم مِّنَ ٱلنِّسَآءِ إِلَّا مَا قَدْ سَلَفَ ۚ إِنَّهُۥ كَانَ فَٰحِشَةً وَمَقْتًا وَسَآءَ سَبِيلًا).

[13]Ibn Kathīr (1999b), p. 240; Al-Ālūsī (1994), vol. 3, p. 488.

[14]Al-Āmidī (n.d.), p. 91.

Quran. He believed that it is indecent to punish people for an offense that they were not informed about before they committed it. The concept of this maxim developed and is recognized as a foundation for the principle of legality of crime and punishment among Muslim scholars, especially in the Shia school of thought.[15]

Thus, the principle of legality is fully accepted by the Islamic legal system. Sharia clearly declares that there should be no punishment without law. This principle has been reflected in many Islamic legal sources, including the Holy Quran, and was widely practiced by Prophet Mohammad and his followers. This principle is accepted by Sunni and Shia jurists as well. Furthermore, it has been developed and considered to be a foundational principle applied in legislative processes throughout the long history of Islamic legal systems, and judges are required to respect this principle when they make decisions. Ignoring this principle in judicial processes violates the fundamental rights of citizens and the norms accepted by Sharia.

4.3 The Principle of Legality in Afghan Law

The principle of legality is also reflected in the 2004 Constitution and the Penal Code of Afghanistan. Article 27 of the Afghan Constitution includes the principle of legality and states:

> No deed shall be considered a crime unless ruled by a law promulgated prior to commitment of the offense. No one shall be pursued, arrested, or detained without due process of law. No one shall be punished without the decision of an authoritative court taken in accordance with the provisions of the law, promulgated prior to commitment of the offense.[16]

This article clearly accepts the principle of legality and announces that no act is considered a crime unless it is recognized as a crime by law before it is committed.

Article 3 of the Afghan Constitution states:

> No law shall contravene the tenets and provisions of the holy religion of Islam in Afghanistan.[17]

Although Article 3 is ambiguous when it comes to the definition of the terms "tenets" and "provisions" found in the holy religion of Islam, the article rejects any law that contradicts Islamic principles. Also, there is a consensus among all Muslim scholars, both Shia and Sunni, that the principle of legality is one of the fundamental principles of the Holy Quran and Prophet Mohammad's traditions, as well as of the Islamic criminal justice system. Therefore, the principle of legality is also accepted implicitly in light of Article 3 of the Afghan Constitution.

---

[15] Shaykh Ṭūsī (2001), p. 58.

[16] The Constitution of Afghanistan (2004) Art. 27.

[17] The Constitution of Afghanistan (2004) Art. 3.

Furthermore, the Penal Code of Afghanistan also accepts the principle of legality of crimes and punishments as a fundamental standard. The second article of the Penal Code states:

> No act shall be considered crime, but in accordance with the provisions of the law, which has been enforced before commitment of the act under reference.[18]

This article clearly indicates that crimes are those acts that are recognized as such by law. The Penal Code also prohibits the punishment of those who have committed an act not recognized as a crime by law.

> No one can be punished, but in accordance with the provisions of the law, which has been enforced before commitment of the act under reference.[19]

This article prohibits any kind of punishment for any act that is not criminalized under the laws of Afghanistan. So the principle of legality of crime and punishment is accepted by the Afghan legal system and must be respected by the courts and law enforcement. Thus, the courts must consider this principle when they make a decision.

4.4 Analysis of the Application of Article 130 of the Afghan Constitution

According to Article 130 of the 2004 Constitution of Afghanistan, in the case of a legal lacuna, the Afghan courts are allowed to make decisions based on the provisions of the Ḥanafī school of thought concerning a case under consideration. Although there is no consensus among Afghan judges and legal experts on the general implementation of Article 130 of the Afghan Constitution, it has been practically applied in a variety of criminal cases. Generally, there are two groups of judges and legal experts that have different interpretations when it comes to the implementation of Article 130. One group believes that the article must be implemented only in civil cases. Other judges and legal experts believe that all cases, including criminal cases, should be subject to the said provision. Both parties have their own justifications for their argument.

First, this chapter will examine the view of those who limit the implementation of the article to only civil cases, and then it will go on to discuss the opposing group's argument. One of the members of the Supreme Court of Afghanistan, Justice Barat Ali Mateen,[20] believes that Article 130 must be applied only to civil cases because

[18] Penal Code of Afghanistan (1976) Art. 2.

[19] Penal Code of Afghanistan (1976) Art. 3.

[20] Judge Barat Ali Mateen graduated from Rohol Madaris "Dār al-ʿUlūm RūḤānī Baba" in Gardez City of Paktia Province in the south of Afghanistan. Then he graduated from the Kabul University Sharia faculty with a BA with honors in Islamic law in 1984. After 30 years' experience as a judge, he was appointed as a member of the Supreme Court of Afghanistan in 2013.

the application of Article 130 in criminal cases contradicts the principle of legality of crimes and punishments. Furthermore, applying this article to criminal cases is unconstitutional because the principle of legality is accepted by both the Afghan Constitution and the Penal Code.

Justice Mateen references specific provisions of the Penal Code. Article 2 states: *No act shall be considered crime, but in accordance with the law.*[21]

Article 3 of the Penal Code guarantees that no one shall be punished without law:

> No one can be punished but in accordance with the provision of the law which has been enforced before commitment of the act under consideration.[22]

For these reasons, Justice Mateen believes that only civil cases should be subject to Article 130 of the Constitution. He believes that in order to respect the principle of legality, Article 130 should not be applied in criminal cases.[23]

Dr. Mohammad Amin Ahmadi, former member of the Independent Commission for Overseeing the Implementation of the Constitution (ICOIC), also believes that Article 130 should only be applied to civil cases, not to criminal cases. He said Article 130 includes a condition about when the Ḥanafī doctrine should be applied to a case: *within the limits set by this Constitution*. One of the limits in the Constitution is Article 27, which accepts the principle of legality. Thus, according to Ahmadi, applying Article 130 to criminal cases should be considered a violation of the Constitution.[24]

Mohammad Ashraf Rasooli[25] believes that Article 130 of the Constitution must not be used in criminal cases at all because it is unconstitutional as it violates Article 27 of the Constitution and many provisions of law, like Articles 1, 2, 3, and 27 of the Penal Code, and provisions of international law.[26] He maintains that Afghanistan has a presidential system, in which the principle of separation of powers is strictly observed. So only the legislature has the power to enact laws and criminalize an act. If an act is not considered a crime by law and there is no punishment for such an act under the law, courts cannot function as lawmakers and criminalize an act.[27]

[21] Penal Code of Afghanistan (1976) Art. 2.

[22] Penal Code of Afghanistan (1976) Art. 3.

[23] Interview with Barat Ali Mateen, justice at the Supreme Court of Afghanistan. Dated 1 April 2016.

[24] Interview with Dr. Mohammad Amin Ahmadi, former member of the Independent Commission of Overseeing the Implementation of the Constitution (ICOIC) and current chancellor of Ibn Sina Private University in Kabul. Dated 5 March 2016.

[25] Mohammad Ashraf Rasooli is a famous lawyer in Afghanistan with many published work in the field of Afghan law. He served more than 45 years in the justice sector: 15 years as a judge at the Afghan Supreme Court and for several years the head of the *taqnīn* (Drafting Laws) Department and then the deputy minister of the Ministry of Justice (MoJ). In addition, he was the chairman of the drafting committee on the new Penal Code of Afghanistan and currently serves as a senior advisor for MoJ.

[26] Interview with Mohammad Ashraf Rasooli. Dated 5 April 2016.

[27] Rasooli (2015), p. 83.

Furthermore, Mr. Ruhullah Qarizada,[28] president of the Afghan Independent Bar Association, disagrees with the use of Article 130 of the Afghan Constitution. He maintains that Article 130 must be limited to noncriminal cases because making decisions in criminal cases based on Article 130 of the Constitution contradicts the principle of legality.[29]

Furthermore, Dr. Allamah, deputy at the General Attorney Office and one of the drafters of the new Penal Code, also maintains that Article 130 of the Afghan Constitution shall not be used in criminal cases because it is a violation of the principle of legality, which is recognized by the Constitution and the Penal Code of 1976 of Afghanistan.[30]

Also, Dr. Ahmad Reza Sadeqi, legal advisor for the Ministry of Justice and member of the drafting committee of the new Penal Code, believes that the principle of legality is accepted in the legal system of Afghanistan, so the use of Article 130 is a violation of this principle; hence, this article shall not be used in any criminal case at all.[31]

Moreover, Mr. Muhsin Farid, chancellor of Tabish Private University and member of the Penal Code committee, believes that using Article 130 of the Constitution is unconstitutional and against the principle of legality.[32]

On the other hand, some other judges and legal experts believe that Article 130 is applicable to all cases, including criminal matters. For instance, the former Supreme Court of Afghanistan Chief Justice Abdul Salaam Azimi says that Article 130 should be applied because state law does not include all crimes occurring in society; in contrast, Sharia—particularly the Ḥanafī school of thought—comprehensively covers all aspects of life in society. Thus, it is necessary that courts fill the legal gaps by using the Ḥanafī doctrines. He said there are five main purposes for the implementation of Sharia: the preservation of (1) religion/faith (Arabic: *dīn*), (2) life (Arabic: *nafs*), (3) lineage/progeny (Arabic: *nasl*), (4) intellect (Arabic: *ʿaql*), and (5) property/wealth (Arabic: *māl*). The main goal for the implementation of Sharia is to protect these objectives. If any act contradicts the above purposes, it is punishable. Thus, Sharia is more comprehensive and covers many aspects of life that may not be criminalized in state laws.[33] Furthermore, a Supreme Court of Afghanistan justice, Deen Mohammad Gran,[34] also said that Article 130 should be applied to all cases, including criminal matters. He also believed that Sharia, not state law, adequately

---

[28] Mr. Ruhullah Qarizada has served as President of the Afghan Independent Bar Association since 2008. He was one of the core members of the drafting committee of the new Penal Code.

[29] Interview with Mr. Ruhullah Qarizada. Dated 5 December 2018.

[30] Interview with Dr. Ghulam Haidar Allamah, Deputy of General Attorney Office and member of the drafting committee on new Penal Code. Dated 9 February 2017.

[31] Interview with Dr. Ahmad Reza Sadeqi. Dated 19 Feb 2016.

[32] Interview with Mr. Muhsen Farid. Dated 27 Aug 2016.

[33] Interview with Prof. Abdul Salaam Azimi, former Chief Justice of Afghanistan. Dated 29 September 2017.

[34] Deen Mohammad Gran graduated from the Kabul Sharia Faculty and obtained his master's degree in Comparative Islamic Jurisprudence from al-Azhar University in Egypt. He was a professor of the Sharia faculty at Kabul University and served as the dean of the Kabul Sharia faculty for 7 years and then became a member of the Afghan Supreme Court.

covers all activities that are harmful to society. Therefore, in the case of a legal lacuna, the case should be referred to Sharia.

Additionally, Abdul Karim Qanit,[35] a senior judge, has the same opinion and believes that Afghanistan's state law is not complete; on the other hand, Sharia is much more inclusive and can address any kind of legal problem. So the use of Article 130 allows judges to have access to tremendous sources of laws and legal principles to find a solution for almost any kind of legal question. He also claims that Article 130 does not violate the principle of legality of crime and punishment because the inclusion of Article 130 in the Constitution means that the Constitution specifically recognized the Ḥanafī school of thought as law. Therefore, according to Article 130, the Ḥanafī school of thought has the same status as law in the legal system of Afghanistan.[36]

Although the application of Article 130 of the Afghan Constitution to criminal cases has been shown to be a controversial issue, almost all Afghan legal scholars and judges agree that the Penal Code of Afghanistan, which was enacted on October 7, 1976, is out of date and does not match some of the needs of today's Afghan society. There are many acts that should be considered a crime to prevent harm to citizens and bring harmony to society.[37] Nevertheless, to some extent, the 1976 Penal Code and other laws that deal with criminal matters are not capable of providing answers for all the needs in this regard. This deficiency of law forces judges to use Article 130 when there is a gap in state law.[38]

Indeed, although some judges disagree with using the Ḥanafī school doctrine in criminal cases, gaps in existing criminal law force them to use the Ḥanafī school of thought in case of a legal lacuna. For example, Judge Said Murad Sharifi, the current Secretary-General of the Supreme Court High Counsel, also believes that Article 130 of the Constitution should not be used in criminal cases. In a Supreme Court seminar for provincial chief judges in 2007, he proposed that Article 130 of the Constitution shall not be applied to criminal cases because it is a violation of the principle of legality, which is accepted in the Constitution and the Penal Code of Afghanistan; however, due to the gaps in the Penal Code and other related laws, his proposal was rejected and the Supreme Court allowed lower courts to apply Article 130 in the case of a legal lacuna.[39] He also added that recently there was a case regarding a judge that violated the principle of impartiality. He provided first a fraudulent document for one of the parties (the plaintiff) and then decided the case

---

[35] Mr. Abdul Karim Qanet has served as a judge for more than 40 years, and now he is a counselor judge for the justices of the Supreme Court.

[36] Interview with Judge Abdul Karim Qanet. Dated 13 June 2016.

[37] Interview with former Chief Justice Abdul Salam Azimi. Dated 25 April 2016. Interview with Judge Said Murad Sharifi, Secretary-General of the Supreme Court High Council. Dated 11 June 2016.

[38] Interview with retired Senior Judge Abdul Kareem Qanet. Dated 25 June 2016/ Interview with Abdul Salam Qāḍizadah, former chief judge of Kabul appellate court. Dated 13 June 2016.

[39] Interview with Said Murad Sharifi, secretary General of High Counsel of the Supreme Court of Afghanistan. Dated 11 June 2016.

based on that document in favor of the plaintiff. According to law, if a judge is accused of a crime, his case will be investigated and adjudicated by the High Counsel of the Supreme Court.[40] The judge in this case acted in a way that the High Counsel of the Supreme Court considered a violation of the code of conduct. However, since there was no provision of law to punish him, the High Counsel of the Supreme Court made its decision based on Article 130 of the Constitution. Even though some justices and Judge Sharifi clearly said that they disagree with applying Article 130 in criminal cases, the lack of provision in the laws regarding certain harmful acts in society convinced them to promulgate the decision based on Article 130 of the Constitution.[41]

Considering both parties' points of view, it seems that there are some weaknesses and strong points in both of their arguments. On one hand, the since Penal Code of Afghanistan was enacted on October 7, 1976, there have been many gaps in the field of criminal law in Afghanistan; on the other hand, there are some fundamental principles that must be considered to guarantee justice and fairness when a criminal case is under consideration in court. Generally speaking, it is not legal to punish someone based on an act that is not a crime in the law. The author prefers that Article 130 should not be applied to criminal cases at all because of the following reasons:

1. Historically, the concept of this article is derived from the first article of the Egyptian Civil Code, written by ʿAbd al-Razzāq al-Sanhūrī in 1949.[42] The first article of the Sanhūrī Code only talks about a legal lacuna in civil cases, not in criminal cases. Since this concept was originally built for civil cases, not for criminal cases, it should be limited only to what it was made for.
2. The article only authorized the courts to make a decision according to the Ḥanafī school of thought in case of a legal lacuna. According to the civil procedure of Afghanistan, the parties can go directly to court and start a legal action. The code defines a claim as demanding a right from another before a court.[43] Also, the code says that the petitioner can request the court directly or through legal bureaus, such as the Law Department of the Ministry of Justice (*ḥuqūq*), for a legal proceeding and to make a decision regarding it.[44] Thus, according to the law, the parties can go directly to the court and start their claim before a judge. I believe that if there is a gap in the laws regarding a case in court, the judge can refer to the Ḥanafī school of thought and make a decision on the case accordingly.

[40] Law on Organization and Jurisdiction of the Judiciary of Afghanistan (2013) Art. 91.

[41] Interview with Said Murad Sharifi, secretary General of High Counsel of the Supreme Court of Afghanistan. Dated 11 June 2016.

[42] Civil Code of Egypt (1949) Art. 1.

[43] Civil Procedure of Afghanistan (1990) Art. 5, official Gazette No: 722.

[44] Civil Procedure of Afghanistan (1990) Art. 12.

3. Criminal law procedure provides for the process for resolving a criminal case, starting from the discovery of a crime by the police, followed by the investigation of the prosecutor,[45] and finally the submission of the case to court for adjudication. According to criminal procedure, criminal cases never go directly to court as there must be a pretrial proceeding. If an act is not criminalized, how can a police officer make an arrest and charge a citizen with an offense that is not considered a crime according to law? Furthermore, how can the prosecutor initiate a case and conduct an investigation regarding an act that is not a crime under the law? Due to a defined legal procedure, the judges, on one hand, cannot hear a case directly from the victim as it has to come from the prosecutor's office; on the other hand, the police and the prosecutor have no respective authority to arrest and investigate someone because of an act that is not considered a crime under the law. So it means Article 130 of the Afghan Constitution cannot be applied to criminal cases.
4. There are conditions in the article that limit its application by the court. According to the article, first, the case must be under the consideration of the court. Second, the priority is the provisions of the Constitution and other laws; it states that if there is no provision in the laws, including the Constitution, regarding a case, the court shall make a decision according to the Ḥanafī school of thought, but this decision must be within the limits provided by the Constitution to provide justice in the best way possible. To make it more clear, it would be best to analytically examine what the conditions mean:

   - The first issue is that the case must be under the consideration of the court. The *Law on Organization and Jurisdiction of Judiciary Branch of Afghanistan* defines a case as an issue of a criminal, civil, public, family, or commercial nature that parties submit to the court for a decision.[46] So the court is mandated to decide a case if it is officially referred to it for consideration. However, Article 130 does not give any hint as to whether aside from the court any other institution, like the police department or prosecutor's office, can take action against a citizen based on Article 130 of the Afghan Constitution. It will be discussed when we analyze the cases in which Article 130 of the Constitution has been applied.
   - The court cannot apply Article 130 of the Afghan Constitution if there is no provision in the Constitution or other laws. So since the priority is the Constitution and state law, the court must refer to them first. If there is no provision in these laws, the court can then apply the Ḥanafī school of thought to the case. It will be examined in the case study how the courts have dealt with this condition.

The limits set by the Constitution are significant because they guarantee the basic rights of the citizens and prevent the state to exercise its power to violate citizen's

[45] The Constitution of Afghanistan (2004) Art. 34.

[46] Law on Organization and Jurisdiction of the Judiciary Branch of Afghanistan (2013) Art. 4, clause 15.

rights. In addition, in the Constitution, there are principles that are important and almost all civilized nations accept as the foundation for their legal system, particularly the criminal justice system. This paper will study how the Ḥanafī school of thought plays a role in the criminal justice system of Afghanistan within the limits set by the Constitution.

Although there is no consensus among Afghan judges and legal experts on the application of Article 130 to criminal cases, in practice, whenever there is no provision of law regarding an act that judges consider harmful to society and damaging to the social order, they make decisions according to Article 130.

Analyzing these arguments, there are weaknesses and strengths on both sides. On one hand, the current Penal Code does not respond to the needs of society because it was enacted in 1976. There are many laws[47] that adopted to fill the gaps, but gaps remain. On the other hand, the Afghan Constitution and the Penal Code adopt the principle of legality of crimes and punishments, which prevents punishing someone for an act that is not criminalized under the law.[48] Article 130 has been widely used in practice by the Afghan courts in criminal cases, which is a clear violation of the principle of legality.

Although it could be argued that since the Ḥanafī school provisions have been specifically included in the text of Article 130, it should not be considered a violation of the principle of legality. The text of the article, however, reveals that there are some conditions that limit the use of Article 130 in criminal cases. One condition is that this article must be used within the *limits set by the constitution*, and Article 27 of the Constitution, which supports the principle of legality, is a limitation and should be considered a firewall to limit the applicability of Article 130 only to noncriminal cases.

Obviously, since 1976, when Afghanistan's current Penal Code was enacted, there have been many changes in the criminal law field and norms of Afghan society that consequently changed the concepts of crime and punishment in society. Accordingly, there are many gaps in the criminal law of Afghanistan that must be taken into consideration. Those who are in favor of using Article 130 in criminal cases believe that because the current criminal law provisions are inadequate to cover new offenses emerging in society, judges must control the harm done to society and be authorized to punish wrongdoers using Sharia law.

On the other hand, theoretically, there are some fundamental principles and norms that must be taken into account to guarantee justice and fairness when a criminal case is under judgment. One of these standards is the principle of legality of crime and punishment. This principle has deep roots in Sharia and Islamic main sources, the Quran and Prophet Mohammad's traditions. Furthermore, it is accepted

[47]More than 50 laws, besides the Criminal Code, in Afghanistan have criminal provisions, such as the Law on Crime Against Internal and External Security, Anti-Bribery and Corruption Law, Law on Elimination of Violence Against Women (EVAW), Anti-Money Laundering and Proceeds of Crime Law, Law Against Terrorism Crimes, Counter Adduction and Human Trafficking Law, Law Against Intoxicating Drinks and Drugs as well as Controlling them, etc., but still a hole remains.

[48]The Constitution of Afghanistan (2004) Art. 27/ Penal Code of Afghanistan (1976) Art. 2.

by the legal system of Afghanistan through both the Constitution and the Penal Code.

4.5 Criminal Procedure in Accordance with Law and Sharia

The procedure for criminal cases is different according to Afghan law and Sharia principles. Although there are some similarities between both systems, they have considerable differences that have a significant impact on the perceived legitimacy of court decisions. Some of the common standards that both systems have include respect for individuals' property, equality before the law, nonretroactive application of laws, presumption of innocence,[49] and the principle of legality.[50] There are also considerable differences that should be taken into account, particularly due to the fact that courts are applying the Ḥanafī school provisions to criminal cases based on Article 130 of the Constitution.

In terms of institutional structures, according to Sharia, there are no police and prosecutor offices to respectively conduct a primary investigation and file a case in court. However, it is unconstitutional if a case has not been processed according to law.[51] Having such institutions is not contrary to Sharia, but it can affect the outcome of the case if it is processed under a different procedure. For example, if a court uses Article 130 of the Afghan Constitution as a basis for its decision regarding a case that is not considered a crime under the law, courts applying (a) the Penal Code or (b) Sharia would reach different results. Each system, state law and Sharia, has its own norms and standards that must be considered when a criminal case is processed. If these standards do not reflect due process of law, the legitimacy of the process and the decision of the court should be challenged.

The norms set by Islamic jurists are not the same as those established by state law. For instance, state law provides a list of incriminating evidence that must be collected by the police and the prosecutor; however, it is not the same in Sharia because there is no role for the prosecutor in the Sharia. To explain these similarities and differences, the procedures in each system will be discussed briefly.

Before analyzing the criminal procedures in the legal systems of Afghanistan, it should be noted that the cases examined in this work have not been processed through one single law on criminal procedure. Afghanistan has had three criminal

---

[49] Lippman (1989), pp. 46–47.

[50] Id., pp. 57–60.

[51] The Constitution of Afghanistan (2004) Art. 27: "In cases under consideration, the courts shall apply provisions of this Constitution as well as other laws. If there is no provision in the Constitution or other laws about a case, the courts shall, in pursuance of Ḥanafī jurisprudence, and, within the limits set by this Constitution, rule in a way that attains justice in the best manner."

procedural laws since 1965: the first one was enacted in 1965;[52] the second, the *Interim Criminal Procedure Code for Courts,*[53] was enacted on February 25, 2004; and the current *Criminal Procedure Law*, which has 382 articles, was enacted on May 05, 2014. The cases under study in this research deal with the two most recent laws because some of these cases happened before May 2014.

In addition, there are two police laws in Afghanistan: one enacted on September 22, 2005, and the current police law, which is applicable from August 27, 2009. Furthermore, there are two laws on the *Structure and Authority of the Attorney General Office* (the current law was enacted on October 07, 2013) and two laws on the *Organization and Jurisdiction of the Judiciary* (the current law was enacted on June 30, 2013), which have been applied in different times. Thus, in the section discussing the case studies, different laws will be referred to in the different cases based on which was enacted and applied at the time.

4.5.1 *Criminal Procedure According to the Law of Afghanistan*

Constitutionally, criminal procedure in Afghanistan has been divided among three different governmental organizations: the police, the Attorney General's Office, and the courts. The first step in criminal procedure involves the police department: to discover the crime and criminal. The second stage pertains to the Attorney General's Office: to conduct the investigation, file the case, and then submit it to the courts for adjudication, which is the final step. Article 134 of the 2004 Afghan Constitution states:

> Discovery of crimes shall be the duty of police, and investigation and filing the case against the accused in the court shall be the responsibility of the Attorney's Office, in accordance with the provisions of the law....[54]

Article 134 provides that the police have the duty to discover crimes in accordance with law. The police department therefore has the authority to deal with any criminal act and stop people from committing crimes.

It is important to note that criminal procedural law in Afghanistan has been designed for law enforcement institutions to regulate the procedure only for those crimes that are defined by law. This criminal procedure does not cover cases that are not criminalized by the Penal Code or other laws. The Afghan Penal Code states:

---

[52] The 1964 Criminal Procedure Code was published in four volumes and had more than 480 Articles. It was in place until February 2004.

[53] The Interim Criminal Procedure Code was composed of 15 chapters and 98 articles. Since it was too short, there were some gaps in this law that the Afghan government allowed the prosecutor's office and the courts to fill by referring back to the 1965 Criminal Law and its amendments.

[54] The Constitution of Afghanistan (2004) Art. 134.

> This law regulates the "taʿzīrī" crimes and punishments. Those committing crimes of "Ḥudūd", "qiṣāṣ" and "diya" shall be punished in accordance with the provisions of Islamic religious law (the Hanafi religious jurisprudence).[55]

In *taʿzīr* cases, the court must rely only on evidence recognized by law. If the evidence is not collected in a manner prescribed by law, the court is not permitted to issue a decision based on it. For instance, the law states:

> The court cannot make a decision based on evidence and reasons collected not in accordance with the law.[56]

In addition, the current criminal procedure indicates that the court cannot issue a decision against an accused person based on doubtful evidence:

> The court cannot issue a decision to convict the accused person based on suspicion or if there is doubt in reasons or evidence.[57]

The court is therefore obligated to formulate its decision based on due process of law and ensure that all reasons are supported by law and all evidence is collected legally.

Examining police laws[58] reveals that the police have a wide-ranging authority. These laws have not drawn a specific circle for police to practice their power against citizens within a limited boundary. For example, there are some vague terms in police laws, like *ensuring and maintaining public order and security*, *counter moral deviations*, *moral social behavior*, that could be defined in many ways. On one hand, this ambiguity affects the freedom of the citizens in their daily life; on the other hand, it causes some problems in the implementation of the law and the authority of the police to take preventive actions to stop people from committing crimes. For instance, the *Police Law of 2005*[59] gave 21 duties to the police. Some of these do not have clear boundaries that specify the exact obligations. Here are examples:

1. Ensure and maintain public order and security
2. Ensure individual and societal security and protect their legal rights and freedoms
3. Take preventive actions to stop crimes from happening
4. Timely discover the crimes and arrest the suspects and perpetrators according to the provisions of the law
5. Counter moral deviations, in moral social behavior and actions that disturb public tranquility
6. ………[60]

[55] Penal Code of Afghanistan (1976) Art. 1, official gazette no. 347. Each of these types of crimes will be discussed in greater detail in upcoming chapters.

[56] The Interim Criminal Procedure Code for Courts (2004) Art. 7, official gazette no. 820.

[57] Criminal Procedure Code (2014) Art. 19, official gazette no. 1132, clause 4.

[58] Both Laws, Police Law of Afghanistan (22 September 2005), which is not enacted anymore, and the enacted current Police Law published on official gazette no. 994 on 27 August 2009.

[59] Parwīz Kāmbakhsh case, discussed in the related chapter, has been processed under this law; however, on 27 August 2009, a new law was passed by the parliament and is still enacted.

[60] The Police Law of Afghanistan (2005) Art. 5.

The third clause indicates that the police have the authority to take preventive actions to preclude a crime or to discover a crime if it has already happened. Some of these clauses, however, can be widely interpreted by the police; e.g., any act that harms public order and security requires police action. Since the law provides no definition for these terms, it may give unlimited power to the police department to react against any act that they consider harmful to society and can limit the citizens' freedoms. But the law limits the authority of the police when it comes to keeping people under surveillance. The police law states that when discovering aspects of a crime and examining a suspect, the police can keep him under surveillance for up to 72 h only.[61]

The 2014 *Criminal Procedure Code* puts responsibility on the police and national security operatives to detect crime and arrest the accused person, as well as collect evidence:

(1) Detection of a crime, according to circumstances, shall take place by the police and national security operative.
(2) The police and national security operative after receiving notification about a crime or noticing the signs and traces of a crime shall go to the crime scene observing other conditions contained in this law and carry out the following activities:

  1-. Observing the crime scene and photographing and identifying the circumstances and conditions that reveal the occurrence of the incident.
  2-. Identifying the type of crime, perpetrator and victim.
  3-. Arresting and searching the suspect, if necessary.
  4-. Identifying evidence, proofs, traces and signs related to the crime, perpetrator and its consequences.[62]

It is important that the law assign the job of discovering a crime and identifying the type of crime etc. to the police and national security officers. Because specific crimes are defined in the Criminal Code, they can react only against those acts that are criminalized by such code:

> An act or omission of an act contrary to the law, such that the act should result in a criminal effect and a cause relationship be established between the act and the effect, is the material element of crime.[63]

Thus, the police can take an action against a person if he commits an act that is already recognized as a crime under the law. If someone acts in a manner that is considered a crime by law, the police can make an arrest. If a crime has occurred, after the discovery of such crime, the police are mandated to make an arrest and provide an arrest registry for the suspect and include all the necessary elements for the further processing of the case. The Criminal Procedure Law provides:

---

[61] The Police Law of Afghanistan (2005) Art. 25.

[62] Criminal Procedure Code (2014) Art. 80, official gazette no. 1132.

[63] Penal Code of Afghanistan (1976) Art. 27.

(1) Police and national security operative shall be duty-bound to prepare a registry for the suspect's arrest. The registry shall contain the following:

1-. Reason for arrest.
2-. Date of arrest (time, day, month, and year).
3-. Place of arrest.
4-. Primary statements of the arrested person.
5-. Details of the incident

(2) Arrest registry shall be signed by the person who prepares it and other people who were present during the arrest and the suspect's fingerprint shall be obtained.[64]

The *Interim Criminal Procedure Code* specifies that upon receiving information regarding a crime, the police shall report the case to the primary prosecutor's office within 24 h.[65] When the primary attorney's office receives the case from the police, it should complete the investigation and submit the case to the primary court for adjudication. The police are also mandated to officially submit the file, including the arrest registry and the collected evidence related to the crime, to the prosecutor within 72 h after the arrest:

(1) Police are obligated to officially send the registry of performance along with collected documents, evidence and grounds to the prosecutor's office and also hand over the suspect to the relevant prosecutor's office within 72 hours for investigation, after the suspect is arrested.[66]

When the primary prosecutor's office receives a report regarding a crime committed in its territorial jurisdiction, within 48 h, it shall start a further investigation and file a criminal case. The prosecutor's office cannot reject or stop the proceedings of a criminal case referred to them unless the law states otherwise.[67] The main goal of the investigation by the primary attorney's office is to conduct a comprehensive assessment of the evidence, uncover the facts of the case, and determine the responsible person or persons in the case. In addition, during the investigation, the prosecutor must collect both compelling reasons for prosecution and reasons for acquittal and evaluate them equally.[68]

According to law, one of the duties of the attorney's office is to investigate and start litigation against the accused before the court.[69] The prosecutor must do an investigation regarding felonies and misdemeanor crimes to find the facts of the case, make sure that a crime happened, and identify the criminal.[70] After the prosecutor

[64] Criminal Procedure Code (2014) Art. 86, official gazette no. 1132.

[65] The Interim Criminal Procedure Code for Courts (2004) Art. 21, official gazette no. 820.

[66] Criminal Procedure Code (2014) Art. 87, official gazette no. 1132, clause 1.

[67] The Interim Criminal Procedure Code for Courts (2004) Art. 22/ Art. 33, official gazette no. 820.

[68] The Interim Criminal Procedure Code for Courts (2004) Art. 33, official gazette no. 820.

[69] The Law on Structure and Authority of Attorney General Office (2013) Art. 3, official gazette no. 1117.

[70] Criminal Procedure Code (2014) Art. 145, official gazette no. 1132.

completes the investigation,[71] he should provide an accusation letter (charge sheet),[72] and after confirmation, the prosecutor is obligated to file a criminal case and officially submit it to court.[73] Courts have the authority to process all criminal cases and make a decision within the limits provided by law.[74] When a criminal case is referred to courts, the relevant court must adjudicate the case within the time limit provided by law.[75]

Finally, the court must issue a decision in accordance with law and based on the reasons and evidence provided under the criminal procedural law. The criminal procedural law provides a list of incriminating evidence that should be relied on when a decision is made. The most important pieces of incriminating evidence are the following: the confession of the accused, testimonies of witnesses, relevant documents, the identification of the suspect via a random lineup, different signs that have been scientifically proven by experts to be effective in detecting crimes, and criminal identification. All relevant evidence can be applied in all steps of a criminal case proceeding. The court cannot make a decision regarding a criminal case based on suspicion, doubtful reason, or doubtful evidence.[76]

This is a brief explanation of the procedure followed in criminal cases in Afghanistan, from the discovery of a crime until a decision is made by the relevant court. None of the authorities (neither the police, the prosecutor, nor the courts) are allowed to criminalize an act that is not considered a crime under the law. The police and the prosecutor are obligated to take action when a crime happens. All the

[71] Criminal Procedure Code (2014) Art. 163, official gazette no. 1132.

[72] Criminal Procedure Code (2014) Art. 164, official gazette no. 1132.

[73] Criminal Procedure Code (2014) Art. 175, official gazette no. 1132: (1) If the charge sheet is confirmed, the prosecutor is obligated to file a criminal case against the accused person and prepare the indictments for all the accused persons considering the contents of the charge sheet and give a copy of the indictment to each of the accused persons or their defense attorney. The file should be submitted to the competent court within the time limits stipulated in law.

(2) The prosecutor is duty-bound to prepare the list of investigation papers attached to the criminal case file and submit them to the competent court. (3) The prosecutor is obligated to notify the accused, victim, plaintiff and claimant about submission of the case to the court with details of case number and date.

[74] Criminal Procedure Code (2014) Art. 178, official gazette no. 1132: "All criminal cases shall be processed by the authorized court, unless provided otherwise by another special law."

[75] Criminal Procedure Code (2014) Art. 101, official gazette no. 1132: (1) Once the case is referred to the court, the fate of the accused person in detention is decided by the relevant court. The relevant court can issue the accused person's detention order during the court proceeding according to the following: 1–During the court proceedings in a primary court up to 30 days. 2–During the court proceedings in an appeals court up to 30 days. 3–During the court proceedings in the Supreme Court up to 60 days. (2) If the case is returned to the prosecution office by the court based on some deficiencies in investigation, the court is obliged to determine the fate of the accused person according to the authorities stated in paragraph (1) of this article.

[76] Criminal Procedure Code (2014) Art. 19, official gazette no. 1132. This Article of the Criminal Procedure Code categorizes the incriminating evidence used by the court. The court cannot convict the accused in a case based on doubtful evidence or without reliable evidence; the evidence which can be deemed reliable is heard in the law.

activities of the police and the prosecutor must be in accordance with law and must deal with crimes that are only specified by law.[77] If an act is not criminalized under the law and judges make a decision based on the Ḥanafī school provisions in accordance with Article 130 of the Afghan Constitution, the legitimacy of the court decision may be challenged. The following section will briefly explain the criminal procedure according to Sharia.

4.5.2 Criminal Procedure According to Sharia

Generally speaking, Sharia accepts some common principles of criminal procedure; these have been implemented from the first century of Islam. However, there are some differences that should be taken into account. This section will briefly discuss a variety of crimes from the Sharia perspective, followed by a discussion on the differences between criminal procedures under the law and Sharia, and conclude with an analysis about why this is important in Afghanistan.

Based on Sharia, crimes are classified into three groups: *Ḥudūd*, *qiṣāṣ*, and finally *taʿzīr*. Ḥudūd crimes have been defined in the Quran or Sunnah and, according to the Ḥanafī doctrine, include theft,[78] adultery,[79] defamation,[80] highway robbery,[81] and drinking wine.[82] Qiṣāṣ literally means "equality or equivalence" and is divided into two categories: crimes against persons (intentional murder) and crimes against the body (physical injuries). These crimes are punishable by death, in the case of intentional murder, or in the form of blood money (*diya*), in the case of physical assault resulting in injuries.[83] The third type of crime is *taʿzīr*, the discretionary punishment fixed by a ruler or an authorized judge.[84] It is not necessary to go deeper

[77] Criminal Procedure Code (2014) Art. 87, 89, and 91, official gazette no. 1132.

[78] Theft "*sariqa*" according to the Ḥanafī school doctrine is taking away someone's property with a value of 10 or more silver coins.

[79] Adultery "*zinā*" is having sexual intercourse without a marriage contract between the man and the woman.

[80] Defamation "*qadhf*" Some people write it "Qazaf", which is wrong. *Qadhf* means, for example, that someone accuses someone else of committing adultery but cannot prove it. Defaming someone with no proof is considered a punishable crime in the Sharia.

[81] Highway Robbery "*hirāba*" is also considered a serious crime and punishable by execution and amputation. This might be the most severe punishment in Islamic law in order to prevent threats and fear among commerce and travelers.

[82] Drinking wine "*khamr*" is also one of the *Ḥudūd* crimes, but the Ḥanafī school of thought believes that only drinking wine is considered as a *Ḥadd* crime, not any other kind of alcohol. The other schools? Believe that drinking any kind of intoxicating alcohol is considered *Ḥadd* crime and shall be punished the same as drinking wine.

[83] In the case of *qiṣāṣ* crimes, the victim is authorized to waive the original punishment and ask for blood money or money to compensate for their bodily injuries defined in Sharia.

[84] Lippman (1989), p. 38.

into discussing the classification of the crimes because there is much literature regarding this topic.[85]

Generally speaking, there are no official stages in Sharia criminal procedure as there are in Afghan criminal law procedure. In Islamic classical legal texts, the concept of judgment and related matters has been discussed in a separate section under the topic of *Adab al-Qāḍī* or issues related to witnesses;[86] however, there are some books that offer detailed discussions of issues related to judges and judgment in according to the Islamic judicial system.[87] In early Islam, there is no hint of the existence of official institutions for the police and/or prosecutor to deal with crimes and criminals; instead, it is the duty of every citizen to remain responsible in order to prevent harm to society. The Quran says: *And let there be among you a community to of virtue, and advocating righteousness, and deterring from evil. These are the successful.*[88] It means that citizens should prevent each other from doing wrongful things. Also, there are other Quranic verses that place the obligation on the shoulders of Muslim citizens to prevent other Muslims from doing harmful acts.[89]

Furthermore, there are several traditions of Prophet Mohammad that confirm that every Muslim has the responsibility to observe other Muslims in a way to prevent potential harm to society.[90] Although there was no office or person designated as the police in early Islam, one of the disciples of the Prophet, Anas ibn Mālik, narrated that Qiyās ibn Saʿd was like a policeman for Prophet Mohammad.[91] A famous commentator, Zayn al-Dīn ʿAbd al-RaḤmān, on al-Bukhārī's book *Fatḥ al-Bārī* said that the concept of establishing an official police department was established for the first time in the Umawī rulers' era (early eighth century) and did not exist during the Prophet's time. The statement of Anas ibn Mālik shows that the concept of police became common during his era.[92]

[85] For further study, please see Bassiouni (2014), Rohe (2014a), Sharif (1985), and Siddiqui (2010).

[86] Rohe (2014b), p. 43.

[87] For example, two famous books called, Adab al-Qāḍī, one is written by Abū Bakr al-Khaṣṣāf and another is written by al-Māwardī. Also, there is another book, *Muʿīn al-Ḥukkām fī mā yataraddadu bayna al-khaṣmayn min al-aḤkām*, written by a famous Ḥanafī scholar, ʿAlāʾ al-Dīn ʿAlī ibn Khalīl al-Ḥanafī.

[88] The Holy Quran, Sura Āl ʿImrān, Āya 104.

[89] The Holy Quran, Sura Luqmān, Āya 17 "O my son, observe the prayer, advocate righteousness, forbid evil [...]". The Holy Quran, Sura Āl ʿImrān, Āya 110 "You are the best community that ever emerged for humanity: you advocate what is moral, and forbid what is immoral [...]".

[90] Al-Bukhārī (2001), Hadith No: 893: "All of you are observer and everybody is responsible for their under the guardianship custodian people; the ruler is responsible for the citizens, the man is responsible for his family members, the wife is responsible in the house of husband, and the worker is responsible for his/her boss property, so all of you are observer and everybody is responsible."

[91] Al-Bukhārī (2001), Hadith No: 6622.

[92] ʿAsqalānī (2000).

One of the main principles in Islamic law that provides a framework for the entire process of a case is that Plaintiff must provide proof for his claim. If the plaintiff cannot, the defendant must take an oath to reject the claim and deny guilt.[93] These are the key procedures according to Sharia. In terms of proof, there are seven ways to prove a case based on the Ḥanafī school: through (1) witness testimony, (2) confession, (3) oath, (4) refusal to make an oath (*nukūl*),[94] (5) *al-qasāma*,[95] (6) knowledge of the judge regarding the case, and (7) circumstantial evidence.[96] These are general Ḥanafī guidelines that have been used by judges in making decisions in both civil and criminal cases.

In contrast to Afghan formal criminal law procedure, there are some differences from Sharia criminal procedure. The first difference is making an oath, which is not included in Afghan criminal law; the second difference is the defendant's refusal to make an oath; the third is *al-qasāma*;[97] and the last one is knowledge of the judge regarding the case. Briefly looking at these differences, it is clear that the procedure for every case will not be the same. On the other hand, none of the incriminating evidence listed under the Criminal Procedure Code would be accepted as proven evidence in the Islamic criminal law procedure, especially in the *ḥudūd* cases.

Using an adultery case as an example, in accordance with Islamic criminal law, there are only two ways to prove the case: (a) the confession of the adulterer or (b) the testimony of four eyewitnesses who saw the act of sexual intercourse with their own eyes. Each of these four eyewitnesses must give their testimony one by one before the court with no differences in the facts of the case; they must have consistency in their words, the place of the crime, and the time of the act. If there is any difference in the eyewitnesses' testimonies, even if only one of them gives a testimony different from the other three, the case would be dismissed.[98] Other evidence, such as video recording or forensic tests, would not be acceptable to prove an adultery case according to Sharia. Proving an adultery case in accordance with Sharia standards through the testimony of eyewitnesses seems almost impossible; however, there are some cases of adultery that have been proven through confession.[99]

Another significant difference between Islamic criminal procedure and criminal procedural law is that the plaintiff cannot testify as a witness in the same case. In all

[93] Al-Sarakhsī (1993b), vol. 11, p. 82; Ibn al-Ḥajāj (n.d.), Hadith No: 1711.

[94] There are situations in which the plaintiff cannot provide a witness and the defendant must take an oath but refuses to do so. Such refusal of the defendant is called *nukūl.*

[95] According to the Ḥanafī school, this term is used when a dead body is found and no one knows for sure who the murderer is, in which case 50 people from the victim's family must make oath that the accused person is the murderer. This is one of the approaches to prove a case.

[96] Al-Ṭarābulusī (1973), pp. 65–143.

[97] *Al-qasāma* (Arabic: القسامة) refers to a situation where a dead body is found close to a village or the living area of a tribe but no one knows the murderer. In this case, 50 people of the village or the tribe must take an oath that they did not kill the person and do not know who the murderer is.

[98] Al-Marghīnānī (n.d.), p. 339; Al-Sarakhsī (1993a), vol. 9, pp. 91–92.

[99] Ibn al-Ḥajāj (n.d.), Hadith No: 1692.

criminal cases, it is the duty of the prosecutor to investigate the case and issue an accusation letter against the suspect,[100] but in accordance with law, the prosecutor cannot be involved in a case if he already participated in it through a different role:

> The prosecutor cannot participate in stages of legal prosecution in the following situations:
>
> 1-. ....
> 2-. ....
> 3-. If he/she has previously participated in the same case as lawyer, judge, legal advisor of a party, expert, or witness.[101]

In such a situation, the prosecutor is prohibited from acting as a witness if he already played a role in the case as a plaintiff. The prosecutor charges the accused with a crime, and he must demonstrate his claim by using witnesses, as with any other kind of proof. Legally, the prosecutor cannot accuse someone and then give testimony as a witness against him in the same case.

According to Islamic criminal procedure, however, the victim can also serve as a witness in the same case, especially in *Ḥudūd* crimes. To be more specific, according to Sharia, when a witness gives testimony against a person in front of the court, he directly becomes an accuser and starts a claim against that person as a plaintiff. For example, in a robbery case, when witnesses give testimonies in front of the court, they accuse a person of committing robbery and are thus considered plaintiffs in this case. In fact, in this case, the witness plays a double role in the same case: he is a witness in the case, and he also accuses the defendant by testifying that he committed the crime and there is no role for the prosecutor. It is noteworthy to mention that having a prosecutor's office is not against Sharia, however according to Sharia classical sources, there is no need for someone in the role of prosecutor to proceed with a criminal case.

Another remarkable dissimilarity between the two criminal procedures is the lack of official courts in Sharia. At the time of Prophet Mohammad and early Islam, there was no official court with a regulated, detailed procedure.[102] Cases were submitted directly to the Prophet in the mosque or anywhere else, and then he made decisions. There were no police, prosecutor offices, or an official court system. The court system was developed later on, during the Abbasid rulers' era.

In accordance with Sharia principles, generally there are two types of obligations in Muslim society that should be taken into consideration: one is private right, *Ḥaqq al-ʿabd*, and another is public right (right of Allah, *Ḥaqq Allāh*). This Sharia principle is reflected in the criminal procedural law of Afghanistan. Chapter 4 of the Penal Code, which is composed of 13 articles, discusses this issue.[103]

---

[100] The Law on Structure and Authority of Attorney General Office (2013) Art. 3, official gazette no. 1117, clause 1.

[101] Criminal Procedural Code (2014) Art. 14, clause 3.

[102] Rohe (2014b), p. 43.

[103] Criminal Procedural Code (2014) Articles 189–201.

The first type of case, *Ḥaqq al-ʿabd*, is related to an individual's rights. In this case, the victim can directly claim his rights. The second one is considered the rights of society, which is represented by the prosecutor. In the first case, the claim should be proven by evidence, including oral testimony (*shahāda*). Evidence in the form of witness testimony carries the most weight in the law of evidence in Islamic jurisprudence; because of the lack of written standards in Arab society, documentary evidence was not common in early Islam.[104]

In the second type, *Ḥaqq Allāh*, the prosecutor should file a case against the accused person and should prove the claim against him. The prosecutor cannot accuse someone and give testimony against him. However, according to the Islamic criminal procedure, as discussed above, it is possible for one person to play this double role, especially in the case of *Ḥudūd*.

These points raise the following question: how can an act that is not criminalized under the law but considered a crime in Sharia be processed according to state criminal procedure, and how can the judgment be legitimate? The main concern under the Criminal Procedure Code is that the prosecutor and police officers only investigate acts that are already criminalized by law. If the basic proceeding of a case is not processed in accordance with the provisions of law, the court shall issue an order to nullify the proceedings and overrule the decision. The basic proceedings refer to the court formation and its jurisdiction. There are two kinds of jurisdictions of the court, one is territorial jurisdiction and the other is subject matter jurisdiction. All pretrial processes of a criminal case must be done by the police and prosecutor offices and then the case should be submitted to the relevant court for adjudication.[105] Particularly, when state courts apply the Ḥanafī school provisions to a case, they still try the case according to state criminal procedures, even though these procedures do not align with those provided by the Ḥanafī school provisions. These discrepancies therefore challenge the legitimacy of state court decisions made in reliance on the Ḥanafī school provisions.

Another big difference between the two systems is that under the Criminal Procedure Code, judges cannot make a decision based on their own knowledge regarding a case without considering the incriminating evidence listed in Article 19 of the Criminal Procedure Code. Under the Ḥanafī school principles, however, the judge can make a decision regarding a case based on his own knowledge under specific circumstances. The author of *Muʿīn al-Ḥukkām*, a famous Ḥanafī book, said that a judge can make a decision based on his own knowledge if the case happened

[104] Rohe (2014b), p. 49.

[105] Criminal Procedure Code (2014) Art. 289, official gazette no. 1132: "(1) Noncompliance with provisions of the law during one of the basic proceedings will result in its nullification. (2) Basic proceedings involves observing the provisions of the law regarding the court formation, its territorial or subject matter jurisdiction, arrest, search, investigation, expert examination and the right to have an attorney. (3) In case of non-compliance with the law regarding one of the matters stipulated in paragraph (2) of this article, the court is obligated to issue an order to nullify the proceedings and overrule the decision – even though no request was made concerning the matter. The previous proceedings will be nullified and new proceedings according to the provisions of the law will be conducted."

within his jurisdictional authority.[106] Jurisdictional authority refers to a region in which a judge can exercise his judicial powers.

Sections (2)–(4) of Article 19 of the Criminal Procedure Code states:

- Relevant evidence set forth in this chapter is applicable in all stages of the criminal case proceedings.
- Signs may provide the basis for an accusation only when they make an accurate and compatible chain of relevant facts and they prove criminal elements with certainty.
- The court cannot issue a decision to convict the accused person based on suspicion or if there is doubt in reasons or evidence.[107]

Afghanistan's Criminal Procedure Code does not contain any provision requiring a judge to make a decision based on his own knowledge; the law says the court must make a decision according to the reasons listed by law. Therefore, if a case is adjudicated in light of Article 130 based on the Ḥanafī school provisions, it is problematic because it is not clear which procedure should be implemented by the court. If the court implements the Criminal Procedure Code, it will not match the standards of the Ḥanafī school; on the other hand, if the Ḥanafī school norms have been applied, it will challenge the legitimacy of the court's decisions due to failure to apply the appropriate procedural law.

Thus, the criminal procedures in state law and Sharia have some common standards and norms; however, there are major differences between these two procedures, too. Furthermore, the classification of crimes is also different, and each procedure has been designed to facilitate specific types of crimes. The criminal procedural law only deals with *taʿzīr* crimes, which are criminalized by law, while the Sharia procedures comprehensively deal with several types of criminal acts, namely *Ḥudūd*, *qiṣāṣ*, *diya*, as well as *taʿzīr*. Also, the standards of proof are different between the two systems, and each one has its own process and types of permitted evidence that give legitimacy to the court's decisions. Finally, there are some considerable differences between the two procedural systems that must be taken under consideration when a criminal case is being processed.

4.6 *Taʿzīr*

In Islamic criminal law, generally, there are four kinds of crimes and punishments: *Ḥudūd*, *qiṣāṣ* or *diya*, and *taʿzīr*. Islamic criminal law has specific definitions and punishments for all kinds of crimes, except *taʿzīr* crimes. The first two have been mentioned in the Quran or Sunnah, but *taʿzīr* punishment refers to the wish of the ruler. Under Sharia, *taʿzīr* punishments are not considered a principal punishment

[106] Al-Mawṣilī (1937), p. 121; Al-Ṭarābulusī (1973), p. 122; Ibn Simnānī (1984), p. 361.

[107] Criminal Procedure Code (2014) Art. 19, official gazette no. 1132, clauses 2, 3, and 4.

applicable to *ḥudūd* crimes. They are mainly applied under two conditions: first, as an alternative to principal punishments, for instance, failure to complete the required standard of proof for applying punishments in the case of *Ḥadd* crimes. Second, they are applied as a supplementary punishment, along with the principal punishment.[108]

In almost all the decisions that Afghan courts have made based upon Article 130 of the Constitution, judges have relied upon the concept of *taʿzīr* to legitimize their decisions. To understand and have a clear idea of the limits of the applicability of *taʿzīr*, it is necessary to define what it means and who has the authority to apply it. For a better understanding of the scope of the use of *taʿzīr* in the context of Afghanistan, it is necessary to discuss several questions: What is *taʿzīr*? What is the status of *taʿzīr* crimes in Sharia? What is the relationship between *taʿzīr* and other crimes? When is it applicable? Who has the authority to apply it? Before analyzing specific cases, providing answers for these questions will help address the primary research question of how Afghan courts apply Sharia in their decisions when state law is silent regarding a case.

4.6.1 What Is Taʿzīr*?*

There are different ways of using the term *taʿzīr* in Islamic sources. Some scholars believe that *taʿzīr* means literally *support* and *honor*, as the Holy Quran says: "That you may believe in Allah and His Messenger, and support Him, and Honor Him. . . ."[109] However, some Islamic legal experts disagree with the above definition and say *taʿzīr* in a legal context refers to discipline and correction, even though this meaning is different from what is provided by the dictionaries.[110] In the current and classical conceptions of Islamic jurisprudence, *taʿzīr* means *to discipline, to prevent, to correct, and to chastise*,[111] but in Islamic Sharia, it has been implemented as a punishment for those sins for which there is no specific punishment in Sharia.[112]

The concept of *taʿzīr* was not very common during Prophet Mohammad's era because there are not enough narrations from him that prove the common usage of *taʿzīr* at that time. The only narration that mentions *taʿzīr* is a Hadith of the Prophet that says: "Do not lash people more than 10 lashes, except in *Ḥudūd* crime."[113] This is the only narration from the Prophet regarding the concept of *taʿzīr* that scholars rely upon to allow punishing people based on *taʿzīr*.[114] After Prophet Mohammad's era, the concept of *taʿzīr* became more common, and Islamic rulers, including the

---

108 ʿAwda (n.d.), p. 81.

109 The Holy Quran, Sura al-FatḤ, (48: 9).

110 Ibn ʿĀbidīn (1992a), p. 227.

111 Al Said (1995), pp. 295–296; Ibn Hammām (1970), p. 212.

112 Ibn ʿĀbidīn (1992a), p. 235; Rohe (2014c), p. 177.

113 Al-Bukhārī (2001), Hadith No: 2591, and Ibn al-Ḥajāj (n.d.), Hadith No: 3222.

114 Al-Tirmidhī (1998), Hadith No: 1383.

four Caliphs, punished people based on *taʿzīr*. If a citizen acts in a way that harms society or public and personal safety or violates the lawful rights of other persons, the ruler (*Ḥākim*) or judge (qadi) can criminalize that act and punish the actor based on *taʿzīr*.[115]

There is no minimum or maximum level for *taʿzīr* punishments. It includes any kind of disgrace or discipline that could be used to punish wrongdoers and discourage people from committing future crimes. There are multiple reactions that may be taken by the ruler or judge against the offenders in order to keep the social order and harmony and protect citizens and their property. In fact, *taʿzīr* punishments have been implemented on the wrongdoer based on his social caste.

According to the status of an individual in society, the reaction of the ruler or judge could vary from person to person. For instance, the *taʿzīr* punishment for persons whose status is very high in society or the nobles, including religious scholars (*ʿulamāʾ*), shall be only informing them of the offense. A judge could tell them that he was informed that they committed such an act, which was not expected of them. It was believed that this would be enough to prevent them from repeating that act in the future. The second level of *taʿzīr* punishment applies to common nobles, like governors, businessmen, community leaders, and feudal lords. They could be informed and asked to show up in court. When they show up in court, it will harm their reputation in society, which will be considered a warning to them. The third category of *taʿzīr* punishment is that applied to the populace and common citizens. They could be punished by being asked to show up in court or by imprisonment. The last category covers villainous people, who should be punished by any of the abovementioned punishments, plus lashing.[116] This shows that different approaches have been taken by rulers to criminalize an act that is destructive to social order and harms citizens and their property.

4.6.2 The Differences Between Taʿzīr *and Other Islamic Punishments*

There are differences between *taʿzīr* and other punishments in Islamic law. These differences are based upon the authority of the ruler or judge and the way they seek to prevent people from harmful acts. Understanding the differences between *taʿzīr* and other Islamic punishments will help present a clear picture of the use of Sharia principles when Afghan judges make decisions in light of Article 130 of the Afghan Constitution. The main differences are as follows:

1. The punishments for *Ḥudūd*, *qiṣāṣ*, and *diya* are specific and mandatory if the crime has been proven based on the standards set by Sharia. Judges cannot make

[115]Bassiouni (2014), pp. 141–144.

[116]Mullā Khusraw (n.d.), p. 75.

any change in the type, quality, or quantity of punishment for any of these crimes. These punishments must be applied as they are defined in the texts. The primary legal sources of Islamic law do not describe *taʿzīr* punishments, but it is recognized as a ruler's decision to punish people who commit an act, which is considered harmful for the citizens and social order. Although maximum and minimum punishments may exist for most *taʿzīr* crimes, judges are authorized to choose only one of them based on the situation.

2. The ruler cannot forgive the offender or alter punishment in *Ḥudūd*, *qiṣāṣ* and *diya* cases, but he can make changes in the quality and quantity of *taʿzīr* punishments; however, in some cases, the ruler can forgive the offender and choose no punishment.
3. In *Ḥudūd*, *qiṣāṣ* and *diya* cases, the focus is only on the crime, not on the criminal, but in the case of *taʿzīr* crimes, both the crime and the criminal are considered.[117]
4. Ḥudūd crimes are not applicable to children, but being underage does not prevent the application of *taʿzīr* if the crime relates to the rights of the people (*Ḥaqq al-ʿabd*). For instance, if it contradicts the right of Allah (*Ḥaqq Allāh*), such as adultery or theft, it is forgivable.[118]
5. The punishment for a Ḥudūd crime will be dropped if there is doubt on the guilt of the accused, but *taʿzīr* punishments are applicable even where there is doubt. For example, the case of adultery requires a high standard of proof according to Sharia principles, and if the required proof is not achieved, the *Ḥadd* punishment for this crime will not be applicable because of the doubt on the sufficiency of the evidence. The accused could still be punished by *taʿzīr*, however, because sin was committed and the offender should be punished.
6. Another difference is that only the ruler (amir, imam, *and Ḥākim*) has the authority to impose punishment for a *Ḥudūd* crime, but *taʿzīr* may be applied by an authorized representative of the ruler.[119]
7. Pleading for mercy is not allowed in *Ḥudūd* crimes, and no one, including the ruler, has the authority to forgive a person who commits *Ḥudūd* crimes. But with regard to *taʿzīr* crimes, rulers are allowed to show mercy and forgiveness to wrongdoers; also, other citizens may ask for mercy and forgiveness on behalf of the offenders.[120]
8. *Taʿzīr* crimes can be proven by the testimony of the plaintiff and another person, but *Ḥudūd* crimes require a high standard of proof that goes beyond reasonable doubt.[121]

---

[117] ʿAwda (n.d.), pp. 82–83.

[118] Ibn ʿĀbidīn (1992a), p. 60.

[119] Abū Zuhra (1998), p. 25.

[120] Ibn ʿĀbidīn (1992a), pp. 59–60.

[121] Id., p. 237.

4.6.3 Who Has the Authority to Apply Punishment for *taʿzīr* Crimes?

There are two views regarding who has the authority to punish wrongdoers based on *taʿzīr*. One group of scholars believes that judges have the authority to punish people based on *taʿzīr*,[122] while a second group believes that only rulers have such power.[123]

The first group of scholars believes that if a judge is *mujtahid*, capable of formulating rules of divine law through an independent interpretation of the Qur'an and the Hadith of Prophet Mohammad, such a qualified judge has the authority to punish people based on *taʿzīr*. The judge must be an expert in Islamic jurisprudence and be able to make a fair judgment regarding a case in light of the main sources of Islamic Sharia. However, some experts believe that even the judges (qadis) who do not have this expertise have the power to punish people based on *taʿzīr* offenses because they are in charge of protecting the public welfare.[124]

The second point of view is that it is the authority of the rulers to punish people based on *taʿzīr* crimes.[125] In this case, the judges are not allowed to apply *taʿzīr* punishments independently. The judges must follow the order of the ruler because the ruler is in charge of the community and must protect the public welfare. Sometimes, the judges can also follow the precedents set by previous jurists in similar cases that are well known among legal scholars. Islamic jurists have collected different kinds of *taʿzīr* punishments that were set by the companions of Prophet Mohammad and other independent jurists. These well-known precedents and collections of Islamic jurists' opinions are considered to be the rules and regulations to be followed by imitator judges, who do not have the ability of *ijtihād*; however, they have no authority to ignore the rules and punish people according to their wish.[126]

Since in Afghanistan all the judges are considered to be "imitator judges" because there is not a single judge that has the ability to do *ijtihād* and create rules through an independent interpretation of the main sources of Islamic law, they are not authorized to implement *taʿzīr* punishments based on their will. Also, because *taʿzīr* punishments are within the authority of the ruler, the judges must establish rules based on *taʿzīr* to keep social order and provide safety for the citizens and their property.[127] The Penal Code and other laws regulate the punishment for *taʿzīr*

[122] Id., p. 178.

[123] Id., p. 229.

[124] Lippman (1989), p. 44.

[125] Ibn ʿĀbidīn (1992a), p. 229.

[126] Abū Zuhra (1998), pp. 95–96.

[127] According to the Constitution of Afghanistan, the government and the legislation can draft and pass laws. Article 95 of the Constitution states: "The proposal for drafting laws shall be made by the Government or members of the National Assembly or, in the domain of regulating the judiciary, by the Supreme Court, through the Government. Proposals for drafting the budget and financial affairs laws shall be made only by the Government."

crimes,[128] and judges are authorized to adjudicate cases and make decisions only in accordance with law. There is no document indicating that judges have the authority to criminalize an act and punish people on behalf of the ruler to meet the Sharia requirements.

Furthermore, since the principle of legality is accepted in Sharia and the legal system of Afghanistan, judges are only authorized to implement the provisions of the law for an act that is already recognized as a punishable crime by law. Thus, Afghan judges cannot criminalize an act that is not considered a crime under the law or in Sharia.

It is important to note that according to Sharia principles, the ruler has the power to govern the country, but he is also responsible for the welfare of the citizens and is in charge of their safety and that of their property. In addition, it is the obligation of the ruler to resolve disputes and guarantee justice in society. Although the ruler can appoint people to fulfill his responsibilities on his behalf, the authority of these appointed people must be limited to the scope of their authorization. They cannot go beyond their duties and perform something that is not included in their authority. Since *taʿzīr* crimes and their punishments are already regulated by law, judges must deal only with these crimes and the punishments that are recognized by law. Today in Afghanistan, judicial authorization, which is issued by the President to Afghan judges, only gives them authority to adjudicate cases and make decisions according to law. There is no single document that shows that the President has authorized Afghan judges to criminalize an act based on *taʿzīr* or to punish people beyond the law.

Based on the above reasons, Afghan judges are not authorized to criminalize an act that is not considered a crime under the law, and they cannot punish people based on their personal will. The judges must make decisions regarding a case based on provisions of law and punish the guilty within the limits set by law.

4.7 Making Decisions According to the Dominant Opinion of the Ḥanafī Doctrine

A common feature of Islamic jurisprudential schools is that there is a variety of opinions regarding one legal issue. The Ḥanafī school of thought is not an exception in this regard. To avoid anarchy in decision-making in accordance with the dominant opinion in the Ḥanafī school regarding a case, Ḥanafī scholars have regulated the hierarchy of the sources and opinions within the Ḥanafī school of thought. These regulated principles are widely accepted in the Ḥanafī school and give legitimacy to legal decisions. Ḥanafī school scholars emphasize that it is the obligation of judges to follow the well-established principles of preference and make decisions accordingly.

[128] Penal Code of Afghanistan (1976) Art. 2 and Art. 3.

A Ḥanafī imitator judge is only authorized to rely on a provision of the Ḥanafī school of thought that is accepted as a dominant opinion by the Ḥanafī scholars. In this regard, there are two standards for a Ḥanafī judge: the first one is that a judge must follow the Ḥanafī school doctrines in his decisions; the second one is that he must respect the principle of preference among the Ḥanafī school doctrines. If a Ḥanafī judge does not make a decision in accordance with the Ḥanafī school doctrines or if his decision is based on Ḥanafī school opinions but does not respect the principles of preference within the Ḥanafī school, then the decision is not valid and must not be implemented.[129] Thus, Ḥanafī scholars regulate Ḥanafī school opinions and sources in terms of strong or weak opinions and trustworthy or nontrustworthy sources.

There are concrete principles, which are called *(qawāʿid al-iftāʾ) Principles of Issuing* fatwa *(legal opinion)*, that regulate the preference of opinions within the Ḥanafī school. The hierarchy of scholars and their opinions require judges, when making decisions, to search for the answer among the Ḥanafī scholars' opinions from top to bottom. For example, if there is an opinion from one of the first-class scholars, Imam Abū Ḥanīfa, Imam Abū Yūsuf, or Imam Mohammad, regarding a case, the judge should not make a decision according to the opinion of a second-class scholar (their students). If there is any conflict of opinions within the school, they are resolved by the preference rules.

A Ḥanafī imitator judge cannot go beyond the doctrines of his own school and make a decision based on other schools' opinions. The imitator judges must follow their own school of thought and cannot go against the doctrines of their school.[130] Ḥanafī scholars clearly state that if an imitator judge, like the current judges in Afghanistan, makes a decision not in accordance with the Ḥanafī school doctrines, their decision is not valid and must not be implemented.[131]

To analyze the court decisions in the cases under study in this work, it is necessary to discuss the principles of preference and the hierarchy of the sources within the Ḥanafī school of thought in greater detail and then examine whether the court made its decision in accordance with these norms. Following a brief explanation of the principles of preference among the different opinions of the Ḥanafī scholars, this work will then discuss the hierarchy of the sources in the Ḥanafī school of thought.

---

[129] Ibn ʿĀbidīn M, Risāla fī al-Qawl al-Mukhtār min al-Aqwāl fī madhhab Imām Abī Ḥanīfa. http://www.al-mostafa.info/data/arabic/depot3/gap.php?file=m001527.pdf Accessed 05, 06, 2021.

[130] Al-Dihlawī (1995), pp. 56–82.

[131] Ibn ʿĀbidīn (1992a), pp. 407–408.

4.7.1 *The Principle of Preference Regarding Different Opinions Among Ḥanafī Scholars*

The principle of preference, which is derived from the hierarchy of scholars within the Ḥanafī school of thought, is one of the main bases for choosing the preferred opinion within the Ḥanafī school regarding a controversial issue. As stated above, the opinions of all the Ḥanafī scholars do not have the same weight. Imam Abū Ḥanīfa established the school, Imam Abū Yūsuf played a significant role in developing and expanding the doctrine of the school in the Islamic world, and Imam Mohammad al-Shaybānī collected all the opinions of the founders of the school and made a reliable collection of its main doctrines. In addition to these three pillars of the Ḥanafī school, there are many other scholars who have contributed significantly and have kept the school alive by issuing new fatwas, within the framework of the Ḥanafī school, concerning newly arising problems in society. It is vitally important for judges to understand the hierarchy of opinions in the Ḥanafī school so that they can distinguish between the strong and weak opinions and choose accurately.

According to Ḥanafī school's principles, there are several categories of scholars and sources that each has specific criteria. Having such categories differentiate between the independent and dependent jurists in terms of issuing a legal opinion and recognizing weak and strong opinions within the Hanafi School of Thought.

(1) The first is a collection of the opinions of Ḥanafī school first-class scholars, which consists of six books, called Zāhir al-Riwāya books. These are the most reliable sources in the Ḥanafī school that were compiled by Imam Mohammad al-Shaybānī, the third famous face in the Ḥanafī school. These opinions are called the main principles of the school and all decisions by Ḥanafī judges should be made in accordance with these opinions.
(2) Another category of opinions is called *Shāz*, which are rare opinions narrated by Imam Abū Ḥanīfa, Imam Abū Yūsuf, and Imam Mohammad but not included in the *Ẓāhir al-Riwāya* books. These kinds of opinions are acceptable if they are in accordance with the main principles of the school; otherwise, they are not valid and judges should not rely on them.
(3) The third category of opinions pertains to the opinions of Ḥanafī scholars called *Al-Muta'akhkhirūn*. This term refers to those Ḥanafī scholars who did not meet and learn directly from Imam Abū Ḥanīfa.[132] The latest category of Hanafi scholars inferred these opinions from the Islamic law sources and they have made a consensus that such opinions are accepted.[133]
(4) The fourth category refers to the opinions of new scholars that were not obtained through a consensus. Opinions from this category are acceptable if they are in

[132] Al-Mujaddidī (2003).

[133] The term *al-muta'akhkhirūn* refers to the second-class scholars of Ḥanafī school, who learned indirectly from students of Imam Abū Ḥanīfa.

accordance with the main principles of the school; otherwise, they must be rejected.[134]

These four categories serve as the main attributes of the Ḥanafī school opinions; judges are obligated to respect them when they make a decision. If an imitator judge does not respect this hierarchy, his decision is not valid and must not be implemented.[135]

Some Ḥanafī scholars have looked at the classification of the scholars from different perspectives. The scholars discussed above classified the Ḥanafī scholars into four main groups, while others believe that there are seven categories of scholars in terms of their knowledge and authority to deal with legal issues. A famous Ḥanafī scholar, Ibn Kamāl Bāshā (1469–1534), classified the Ḥanafī school scholars into seven categories: the first one is *mujtahid muṬlaq*, like Imam Abū Ḥanīfa, the founder of the Ḥanafī school. The second category includes Imam Abū Ḥanīfa's students: Imam Abū Yūsuf, Imam Mohammad al-Shaybānī, and Imam Zufar (728–801). The third category is composed of their students and so on.[136]

While some suggest that the Ḥanafī school scholars are categorized into seven main groups,[137] most researchers, however, believe that historically the Ḥanafī school scholars should be categorized into five main groups:[138]

1. The first class of scholars is called the earliest (*al-mutaqaddimūn*) scholars, who directly learned from Imam Abū Ḥanīfa.[139] They include Imam Abū Yūsuf (731–798),[140] Imam Mohammad al-Shaybānī (750–805),[141] Imam Zufar (728–801),[142] and a few others. They are qualified to do *ijtihād* (independent legal reasoning) within the framework established by the founder of the school, Imam Abū Ḥanīfa; however, they also had the power to disagree with Abū Ḥanīfa regarding some secondary issues. Generally, they followed the main principle of *ijtihad*, formed by Abū Ḥanīfa, but sometimes they issued their own opinions and did not always follow Imam Abū Ḥanīfa's opinions.[143]
2. The second category of Ḥanafī scholars is a group of jurists who directly learned from the Abū Ḥanīfa's students. They are qualified to do *ijtihād* involving issues on which first-class scholars did not release any opinions; if there is an opinion issued by first-class scholars, they must follow such opinions. The famous

[134] Al-Dihlawī (1995), p. 52.

[135] ʿUṭwa (1994), p. 61.

[136] Al-Rūmī I, p. 1.

[137] ʿAbd al-Qādir ibn Mohammad ibn Naṣrallāh (n.d.), p. 558.

[138] ʿAbd al-Ḥay (1986), p. 7.

[139] Al-Mujaddidī (2003).

[140] Yaʿqūb ibn Ibrāhīm, the second face of the Ḥanafī school, worked as a chief justice (*Qāḍī al-Quḍāt*) of the entire Islamic Empire.

[141] Abū ʿAbdallāh Mohammad ibn al-Ḥasan al-Shaybānī, the third famous face of the Ḥanafī school, collected all Abū Ḥanīfa opinions in six books, which are called *Ẓāhir al-Riwāya*.

[142] Zufar ibn al-Hudhayl ibn Qays, the fourth famous scholar of the Ḥanafī school.

[143] Al-Tamīmī (n.d.), p. 11.

representatives of this class are Abūbakr al-Khaṣṣāf (797–875);[144] Mohammad ibn Salāma al-ṬaḤāwī (852–321);[145] Abū al-Ḥasan al-Karkhī (874–951);[146] ʿAbd al-ʿAzīz Aḥmad ibn Nāṣir al Ḥalwānī (died in 1057); Mohammad ibn AḤmad ibn Abī Sahl Abū Bakr al-Sarakhsī[147] (died in 1090); ʿAlī ibn Mohammad al-Bazdawī[148] (died in 1089); Ḥasan ibn Manṣūr Fakhr al-Dīn al-Ūzjandī, famous by the name Qāḍī Khān[149] (died in 1196); MaḤmūd ibn AḤmad ibn ʿAbd al-ʿAzīz ibn Māzah al-Bukhārī (1156–1219), the author of famous book *al-MuḤīṭ al-Burhānī*; and some others. It is important to note that they could not create any legal opinion that opposed Imam Abū Ḥanīfa's opinion, involving either the main principles or subsidiary issues.

3. The third category is imitator scholars who are not able to do *ijtihād* but who had comprehensive knowledge about the Ḥanafī school's principles and the earliest scholars' opinions. The famous representative of this group is Abū Bakr AḤmad ibn ʿAlī al-Rāzī (918–981). These third-category scholars were authorized to give more details and explanations to the succinct issues raised by the founders of the school and provide descriptions for the texts to avoid any ambiguity in their opinions.[150]
4. The fourth group is the imitators who have the authority to make a preference (*tarjīḤ*) among the different opinions in accordance with the principles set by the scholars. The famous representatives of this category are Abū al-Ḥusayn AḤmad al-Qudūrī (937–1037) and Burhā nal-Dīn Marghīnānī (1136–1197), the author of a famous Ḥanafī book, *al-Hidāya*. They have sat preference mechanism to select the most reliable opinion among the several opinions of the firstclass jurists of the Ḥanafī School.[151]
5. The fifth group is the imitators who can distinguish between the strong and weak opinions of the earliest scholars. The famous representatives of this group are Mohammad ibn Mohammad al-Kardarī[152] (died in 1424), Jamāl al-Dīn

[144] Abū Bakr al-Khaṣṣāf (died in Baghdad in 875) was a well-known Ḥanafī scholar and writer of many books, one of them is *Adab al-Qāḍī*. Look at *Seyar Aalām Al Nubalā* book.

[145] Abū Jaʿfar AḤmad ibn Salāma al-ṬaḤāwī (852–933) was a follower of the Shāfiʿī school of thought and then became a follower of the Ḥanafī school. He is the writer of the well-known book in the Ḥanafī school *SharḤ Mushkil al-Āthār*.

[146] Abū al-Ḥasan Obaidullah Al Karukhi was a well-known Ḥanafī scholar and is the writer of the famous book *Uṣūl al-Karkhī*.

[147] Mohammad ibn AḤmad ibn Abī Sahl al-Sarakhsī (died in 483 Islamic calendar) was a well-known Ḥanafī scholar. He wrote many books and is especially famous for his book called al-Mabsūṭ, which was written in prison.

[148] ʿAlī ibn Mohammad al-Bazdawī (died in 482 Islamic calendar) has written many books and is especially famous for his book *Uṣūl al-Bazdawī*.

[149] Fakhr al-Dīn al-Ūzjandī (died in 592 Islamic calendar) wrote a famous fatwa book, called *Fatāwā Qāḍī Khān*, which is one of the most reliable fatwa books in Ḥanafī school of thought.

[150] ʿAbd al-Qādir ibn Mohammad ibn Naṣrallāh (n.d.), p. 580.

[151] ʿAbd al-Ḥay (1986), p. 7.

[152] He is the author of *Al-Fatāwā al-Bazāziyya* fatwa book.

MaḤmūd ibn AḤmad al-Ḥuṣarī (1151–1239), and ʿAbdallāh ibn AḤmad ibn MaḤmūd ḤāfiẒ al-Dīn al-Nasafī[153] (died in 1310).[154]

These are the main groups of Ḥanafī scholars. All scholars after the fifth group are called pure imitators. Since the end of the fifth group's era, there have been no individuals who have had a strong influence on the school; all scholars after that must follow all of the above scholars' opinions in their decisions. Because currently all the legal experts and judges in Afghanistan are pure imitators, they are not authorized to issue new opinions against the jurists categorized above; they must respect the hierarchy of the scholars and obey these principles of preference when they make a decision.[155]

After explaining the hierarchy of the Hanafi scholars and their opinions, it is necessary to clarify how preference is determined if there are different opinions from different categories of scholars regarding a single legal issue. The main principle in the Ḥanafī school is that generally the preference goes to Imam Abū Ḥanīfa's opinions and then the opinions of his students. Among his students, Imam Abū Yūsuf has the highest rank; after him, Imam Mohammad is second and then Imam Zufar is third (728–801); and the last one is Ḥasan Ibn Zayād (died). If the opinions of his two students, Imam Abū Yūsuf and Imam Mohammad, contradict Imam Abū Ḥanīfa's opinion, it is up to the Ḥanafī school followers, judges, or Muftis, to follow any of the opinions. If Imam Abū Ḥanīfa and one of his students are on one side and another student is on the other side, the judge must prefer the opinion of Imam Abū Ḥanīfa and the student on his side.[156]

The Ḥanafī scholars have also set a system of preference for different legal issues based on the personal experience of the first-class scholars. For example, Imam Abū Ḥanīfa's opinions are preferred in cases of devotions and worship (*ibādāt*). Imam Abū Yūsuf's opinions are preferred when it comes to the judiciary and judgments because of his long experience in this field.[157] Imām Mohammad's views are preferred in issues involving inheritance law, and there are 17 cases when Imam Zufar's opinions are preferred to be implemented.[158] This means that if there is more than one opinion from the Ḥanafī scholars regarding an issue related to the judiciary, Imam Abū Yūsuf's opinion is the dominant one. If there is an issue regarding worship, Imam Abū Ḥanīfa's opinion must be followed and so on. If a judge does not follow the above rules, his decision is not considered a valid and legitimate verdict.

[153] He is the author of *Kanz al-Daqāʾiq*, one of the important books in the Ḥanafī school of thought.

[154] ʿAbd al-Ḥay (1986), p. 7.

[155] Ibid.

[156] Ibn ʿĀbidīn M Risāla fī al-Qawl al-Mukhtār min al-Aqwāl fī madhhab Imām Abī Ḥanīfa. Available at http://www.al-mostafa.info/data/arabic/depot3/gap.php?file=m001527.pdf Accessed 6 March 2019.

[157] Al-Ḥaṣkafī (2002), p. 464.

[158] Ibn ʿĀbidīn (1992b), p. 76.

4.7.2 The Hierarchy of the Sources Within the Ḥanafī School of Thought

There is a consensus among the Ḥanafī school scholars that it is an obligation of the judges or Muftis (who issue legal opinions) to respect the hierarchy of the sources within the Ḥanafī school when they make a decision. In fact, it is common among the Sunni schools' followers to practice their own preferred doctrine when dealing with a legal issue.[159] Thus, the Ḥanafī scholars classified the sources within the Ḥanafī school based on the reliability of the content collected in the books.[160] It seems that disregarding the hierarchy of the sources had been a problem even in the past, and to avoid this problem, the Ḥanafī scholars fixed the hierarchy of the sources within the Ḥanafī school.[161] There are three categories of sources within the Ḥanafī school of thought that judges must consider when they make a decision. These three categories are (1) *Ẓāhir al-Riwāya*, (2) *Nawādir*, and (3) *al-Waqī'āt*.[162]

The first category of sources, the *Ẓāhir al-riwāya* books,[163] is a collection of the opinions of the founder of the Ḥanafī school, which are narrated directly by Imam Abū Ḥanīfa, Imam Abū Yūsuf, and Imam Mohammad. Sometimes, opinions of other students of Imam Abū Ḥanīfa, such as Imam Zufar (728–801)[164] and Ḥasan ibn Zayād (died in 820),[165] are also considered *Ẓāhir al-riwāya*, but it is mostly the opinions of the first three scholars that are classified within the first category.[166] The reason these opinions are called the principal opinions of the Ḥanafī school is that they are narrated successively from Imam Mohammad without any doubt and collected in six books:

1. *Al-MabsūṬ*:[167] some scholars believe that one of the requirements for *ijtihād* in the Ḥanafī school is to memorize this book.[168] There are several versions of this book, but the most reliable version was narrated by one of the students of Imam Mohammad, named Abū Sulaymān al-Jawzjānī.[169]
2. *Al-Jāmiʿ al-ṣaghīr*: the date of the writing of this book is not clear, but it seems that Imam Mohammad wrote it based on the suggestion of his colleague, Imam

[159] Al-Qarāfī (1995), pp. 82–83.

[160] Al-Dihlawī (1995), p. 52.

[161] Abd al-Ḥay (1986), p. 7.

[162] Ibn ʿĀbidīn (1992b), p. 171.

[163] The *Ẓāhir al-Riwāya* books are the most reliable sources of the Ḥanafī school, which are composed of six books.

[164] Zufar ibn al-Hudhayl ibn Qays, the fourth famous scholar of the Ḥanafī school.

[165] Ḥanān ibn Zayād (died in 820) the famous scholar of the Ḥanafī school and he also learned from Imam Abū Yūsuf and Imam Mohammad.

[166] ʿUṭwa (1994), pp. 8–9.

[167] This is the first book written by Imam Mohammad, also called "al-Aṣl."

[168] Al-Dihlawī (1995), p. 51.

[169] Referred to *Jawzjān*, which is an area in the north of Afghanistan.

Abū Yūsuf. Most of the concepts of the book are narrations from Imam Abū Yūsuf.
3. *Al-Jāmiʿ al-Kabīr*: this book is one of the most important sources of the Ḥanafī school because most key principles and important issues of the Ḥanafī school are collected in this book. Imām Mohammad reviewed this book by himself two times.
4. *Siyar al-Saghīr*: this is the fifth book written by Imam Mohammad and is composed of legal issues concerning war and armed conflicts.
5. *Siyar al-Kabīr*: this is one of the latest books that Imam Mohammad wrote. This book mainly talks about international law principles; thus, he is considered the founder of the international law field in Islamic history.
6. Al-Ziy*ādāt:* this is the last of the *Ẓāhir al-Riwāya* books. Since this book is a collection of issues that are not included in the five books, it is called al-Ziy*ādāt*, which means "extra issues."

All of these six books were written by Imam Mohammad, a famous student of Imam Abū Ḥanīfa, and are considered the main sources of the Ḥanafī school.[170] Some scholars believe that another book called *al-Kāfī*,[171] written by Abū al-Fāḍil Marwazī (*al-Ḥakīm*), should also be considered as a first-category source in the Ḥanafī school alongside the six books of Imam Mohammad.[172]

The second-category sources in the Ḥanafī school are called *Nawādir*. These sources were also narrated by the founders of the school but were not included in the *Ẓāhir al-Riwāya* books. This category also includes those opinions collected from Imam Mohammad's other books, including *al-Kaysāniyyāt*, *al-Ruqiyyāt*, *al-Jurjāniyyāt*, and *al-Hāruniyyāt*, or other books from that era, like *al-Mujarrad*, written by Imam Ḥasan ibn Zayād, one of Abū Ḥanīfa's students.

Furthermore, there are other sources belonging to the second category, like the *Al Aʾmālī*. It was common among Ḥanafī school scholars, especially when Imam Abū Yūsuf was the chief judge, for students to get together and sit around the imam and then ask questions or discuss a topic. At the same time, some of the students wrote down what the imam said in each gathering (*majlis*), and then they collected them into a book and called it *Al Aʾmālī*. Also, there are some collections of the opinions narrated by a single narrator called *al-Nawādir*, such as *Nawādir ibn SamāḤ*, *Nawādir Hishām*, *Nawādir ibn Rustam*, etc.[173]

The third category of the Ḥanafī school sources is called *al-wāqiʿāt*. These are a group of legal opinions issued by the Ḥanafī scholars called *al-mutaʾakhkhirrūn*.[174]

---

[170] Ibn ʿĀbidīn (1992b), p. 171.

[171] A famous Ḥanafī Scholar, Abū al-Fāḍil Marwazī (Ḥakīm Shahīd) collected Imam Mohammad's opinions in one book and named it *al-Kāfī*. The two well-known Ḥanafī scholars, Imam al-Sarakhsī and al-Isbijābī have a description on this book, and Imam al-Sarakhsī book called *al-MabsūṬ al-Sarakhsī*.

[172] Abd al-Ḥay (1986), p. 7.

[173] Ibn ʿĀbidīn (1992b), p. 74.

[174] Abd al-Ḥay (1986), p. 7.

Al-muta'akhkhirrūn referred to those Ḥanafī scholars who were not direct students of Imam Abū Ḥanīfa but who learned from his students, namely Imam Abū Yūsuf, Imam Mohammad, and others, which systematically continued for several decades.[175] When they were asked to provide an opinion regarding a new legal issue and there was no opinion from the founders of the school, Abū Ḥanīfa, Imam Abū Yūsuf, and Imam Mohammad (*al-mutaqaddimūn*), they gave their fatwas (legal opinions) based on the main principle of the Ḥanafī school doctrines.[176] One of the main principles of the Ḥanafī school is that the opinions found in the fatwa books are not reliable and a case must not refer to them unless they are not in conflict with the opinions found in the main sources of the school, or the *Ẓāhir al-riwāya*. If there is an opinion in the main sources, the fatwa books must be ignored and must not even be named as a reference.[177]

These are the main classifications of the Ḥanafī school sources that establish a framework for the judges when making a decision. The question is: what if an imitator judge does not respect the hierarchy of the sources when he makes a decision? The Ḥanafī scholars clearly state that the imitator judge must make a decision in accordance with the main sources (*Ẓāhir al-Riwāya* books) and shall not make reference to an opinion that is uncommon and not well known in the Ḥanafī school.[178] If a judge does not respect the hierarchy of the sources and makes a decision not in accordance with the main sources of the school, his decision is not valid and must not be implemented.[179]

Therefore, the hierarchy of the sources and the scholars is a crucial principle of the Ḥanafī school of thought to measure the validity of an opinion within the school. The Ḥanafī scholars believe that no judge or scholar is allowed to make a decision based on a source that is not part of the Ḥanafī school. Also, it is prohibited to make a decision based on compendium texts that do not have enough clarification regarding the case or were written by an unknown author.[180]

Generally, it is also a common rule among Islamic scholars that reference to a source or an opinion has a significant impact on the weight of an idea. Similarly, when a judge formulates a judgment, he must make reference to the most reliable sources and the first-class scholars' opinion to give value to his decision. If a judge does not respect the hierarchy of the sources and scholars of the Ḥanafī school, his decision should not be enforced. So, according to the Ḥanafī school standards, it is

[175] Ḥafnāwī (n.d.), p. 51.

[176] Ibn ʿĀbidīn (1992b), p. 171.

[177] ʿUṭwa (1994), p. 65.

[178] Id., p. 61.

[179] Id., p. 73.

[180] Among the Ḥanafī school sources, there is a list of books that followers should not rely on when they make a decision. These books are not trustworthy because of different reasons; some of them are not written by well-known scholars like Mulā Miskīn, who wrote an explanatory book on *al-Kanz*, a famous Ḥanafī book. Or some of them do not have enough explanation on cases, like a book called *al-ʿAynī*. This book is an explanatory book of a famous book, called *al-Kanz* (Arabic: الكنز) Durr al-Mukhtār, and of *Tanwīr al-Abṣār*. Please see Ibn ʿĀbidīn (1992b), p. 75.

the obligation of the judges to respect the hierarchy of the opinions and sources within the Ḥanafī school when they make a decision. If they refer to the Ḥanafī school provisions in a case, they must rely on the most reliable sources and doctrines that belong to the first-class scholars of the school.

4.8 Conclusion

The study of the legal framework of Sharia and the historical background of the use of Sharia in the legal system of Afghanistan will pave way for understanding how the Afghan courts apply Ḥanafī school provisions to a case if there is a legal lacuna. Overall, Sharia principles, particularly the Ḥanafī school of thought, have played a significant role in the legal history of Afghanistan. It is noteworthy to say that in the context of Afghanistan, many believe that the terms Sharia and the Ḥanafī school of thought are the same and can be used interchangeably. Historically, Sharia has been considered the main source of law in Afghanistan since Islam came to the region. Afghanistan has a pluralistic legal system, which is composed of Islamic law, customary law, and state law, but Islamic law always has had a strong impact on the two other sources.

Since the majority of Afghan citizens follow the Ḥanafī school of thought, the classical texts of the school have been used as law by Afghan judges for centuries. The principles of Sharia have been recognized as the main law, and courts have made decisions based on them. But after the 1964 Constitution, superiority was given to state law, and Sharia principles have played a backup role in instances of a legal lacuna. Originally, the idea of superiority of law and using Sharia to fill legal gaps was raised by ʿAbd al-Razzāq al-Sanhūrī for the first time when he formulated the Egyptian Civil Code in 1949. The Sanhūrī idea spread very fast among other Muslim countries, and Afghanistan also accepted this provision and included it in its 1964 Constitution. Since then, the supremacy of state law has been recognized in the Afghan legal system, including the current 2004 Constitution.

Article 130 of the 2004 Constitution allows the Afghan courts to apply Ḥanafī school doctrines if there is no legal provision regarding a case. This article has been used commonly by Afghan courts in those cases where judges consider an act a crime but the act is not actually criminalized under the law. Having a close eye on the text of the article reveals that applying this article to a case has some specific conditions and must be done so only within the limits set by law and the Constitution. One of the limits that must be taken into consideration is the principle of legality. This principle is accepted in the Islamic law primary sources, the Quran and the Sunnah of the Prophet Mohammad, and the Afghan Constitution and the Penal Code as well. Another notable issue is the difference between criminal law and Sharia with regard to the procedures for hearing criminal cases. The criminal law procedure and Sharia have different standards, and in most cases, they do not recognize each other as valid norms. The court must scrutinize the variety of applicable standards in both criminal procedures to give legitimacy to its decisions.

Furthermore, when an Afghan court applies Article 130 of the Constitution to a case, it shall be in compliance with the standards that have been accepted in the Ḥanafī school of thought. One of the main principles is the hierarchy of the sources and scholars of the Ḥanafī school of thought. Based on the Ḥanafī school's principles, the decision of a Ḥanafī imitator judge shall not be valid if it was not written in accordance with the first-class sources or if it contradicts the main doctrines of the school.

Moreover, the concept of *taʿzīr* (discretionary punishment) has played an important role in court decisions that have been made in reliance on Article 130 of the Constitution. According to the Sharia principle, only the ruler has the power to punish people based on *taʿzīr* if their act harms other citizens or destroys social order. However, most Afghan judges believe that they have the authority to punish people based on *taʿzīr* if they determine that an act is harmful to society or other citizens. Understanding all of these factors is necessary as they are used as indicators in the following chapters, which concern case studies, to measure whether the Afghan courts respect these norms and standards when they apply Ḥanafī provisions to a case.

References

ʿAbd al-Ḥay I (1986) Muqaddima wa sharh al-jāmiʿ al-ṣaghīr li-MuḤammad ibn Ḥasan al-Shibānī. ʿĀlam al-Kutub, Beirut

ʿAbd al-Qādir ibn MuḤammad ibn Naṣrallāh (n.d.) al-jawāhir al-muḍīʾa fī ṭabaqāt al-Ḥanafīya. Mīr MuḤammad Kutub Khāna, Karachi

Abū Zuhra M (1998) Al-Jarīma wa-l-ʿUqūba fī al-Fiqh al-Islāmī. Dār al-Fikr al-ʿArabī, Cairo

Al Said S (1995) Ḥudūd and Taʿzirāt (translation by Mohammad Mūsa Nuhmat). Saeedi Publication, Kabul

Al Zahabi, Shamsudd īn Mohammad ibe Ahmad ibn Othm*ān ibn Qāimāz (2006) Seyar Aalām Al Nubalā*, Qairo: D*ārul Hadith*

Al-Ālūsī, Shihāb al-Dīn Maḥmūd ibn ʿAbdallāh Al-Ḥusaynī, 1994. Tafsīr Ālūsī= Rūḥ al-Maʿānī, Verified by ʿAlī ʿAbd al-Bārī ʿAṭiyya, Beirut: Dār al-Kutub al-ʿIlmiyya

Al-Āmidī A (n.d.) Al-Iḥkām fī Uṣūl al-Aḥkām, verified by ʿAbd al-Razzāq ʿAfīfī. Al-Maktab al-Islāmī, Beirut, vol 1

Al-Bukhārī M (2001) Ṣaḥīḥ al-Bukhārī, verified by MuḤammad Ẓāhir ibn Nāṣir al-Nāṣir. Dār Ṭawq al-Najāt, Beirut

Al-Dihlawī S (1995) ʿAqd al-Jayyid fī Aḥkām al-Ijtihād wa-l-Taqlīd. Dār al-FatḤ, Emirates: Al Shareqah

Al-Ḥaṣkafī A (2002) Al-Durr al-Mukhtār Sharḥ Tanwīr al-Abṣār wa Jāmiʿ al-AbḤār. Dār al-Kutub al-ʿIlmiyya, Beirut

Al-Marghīnānī ʿA (n.d.) Al-Hidāya: Sharḥ fī Bidāyat al-Mubtadā. Dār Iḥyāʾ al-Turāth al-ʿArabī, Beirut, vol 2

Al-Mawṣilī ʿA (1937) Al-ikhtiyār li-taʿlīl al-mukhtār. al-Maṭbaʿa al-ḥalabī, Cairo, vol 2

Al-Mujaddidī M (2003) Al-Taʿrīfāt Al-Fiqhiyya, term al-mutaʾakhkhirūn. Dār al-Kutub al-ʿIlmiyya, Beirut

Al-Qarāfī A (1995) Al-Iḥkām fī Tamyīz al-Fatāwā ʿan al-Aḥkām wa Taṣarrufāt al-Qāḍī wa-l-Imām. Maktaba al-Maṭbūʿāt al-Islāmiyya, Aleppo

Al-Rāzī M (1999) Tafsīr al-Rāzī, Al-Tafsīr al-Kabīr. Dār Ihyāʾ al-Turāth al-ʿArabī, Beirut, vol 1

Al-Sarakhsī M (1993a) Al-Mabsūṭ li-Sarakhsī. Dār al-Maʿrifa, Beirut, vol 9
Al-Sarakhsī M (1993b) Al-Mabsūṭ li-Sarakhsī. Dār al-Maʿrifa, Beirut, vol 11
Al-Tamīmī T (n.d.) Al-Ṭabaqāt al-Saniyya fī Tarājim al-Ḥanafiyya. Dār al-Rifāʿī, Aleppo
Al-Ṭarābulusī ʿA (1973) Muʿīn al-Ḥukkām fī mā yataraddadu bayna al-khaṣmayn min al-aḤkām. Dār al-Fikr, Beirut
Al-Ṭebarī M (2000) Tafsīr al-Ṭebarī (Jāmiʿ al-Bayān fī Taʾwīl al-Qurʾān). Muʾassasa al-Risāla, vol 17
Al-Tirmidhī M (1998) Sunan al-Tirmidhī, verified by Bashār ʿAwād Maʿrūf. Dār al-Gharb al-Islāmī, Beirut
ʿAsqalānī A (2000) Fatḥ al-Bārī Sharh Ṣaḥīḥ al-Bukhārī. The interpretation of Hadith no. 662. Dār al-Maʿrifa, Beirut
ʿAwda ʿA (n.d.) Islamic and statute criminal law. A comparative study (translation by Ḥasan Farhūdī Nia). Poya Research Foundation, Tehran
Bassiouni MC (2014) The Islamic criminal justice system. In: Ibid. (ed) The Sharia and Islamic criminal justice in time of war and peace. Cambridge University Press, Cambridge, Chapter 3, pp 118–149
Civil Procedure of Afghanistan (1990) Ministry of Justice, Official Gazette No: 722
Criminal Procedure Code (2014) Ministry of Justice, Official Gazette No: 1132
Ḥafnāwī MI (n.d.) Ganjīna IṣṬilāḥāt Fiqhī wa Uṣūlī (translation by Fayż MuḤammad Balūch). Mustaqbal Publisher, Kabul
Ibn ʿĀbidīn M (1992a) Radd al-MuḤtār ʿalā Durr al-Mukhtār (Ḥāshiyya Ibn ʿĀbidīn). Dār al-Fikr, Beirut, vol4
Ibn ʿĀbidīn M (1992b) Radd al-MuḤtār ʿalā Durr al-Mukhtār (Ḥāshiyya Ibn ʿĀbidīn). Dār al-Fikr, Beirut, vol 1
Ibn ʿĀbidīn M (n.d.) Risāla fī al-Qawl al-Mukhtār min al-Aqwāl fī madhhab Imām Abī Ḥanīfa. p 4, http://www.almostafainfo/data/arabic/depot3/gap.php?file=m001527.pdf. Accessed 05 June 2021 file=m002494.pdf
Ibn al-Ḥajāj M (n.d.) Ṣaḥīḥ Muslim, verified by MuḤammad Fawād ʿAbd al-Bāqī. Dār Iḥyāʾ al-Turāth al-ʿArabī, Beirut
Ibn Hammām K (1970) Shar Fatḥ al-Qadīr. Dār al-Fikr, Beirut, vol 5
Ibn Kamāl Bāshā Al-Rūmī (n.d.) Risāla fī Ṭabaqāt Al-Fuqahāʾ. Available at http://www.almostafa.info/data/arabic/depot3/gap.php?
Ibn Kathīr A (1999a) Tafsīr ibn Kathīr, verified by Sāmī ibn MuḤammad Salāma. Dār Ṭayyiba li-l-Nashr wa-l-Tawzīʿ, Saudi Arabia, Riyadh, vol 4
Ibn Kathīr A (1999b) Tafsīr ibn Kathīr, verified by Sāmī ibn MuḤammad Salāma. Dār Ṭayyiba li-l-Nashr wa-l-Tawzīʿ, Saudi Arabia, Riyadh, vol 2
Ibn Simnānī ʿA (1984) Rawḍat al-Quḍāt wa Ṭarīq al-Najāt. Muʾassasa al-Risāla, Beirut
Law on Organization and Jurisdiction of the Judiciary of Afghanistan (2013) Ministry of Justice, official gazette No: 1109
Lippman M (1989) Islamic criminal law and procedure: religious fundamentalism v. modern law. Boston College International and Comparative Law Review, vol 12
Mullā Khusraw M (n.d.) Durar al-Ḥukkām SharḤ Ghurar al-AḤkām. Dār Iḥyāʾ al-Kutub al-ʿArabiyya, Beirut, vol 2
Munir M (2018) The principle of legality in Islamic criminal justice system. Hazara Islamicus 7 (1):107–120
Penal Code of Afghanistan (1976) Ministry of Justice, official gazette No: 347
Rasooli MA (2015) Considering the principle of legality in the constitution of Afghanistan. ʿAdālat, J MoJ Afghanistan 8(45)
Rohe M (2014a) Islamic law in past and present. Brill, Leiden
Rohe M (2014b) The origins of the Islamic state and its legal system. In: Id. (ed) Islamic law in past and present. Brill, Leiden, Chapter 1, pp 25–53
Rohe M (2014c) Overview of the areas governed by classical Islamic law. In: Id. (ed) Islamic law in past and present. Brill, Leiden, Chapter 4, pp 97–211

Sharif M (1985) Crimes and punishment in Islam. Kazi Publications, Chicago
Shaykh Ṭūsī M (2001) Al-Tibyān fī Tafsīr al-Qur'ān. Bunyād Dā'irat al-Ma'ārif-i Buzurg-i Islāmī, Tehran, vol 6
Siddiqui MI (2010) The penal law of Islam. Adam Publishers, Delhi
The Civil Code of the Arab Republic of Egypt (1949). available at http://www.sis.gov.eg/Newvr/Dustor-en001.pdf. Accessed 06, 05, 2021
The Constitution of Afghanistan (2004) Ministry of Justice, Official Gazette No: 818
The Holy Quran
The Interim Criminal Procedure Code for Courts (2004) Ministry of Justice, Official Gazete No: 820
The Law on Structure and Authority of Attorney General Office (2013) Official Gazette No: 1117
The Police Law of Afghanistan (2005) Ministry of Justice, Official Gazette No: 862
'Uṭwa 'A (1994) Qawā'id al-Iftā' - Principle of verdicts (translation by Shāh MaḤmūd Khirad). Afghan Lawyers Association, Kabul

Part II
Case Studies

Chapter 5
Said Parwīz Kāmbakhsh Apostasy Case

5.1 Introduction

Parwīz Kāmbakhsh, a third-year student at Balkh University in the north of Afghanistan, printed an article from the internet that included words deemed insulting to the Prophet Mohammad and the Holy Quran. He distributed the article to his classmates and was subsequently charged with blasphemy and sentenced to death by the Primary Court of Mazar-e-Sharif city. The Kabul Appellate Court then changed the Primary Court's decision to 20 years of imprisonment. Since blasphemy is not criminalized under Afghan law, the courts made their decisions based on Article 130 of the Afghan Constitution, which allows a court to base its decisions on the provisions of the Ḥanafī school of thought if the law makes no provisions for the case under consideration. This section of the chapter analyzes the Kāmbakhsh case in order to determine how the Afghan courts implement Sharia, particularly the Ḥanafī school provisions, in criminal cases not covered by law.

While blasphemy is not a crime according to the law of Afghanistan, such cases must not be processed based on the regular criminal procedure designed for crimes listed in Afghan laws. In fact, a case in which the committed act is only deemed a crime under Sharia but not according to Afghan law is not subject to criminal procedure. Furthermore, it is a challenge to the legitimacy of the court's ruling because criminal procedure deals only with acts that are considered crimes under the law. If an act is not criminalized by law, it is illegal to process it in the law enforcement departments, including the courts of Afghanistan.[1] This analysis will

[1] Art. 27 of the Afghan Constitution and Art. 2 and Art.3 of the Penal Code clearly said: "No deed shall be considered a crime unless ruled by a law promulgated prior to commitment of the offense. No one shall be pursued, arrested, or detained without due process of law. No one shall be punished without the decision of an authoritative court taken in accordance with the provisions of the law, promulgated prior to commitment of the offense." Furthermore, Art. 27 of the Penal Code defines crime as "An act or omission of an act contrary to the law[...]." Besides this, Art. 4, clause 3, of the Criminal Procedure Code (1974) defines a criminal case as "Demand for punishment of the accused

L. Saeed, *Islam, Custom and Human Rights*, Interdisciplinary Studies in Human Rights 7, https://doi.org/10.1007/978-3-030-83086-1_5

also discuss more details about the legality of both pretrial proceedings and the courts' decisions.

Furthermore, the courts' decisions will be analyzed in light of those norms and standards that are discussed in the first part of the study to find out whether Afghan courts respect these principles or not when applying the Ḥanafī school doctrines to a case. Finally, this chapter will examine the consequences of the violation of the principles of Afghan laws and the Ḥanafī school of thought in Mr. Kāmbakhsh's case.

5.2 Analysis of the Parwīz Kāmbakhsh Apostasy Case

Mr. Said Parwīz Kāmbakhsh, a journalist and third-year student at the Faculty of Journalism at Balkh University, printed an article containing words insulting the Holy Quran and Prophet Mohammad. He distributed 11 copies to his classmates and was subsequently arrested by the National Directorate of Security (NDS)[2] office of Balkh Province. The Prosecutor's Office of Mazar-e-Sharif city in Balkh Province charged him with blasphemy and demanded a harsh punishment. In 2007, the Primary Court of Mazar-e-Sharif ruled that he be punished by death in accordance with Article 130[3] of the Afghan Constitution. Mr. Kāmbakhsh's family asked the Supreme Court to adjudicate the case in the Kabul Appellate Court rather than the Balkh Province Appellate Court. The Kabul Appellate Court overruled the decision of the Mazar-e-Sharif Primary Court and reduced Mr. Kāmbakhsh's sentence to 20-year imprisonment based on Article 130 of the Afghan Constitution. The Supreme Court of Afghanistan subsequently confirmed the Appellate Court's decision. He was eventually pardoned by the Afghan government, and in 2009, *Mr. Carl*

by the prosecutor in accordance with the provisions of this law before the court." Also, Art. 4, clause 14, of the Criminal Procedure Code defined the accusation letter as a "written document which is, as a result of investigation, prepared by the relevant prosecutor mentioning proof, reasons and law articles to which the crime and specific punishment has been determined based on which the trial of the accused person is requested." Additionally, the first clause of Art. 7 of the Criminal Procedure Code says that suspects, accused persons, and defendants are entitled to be informed of the crime they are being charged with and receive information regarding the accusation and case proceedings. All these provisions of law declare that no one shall be prosecuted or punished without law.

[2]Since 1978, the National Directorate of Security (NDS) is known as the most powerful institution in the Afghan government. It is well-known for its significant extra-legal activities in the context of assuring security and fighting terrorism. NDS operates without judicial oversight and limited review by parliament. See a report provided by UNAMA (2011) Treatment of Conflict-Related Detainees in Afghan Custody. https://unama.unmissions.org/treatment-conflict-related-detainees-afghan-custody. Accessed 5 Oct 2017.

[3]The Constitution of Afghanistan (2004) Art. 130: "In a case under consideration, the courts shall apply provisions of this Constitution as well as other laws. If there is no provision in the Constitution or other laws about a case, the court shall, in pursuance of Ḥanafī jurisprudence, and within the limits set by this Constitution, rule in a way that attains justice in the best manner."

Bildt, a former Foreign Minister of Sweden—along with *Kai Eide*, the UN High Representative in Afghanistan—smuggled him out of the country using Mr. Bildt's plane and took him to Stockholm. He was then granted asylum in Norway.[4]

The case gives rise to a number of questions: Did the NDS officers have the right to arrest Kāmbakhsh? Since blasphemy is not criminalized in the current laws of Afghanistan, do the police department and the prosecutor's office have the right to process the case in accordance with the provisions of the laws governing criminal procedure? Was the Primary Court's initial decision in accordance with the provisions of the Ḥanafī school of thought? Why did the Kabul Appellate Court overrule the Primary Court's decision and adjudicate differently? In order to answer these and other questions, it is necessary to dig deeper into the case, look closely at every step that was taken, and analyze the findings against the backdrop of the laws of Afghanistan and Sharia.

5.2.1 *Pretrial Proceedings*

Generally, in the Afghan legal system, criminal procedure involves three organizations:[5] (1) police or NDS departments, (2) the prosecutor's office, and (3) the courts. The police or NDS departments are authorized to detect crimes and collect evidence from crime scenes.[6] Since the police or NDS departments' activities provide the foundation for the second procedural phase at the prosecutor's office, the prosecutor cannot process the case if the first step has not been conducted properly:

> If the prosecutor, after receiving the case documents, discovers that legal provisions have not been observed in preparing registries of detection, and collecting evidence and grounds or sufficient evidence have not been collected justifying further actions, they will write down the points and instruct the detection organizations for sound performance.[7]

If the police or NDS departments have violated the law in the course of collecting evidence and conducting a preliminary investigation, the prosecutor's office cannot proceed with the case and, instead, shall report the matter to the relevant authority:

[4] Sveriges Radio (2015) Carl Bildt smuggled journalist out of Afghanistan. http://sverigesradio.se/sida/artikel.aspx?programid=2054&artikel=6074542. Accessed 12 April 2017.

[5] Art. 134 of the Constitution of Afghanistan (2004) states that discovering crimes shall be the duty of the police, while investigation and filing the indictment in court shall be the responsibility of the Prosecutor's Office. Moreover, Art. 122 of the Afghan Constitution states "No law shall, under any circumstances, exclude any case or area from the jurisdiction of the judicial organ as defined in this chapter."

[6] Criminal Procedure Code (2014) Art. 80, official gazette no. 1132.

[7] Criminal Procedure Code (2014) Art. 89, official gazette no. 1132.

> If the prosecutor, during an investigation, discovers that the police and national security operatives have committed legal violations in their handling of a case, he shall report the matter to the concerned competent authority according to the circumstances.[8]

Similarly, the court cannot issue a decision if the prosecutor's office has not collected reliable evidence to substantiate its claims against that accused person. The law states:

> The court cannot issue a decision to convict the accused person based on suspicion or if there is doubt in reasons or evidence.[9]

Throughout this chapter, the process of the case at each stage, based on the above provisions of law, will be examined to ascertain whether the case was processed accordingly. Additionally, the procedure followed in the case is examined from different angles, for instance the prosecutor's investigation, the filing of the case, the submission of the indictment to the court, as well as other activities, with a view to assessing whether or not they were conducted in accordance with law. The chapter will also investigate which Sharia provisions were drawn on in the court's ruling. Finally, some light is shed on the courts' use of Sharia, pursuant to Article 130 of the Afghan Constitution, by investigating whether the legal provisions and Sharia rules, the Ḥanafī school of thought in particular, were properly applied.

The NDS office in Mazar-e-Sharif city received a report and complaint concerning Mr. Kāmbakhsh's activities at Balkh University. The NDS officers arrested Mr. Kāmbakhsh and conducted a preliminary investigation. They then transferred the case to the Prosecutor's Office of Mazar-e-Sharif city for further investigation. It is noteworthy that the NDS office made the arrest when the Constitution states that the police are tasked with discovering the crime and it is the duty of the prosecutor's office to conduct an investigation and file the case against the accused in court.[10] Furthermore, the legislation governing the police and criminal procedure states that the police are responsible for discovering the crime[11] and must thereafter refer it to the prosecutor's office.[12] However, while the laws provide a clear procedure for the discovery and investigation of crimes, the involvement of the NDS in the case is a question that draws the attention of most readers and thus requires closer examination.

Before going deeper into the case, it is necessary to provide some additional information on the NDS in terms of its organization, its background, and its authority. Historically, the NDS, as a powerful institution, was established during the communist party in 1978. However, this institution has been given a variety of names by different governments because since its establishment, it has continuously

[8]Criminal Procedure Code (2014) Art. 91, official gazette no. 1132.

[9]Criminal Procedure Code (2014) Art.19, official gazette no. 1132, clause 4/The Interim Criminal Procedure Code (2004) Art. 7.

[10]The Constitution of Afghanistan (2004) Art. 134.

[11]Police Law (2009) Art. 5.

[12]Law on the Structure and Authority of the Prosecutor's Office (2013) Art. 3.

worked through the Mujahedeen, the Taliban, and the current governments.[13] The NDS is well known for its significant extralegal activities to protect national security and fight against terrorism, which constitute its main obligations.[14] The *Law on Crimes Against Internal and External Security* lists a group of crimes—including terrorism, sabotage, propaganda against the government, treason, espionage, war propaganda, assisting enemy forces, organized activities against internal and external security—that should be investigated by NDS officers.[15]

From a historical perspective, the scope of the NDS' activities is regulated by law in theory, but in practice there is no publicly known scope of authority for the NDS office in the legal system of Afghanistan. Since the NDS law is not publicly available and citizens do not know what activity would be subject to that law,[16] it is difficult to find a clear boundary for the NDS's power and the activities it conducts on a daily basis. Because of the historical background of the NDS office, the common belief among Afghan citizens is that NDS officers can easily arrest and investigate people even without standard norms recognized by laws. Also, it is a common belief among Afghans that if the NDS office is involved in a case, it shows the seriousness of the case.

In the past, this ambiguity in the scope of the objectives and authority of the NDS generated fear in society as it bestowed substantial powers on the NDS staff to arrest and investigate anyone they so choose and to keep them in custody for an unlimited period of time. They could criminalize any act that they thought was harmful to the government. Even during 1979–1987, listening to radio broadcasts from western countries, like BBC, was a serious crime and could constitute grounds for arrest and serious punishment. During 1978 and 1979, the NDS arrested thousands of ordinary people and executed them without a fair trial. Most of these victims were students, teachers, farmers, bus drivers, postmen, traders, and shopkeepers, to list some examples.[17] As a concrete example of the mass killing of Afghan citizens during the communist regime, around 5000 people[18] were executed by the NDS office.[19]

After 2002, and following the enactment of the 2004 Constitution, the situation changed as the Constitution accepted the principles of legality of crime and punishment and the standards for a fair trial. Article 27 of the Constitution states:

---

[13] UNAMA (2011) Treatment of Conflict-Related Detainees in Afghan Custody, pp 14-15. https://unama.unmissions.org/treatment-conflict-related-detainees-afghan-custody. Accessed 5 Oct 2017.

[14] Unpublished Presidential Decree No. 89 (dated 4 November 2001), Law on Crimes Against Internal and External Security (1987) Art. 1-9/ Art. 23.

[15] Law on Crimes Against Internal and External Security (1987) Art. 1-9/Art. 23.

[16] The NDS law was enacted on 04 November 2001, by the unpublished presidential decree no. 89. This law is not publicly available and only some officials of NDS have access to that law.

[17] Ioyn D (2014) The Death List that Names 5,000 Victims. Available via BBC http://www.bbc.com/news/magazine-28645671. Accessed 10 March 2016.

[18] Khaama Press (2016) List of 5,000 Afghan victims killed under the communist regime in the late 1970s. http://www.khaama.com/lists-of-5000-afghan-victims-killed-by-communist-regime-revealed-2398. Accessed 10 March 2016.

[19] The Dutch police released a list of the victims during the investigation of an Afghan individual, Mr. Amānallāh, who was charged to have committed a crime against humanity by the Dutch Police.

> No deed shall be considered a crime unless so ruled by a law promulgated prior to commitment of the offence. No one shall be pursued, arrested, or detained without due process of law. No one shall be punished without the decision of an authoritative court taken in accordance with the provisions of the law, promulgated prior to commitment of the offence.[20]

The Constitution also prohibits applying any form of torture as a means of discovering the truth. The same applies to punishment during investigations. Article 129 of the Constitution states:

> Persecution of human beings shall be forbidden. No one shall be allowed to perform or order torture, not even for discovering the truth from another individual who is under investigation, arrest, detention or who has been convicted to be punished. Punishment contrary to human dignity shall be prohibited.[21]

However, while we have the above constitutional provisions and some additional laws, some studies show that the NDS staff and the Afghan National Police (ANP) do not respect them and continue to keep people in custody beyond the legal limits. Compelling evidence was collected from the provincial NDS facilities in Kabul, Herat, Kandahar, Khost, Laghman, Kapisa, and Takhar provinces.[22] The systematic use of torture and extralegal approaches by the NDS and the Afghan National Police (ANP) for obtaining information was also substantiated in the 2013 and 2015 UNAMA reports regarding the treatment of conflict-related detainees.[23]

While there is no official public definition of what constitutes acting against national security, the *Law on Crimes Against Internal and External Security* of the Democratic Republic of Afghanistan, which is enacted on October 22, 1987,[24] and the *Law Against Terrorism Crimes*[25] provide a list of crimes that must be investigated by the NDS. These crimes are national treason,[26] espionage,[27] terrorism,[28] sabotage,[29] propaganda against the government,[30] assisting enemy forces,[31] as well

---

[20] The Constitution of Afghanistan (2004) Art. 27.

[21] The Constitution of Afghanistan (2004) Art. 129.

[22] UNAMA (2011) Treatment of Conflict-Related Detainees in Afghan Custody. https://unama.unmissions.org/treatment-conflict-related-detainees-afghan-custody. Accessed 11 March 2016.

[23] UNAMA (2013) Treatment of Conflict-Related Detainees in Afghan Custody, pp 29–63 and UNAMA (2015) Treatment of Conflict-Related Detainees in Afghan Custody, pp 42–67. https://unama.unmissions.org/treatment-conflict-related-detainees-afghan-custody. Accessed 12 March 2016.

[24] This law was enacted during the communist regime and mostly targets those who were fighting against the communist regime, but this law has been enforced till now.

[25] Law Against Terrorism Crimes (2008) Art. 8-20, official gazette no. 952.

[26] The Law on Crimes against Internal and External Security (1987) Art. 1.

[27] The Law on Crimes against Internal and External Security (1987) Art. 2.

[28] The Law on crimes against Internal and External Security (1987) Art. 3.

[29] The Law on Crimes against Internal and External Security (1987) Art. 6.

[30] The Law on Crimes against Internal and External Security (1987) Art. 7.

[31] The Law on Crimes against Internal and External Security (1987) Art. 23.

as organized activity against internal and external security.[32] The NDS office has the authority to uncover and investigate these crimes.

Regarding the Kāmbakhsh case, blasphemy is not visibly categorized as a crime in any statutory law of Afghanistan. Arguably, it could constitute part of a violation of national, religious, and ethnic equal rights, which is reflected in Article 11 of the *Law on Crimes Against Internal and External Security*. The article states:

> Anyone who engages in propaganda to stimulate hostility based on national, ethnic, religious, tribal and linguistic reasons, he/she will be sentenced up to three years in prison.[33]

Based on this article, Mr. Kāmbakhsh's activity could be considered a crime because he printed and distributed a document that stimulated hostility based on antireligious propaganda. This kind of activity is regulated by law and the NDS department is in charge of dealing with this crime and, accordingly, the NDS staff should be involved in the case. The above provision of the law gives legitimacy to the NDS's involvement in the case, which should have been processed by the NDS prosecutor's office because according to *The Law on Crimes Against Internal and External Security*, all crimes listed in that law must be investigated and prosecuted by the NDS, except crimes stated in Articles 25 and 26, which remain the responsibility of the police and the prosecutor's office. Therefore, several questions were raised regarding Mr. Kāmbakhsh's case during the pretrial proceedings: If Mr. Kāmbakhsh's act is subject to Article 11 of the *Law on Crimes Against Internal and External Security* and according to that law it is the authority of the NDS office to process such cases, why did the NDS office in Mazar-e-Sharif forward the case to the prosecutor's office? Why has the case not been processed in the NDS prosecutor's office?

From the Sharia perspective, Mr. Kāmbakhsh's act was considered blasphemy and counted as a serious crime and shall be prosecuted; however, blasphemy and apostasy are not criminalized in the law. According to the law, the prosecutor's office has the authority to investigate and process only those acts that are criminalized by law. So there appears to be no legal basis for the police and the prosecutor's office to investigate and prosecute Mr. Kāmbakhsh. In any case, the processing of Mr. Kāmbakhsh's case by the prosecutor's office is challenged by the due process of law principle, which is guaranteed by the Constitution and the laws of Afghanistan.[34]

---

[32] The Law on Crimes against Internal and External Security (1987) Art. 9.

[33] The Law on Crimes against Internal and External Security (1987) Art. 11.

[34] The Constitution of Afghanistan (2004) Art. 27/ Penal Code of Afghanistan (1976) Art. 2/Art. 3.

5.2.2 Police Department

Constitutionally, the police have the authority to discover crimes that are defined in the laws of Afghanistan,[35] but it is illegal for the police to make an arrest for an act that is not considered a crime in the laws of Afghanistan. So, on one hand, the police made an arrest for an act that is not criminalized, while on the other hand, Article 27 of the Afghan Constitution and Articles 2 and 3 of the Penal Code expressly declare that there shall be no crime and no punishment without law.[36]

The abovementioned articles explicitly accept the principle of legality and provide that no action shall be considered a crime unless it has already been legally defined as such before the act was committed. Furthermore, the article prevents arrest and detention without due process. Moreover, the Penal Code of Afghanistan recognizes the principle of legality by preventing anyone from being punished for a behavior that is not defined as a crime by law:

> No act shall be considered a crime, but in accordance with the law.[37]

The legal basis for the police's involvement in the Kāmbakhsh case is not clear because the police are authorized to act on and process a case that is covered by their duty, but Kāmbakhsh's act is not listed as a crime under the law and so could not be included in the police's responsibility. Thus, the police act in the Kāmbakhsh case lacks legitimacy and legal basis under the law of Afghanistan. However, Kāmbakhsh committed a crime according to Sharia, so he must be prosecuted according to Sharia criminal procedure, which follows different norms and standards.[38] The Afghan legal system has many of these norms and standards, but more often there is no clear designation of authority for the exercise of power by law enforcement institutions within the limits set by law. This ambiguity creates problems in the implementation of laws. For instance, Article 5 of the *Police Law of 2005* defines 21 duties for the police, of which some do not provide clear boundaries or properly specify the obligations they imply. Here are examples:

1. Ensure and maintain public order and security
2. Ensure individual and societal security and protect legal rights and freedoms
3. Take preventive actions to stop crimes from happening
4. Discover crimes and arrest suspects and perpetrators in a timely manner and in accordance with the provisions of the law

---

[35]The Constitution of Afghanistan (2004) Art. 134.

[36]The Constitution of Afghanistan (2004) Art. 27: "No deed shall be considered a crime unless ruled by a law promulgated prior to commitment of the offense. No one shall be pursued, arrested, or detained without due process of law. No one shall be punished without the decision of an authoritative court taken in accordance with the provisions of the law, promulgated prior to commitment of the offense."

[37]Penal Code of Afghanistan (1976) Art. 2.

[38]The differences between criminal procedure in accordance with that law and Sharia have been discussed in Chap. 4 in footnotes 38 and 62.

5. Counter moral deviations, immoral social behaviour and actions that disturb public tranquillity
6. ....[39]

Since the court should only proceed in cases in which the pretrial proceedings have been conducted in compliance with the standards stated in the Code of Criminal Procedure, it is worth touching on the issue of the legality of the arrest and investigation process. Analyzing some related clauses of the above article will help us discover the ambiguity of the law regarding the authority of the police. This vagueness gives rise to the extralegal activities of the police and, in many cases, gives them almost unlimited power to curtail citizens' freedoms. For example, Article 5 refers to *ensuring and maintaining public order and security*.[40] The terms "public order" and "security" are very broad and thus give the police much discretion on how to control the behavior of citizens in order to maintain public order and security.

The third clause of Article 5 authorizes the police to prevent citizens from committing acts that are legally defined as criminal. This clause seems reasonable in theory, but it is important to examine how it is reflected in the daily activities of the police. In practice, police officers deem this clause as a form of permission to stop people and even take them into custody in order to prevent a possible crime from being committed.[41] In practice, this clause has been used to justify the infringement of individual liberty.

Moreover, the law prescribes that discovering crimes and arresting suspects must occur in accordance with law.[42] This mandate originally comes from the Afghan Constitution, which states that the "discovery of crimes shall be the duty of the police...."[43] The clause thus limits the authority of the police to perform their duty within the boundaries of law and deal only with acts that are defined as criminal by law. Breaching those legal boundaries would constitute a breach of the basic rights of citizens guaranteed in the second chapter of the Constitution.

The fifth clause of Article 5 refers to moral deviations and moral social behavior,[44] two terms that are not legally defined. There are no indicators for distinguishing between moral and criminal activities in society. According to this clause, the police are authorized to stop or limit any behavior by citizens or to arrest them on grounds of immorality.

These are the main duties of the police in the context of dealing with criminal acts that occur in society. The next step is to observe how these norms are applicable in Mr. Kāmbakhsh's case.

[39]Police Law of Afghanistan (2005) Art. 5.

[40]Police Law of Afghanistan (2005) Art. 5, clause 1.

[41]Police Law of Afghanistan (2005) Art. 5, clauses 1–5.

[42]Police Law of Afghanistan (2005) Art. 5, clause 4.

[43]The Constitution of Afghanistan (2004) Art. 134.

[44]Police Law of Afghanistan (2005) Art. 5, clause 5.

There is no doubt that Mr. Kāmbakhsh violated the principles of Sharia by distributing an article that included words that are insulting to Prophet Mohammad and the Holy Quran. Since the law makes no provision as regards such behavior, processing a case in accordance with the Code of Criminal Procedure constitutes a major challenge for the law enforcement agencies. Thus, soon after Mr. Kāmbakhsh's arrest by the NDS office, the case was transferred to the police department of Balkh province for further investigation as the NDS had no legal authority in the case.[45] As has already been mentioned, Article 5 of the Police Law authorizes the police to act upon any behavior that is harmful to public order and security. Therefore, as actions were taken against behaviors that were harmful to public order and security, these actions by the police department in the case of Mr. Kāmbakhsh had a legal basis under the Police Law and thus could not be deemed a violation of the law. However, it should not be forgotten that it is the task of the prosecutor's office to determine whether a case should be dismissed or further proceeded. Therefore, now it is necessary to look at the activities of the Prosecutor's Office of Balkh Province in the case against Mr. Kāmbakhsh and assess whether or not the process was conducted in accordance with law.

The Code of Criminal Procedure does not provide a clear process to deal with blasphemy accusations because blasphemy is not criminalized in the current laws of Afghanistan. Moreover, law enforcement agencies (which include the prosecutor's office) do not know how to approach serious issues that are not criminalized by law. On the other hand, the police department has the authority to arrest persons suspected of having committed a crime according to law. However, Mr. Kāmbakhsh was not accused of any act deemed a crime under Afghan law, so the following question must be raised: Does his arrest have a legal basis? If he committed a crime according to Sharia, particularly the Ḥanafī school of thought, he should be prosecuted in accordance with the Sharia criminal procedure, not according to the Code of Criminal Procedure because his act is not considered a crime under the law of Afghanistan.

5.2.3 Prosecutor's Filing of the Indictment at Mazar-e-Sharif City Primary Court

The Balkh Province Prosecutor's Office filed an indictment against Parwīz Kāmbakhsh at Mazar-e-Sharif Primary Court for insulting the holy religion of Islam and cursing Prophet Mohammad. The prosecutor charged Mr. Kāmbakhsh with five crimes and requested that he be put on trial because:

[45]For more details, please visit these websites: http://www.aihrc.org.af/home/article/435 & http://www.aihrc.org.af/home/article/4311.

1) [T]he police found an article composed of anti-Islamic ideas. The initials of Saʿīd Parwīz Kāmbakhsh (S.P.K.) were written at the end of the article.
2) [O]ther books and articles with similar content that the accused had distributed among his classmates were also found.
3) Mr. Kāmbakhsh confessed to having downloaded the article from the internet and distributing it among his classmates.
4) [T]he accused engaged in anti-Islamic discussion with his professors and his classmates in the classroom and posed questions about women's rights in Islam.
5) [O]f the opinion of the Balkh religious leaders' council (*Shūrā ʿUlamāʾ Balkh Province*) concerning Mr. Kāmbakhsh that was issued and signed as a "fatwa" by some religious leaders of Balkh province.

These are the main reasons behind the prosecutor's indictment, for which he demanded that the court punish the accused by death. The question is whether there was sufficient evidence to prove the charges and to convince the court to make such a decision regarding the case. Evidence that is not collected in accordance with the legal requirements is invalid under the law, and the court cannot proceed with and render a decision in a case that involves invalid evidence: *The evidence which has been collected without respect of the legal requirements indicated in the law is considered invalid and the court cannot base its judgment on it.*[46] Let us now examine the reasons and the evidence and compare them against what is stated by law.

5.2.4 Fatwa of the ʿUlamāʾ Council of Balkh Province

The fact that the Religious Leader's Council (*shūrā-i ʿulamāʾ*) of Balkh Province was asked for an opinion regarding the case should be taken into account. The legal basis for this inquiry and what role the *ʿUlamāʾ* Council opinion played in the case need to be clarified. According to the Criminal Procedure Code, prosecutors and courts are allowed to draw on expert opinion regarding a case under consideration.[47] The question is whether the *ʿUlamāʾ* Council can be considered an expert or not. Or rather, what impact would the *ʿulamāʾ* fatwa have on the investigation process and the court's decision? The Criminal Procedure Code defines an "expert" as a *professional or technical person who specializes and has enough knowledge and experience in a certain field.*[48] The *ʿUlamāʾ* Council is a group of religious leaders assigned by the government that deals with religious matters in society. According to this definition, *ʿulamāʾ* (religious leaders) can be classified as experts, who the prosecutor and the courts can approach and ask for their view regarding a case. The prosecutor's

[46] Interim Criminal Procedure Code for Courts (2004) Art.7.

[47] Interim Criminal Procedure Code for Courts (2004) Article 32/Criminal Procedure Code (1976) Art. 44, official gazette no. 1132.

[48] Criminal Procedure Code (2014) Art. 4, official gazette no. 1132, clause 33.

office and the courts can also approach other professionals who are not registered as such with the court in order to rely on their knowledge and get their views regarding the issue at hand. Article 44 of the Criminal Procedure Code states:

(1) ………
(2) The judicial police officers, Prosecutor's Office and the courts are obligated to identify the type of investigation and other matters when filing their request for expert opinion.
(3) The Prosecutor's Office and the courts can consider the views of other people who have the requisite expertise, knowledge and experience pertaining to the issue, in addition to the experts who have already provided views and who are registered with the courts

Thus, the law allows the prosecutor's office and the courts to request opinions from experts who have knowledge and experience pertaining to the case. Furthermore, according to a Ḥanafī school doctrine, the judge can consult *ʿulamāʾ* and *fuqahāʾ* for advice regarding a case. Even the Ḥanafī scholars believe that it is better for a judge to consult other jurists (*fuqahāʾ*) regarding the case to find a reasonable solution for the case.[49] Therefore, asking the *ʿUlamāʾ* Council for their fatwa regarding the Kāmbakhsh case was in accordance with Afghan law or the principles of the Ḥanafī school.

5.2.5 The Application of Article 347 of the Penal Code

Before examining the reasons listed by the prosecutor more closely, it is necessary to mention the applicability of Article 347 of the Penal Code to Mr. Kāmbakhsh's case. The first noteworthy issue in the primary court's decision is that it relied on two sources—Article 347 of the Penal Code[50] and Article 130 of the Afghan Constitution. However, Article 130 of the Afghan Constitution clearly states that when there is a loophole in the laws or the case is not covered by any law, the court shall make its decision within the limits set by the Constitution based on the Ḥanafī school of thought.[51] The question here is: If the Penal Code contained provisions that were applicable to Mr. Kāmbakhsh's case, why did the Mazar-e-Sharif Primary Court apply Article 130 of the Constitution and base its decision on the Ḥanafī school of thought? However, Article 347 of the Penal Code should in fact not even have been mentioned in the Mazar-e-Sharif city Primary Court's decision because it is not applicable to the case. The article states:

[49] ʿAlāʾ al-Dīn (1986), vol. 14, p. 416.
[50] Parwiz Kāmbakhsh case, p. 17.
[51] The Constitution of Afghanistan (2004) Art. 130.

> The following persons shall be sentenced to a medium term of imprisonment[52] and a fine of not less than twelve thousand and not more than sixty thousand Afghanis:
>
> a. Persons who, forcefully and with aversion, disturb or prevent the conduct of religious rituals or rites of any religion;
> b. Persons who destroy or damage the permitted places of worship where religious rituals of any religion are conducted, or who destroy or damage any other signs or symbols respected by followers of any religion.[53]

The article is contained in the chapter that covers crimes against religion in general. There are several conditions in the article that must be met. First, it must refer to religious ceremonies. Second, it must refer to persons who forcefully disturb or stop religious ceremonies. Third, the act should involve the destruction or damage of approved places of worship. Since Mr. Kāmbakhsh did not forcefully disturb or stop a religious ceremony of any religion and did not destroy or damage a place of worship, his actions clearly should not be subject to this article. While a careful reading of the article proves that it is not relevant to the case, the primary court should have nonetheless mentioned Article 348 of the Penal Code, which reads:

> A person who attacks a follower of any of the religions, who performs his religious rituals "publicly", by word, action, writing, and other public means, shall be sentenced to a short term of imprisonment of not less than three months and a fine of not less than three thousand and not more than twelve thousand Afghanis.[54]

Although this article concerns attacks on followers of any religion through words, actions, writing, and other means, it in fact seems as though the article is referring to the followers of religions other than Islam, like the Hindu, Sikh, Christian, and Jewish minorities. The majority of such followers left Afghanistan in the course of the three decades of war. If the court had applied this article to the case under investigation because Mr. Kāmbakhsh committed a written attack on Prophet Mohammad and the religion of Islam, he would have been punished by a short-term imprisonment of at least 24 h and not more than 1 year.[55]

Since more than 99% of the population of Afghanistan is Muslim,[56] the above articles can be interpreted as applying to attacks by Muslims on other religious minorities and not attacks against Muslims because the article uses the term *place of worship* rather than *mosque*. In addition, the articles talk about religious ceremonies

[52] Article 101 of the Penal Code of Afghanistan defines medium imprisonment as a term of not less than 1 year and not more than 5 years.

[53] Penal Code of Afghanistan (1976) Art. 347.

[54] Penal Code of Afghanistan (1976) Art. 348.

[55] Penal Code of Afghanistan (1976) Art. 102.

[56] The United States Commission on International Religious Freedom (USCIRF) Annual Report revealed that 99% of the Afghan population is Muslim and that 80% of them are Sunni Muslims and 19% of the population are Shi'a Muslims (p. 135). For further information, please see USCIRF 2015 Annual Report available via https://www.uscirf.gov/publications/uscirf-2015-annual-report. Accessed 14 Sep 2017. Also, see Religion in Afghanistan available via http://www.afghanistans.com/Information/People/Religion.htm. Accessed 14 Sep 2017.

and destroying any respected sign or symbol belonging to the follower of any religion, not apostasy. Therefore, this article should not be applied to an act that does not forcefully and with aversion disturb or prevent the conduct of religious rituals. Mr. Kāmbakhsh did not disturb or prevent people from attending a religious ceremony or a place of worship. So Mr. Kāmbakhsh's act cannot be subjected to this article, and the case should be made to apply the doctrine of the Ḥanafī school of thought.

5.3 Examining the Prosecutor's Charges in Light of Afghan Criminal Procedural Law

To analyze the charges contained in the indictment against the backdrop of the Afghan laws, we first have to see how Afghan law defines a crime. Then law enforcement institutions should take an action against such an act that is considered under the law to be a crime. In fact, there is no explicit definition for a criminal act in the Afghan Penal Code, but its Article 27 defines the *material element* of a crime and gives clarification to the concept of crime as well. It states:

> An act or the omission of an act contrary to the law, such that the act should result in a criminal effect. The causal relationship between the act and the effect constitutes the material element of a crime.[57]

According to the Penal Code, omitting or committing an act that is contrary to law is considered a crime. This ambiguity[58] may be derived from a mistranslation of the Arabic text because during the presidency of Dāwūd Khān in 1976, there were two main sources of the Penal Code: one is the Penal Code of Egypt, and another is the Penal Code of Iraq. These two codes were in Arabic and were considered the main sources of the Afghan Penal Code of 1976.[59]

In light of this definition, in the Kāmbakhsh case, finding the article containing anti-Islamic ideas was not considered a crime as the act in question was not and is not criminalized by law. The Penal Code of Afghanistan states that there is no punishment for acts that were not recognized as crimes in the laws before they were committed.[60] Based on this provision of law, the question arises whether the acts for which the prosecutor issued an indictment for Mr. Kāmbakhsh constituted crimes pursuant to the definition provided under the Penal Code or not.

---

[57] Penal Code of Afghanistan (1976) Art. 27.

[58] In fact, the current Penal Code was written in Arabic, and then it had been translated to the Dari language. The text of Art. 27 of the Penal Code is problematic because it says "An act or the omission of an act contrary to the law," while the omission of an act contrary to law should not be considered a crime.

[59] Interview with Jude Shareefi. Dated 6 Aug 2017.

[60] Penal Code of Afghanistan (1976) Art. 3.

The *Law on the Structure and Authority of the Prosecutor Office* states that the prosecutor's office has the duty and authority to investigate and prosecute criminal cases.[61] It is important to mention that the police and the prosecutor are only authorized to charge and investigate people for acts that are recognized as crimes under the law. There are no legal provisions authorizing those authorities to arrest or investigate a person for an act that does not meet the definition of a *crime* according to law. If we have to look at the case more closely, the charges that the prosecutor brought against Mr. Kāmbakhsh and investigated push us to question whether they actually had a legal basis for their indictment against Mr. Kāmbakhsh.

First, the presence of the article with anti-Islamic content in the room of Mr. Kāmbakhsh does not constitute a crime according to the laws of Afghanistan. Notwithstanding the fact that it might be an act that is not accepted by Islam and some religious leaders may consider it an act that is not acceptable in Islam, the police and the prosecutor's office are not authorized to arrest and investigate Mr. Kāmbakhsh on the grounds of such accusations.

The second charge was that further documents (books and articles) were found in Mr. Kāmbakhsh's room during the search by the police and the prosecutor. As these documents could potentially have had links to the charge of blasphemy brought against Mr. Kāmbakhsh, the police confiscated them. Assuming that having such documents and books is a crime according to Sharia, there is a separate procedure for such instances in Islamic jurisprudence, with no room for the police and the prosecutor to intervene. Therefore, this charge would need to be prosecuted in accordance with the procedure provided in Sharia.[62]

The third charge against Mr. Kāmbakhsh was that he had confessed to writing and printing the article and distributing it to his classmates. However, Mr. Kāmbakhsh denies that, instead claiming that he was tortured by police and NDS officers while in detention and that he did not have a defense lawyer present. It is unconstitutional to torture suspected or accused people just to find the truth about a case:

> Persecution of human beings shall be forbidden. No one shall be allowed to or order torture, even for discovering the truth from another individual who is under investigation, arrest, detention or has been convicted to be punished. Punishment contrary to human dignity shall be prohibited.[63]

Mr. Kāmbakhsh's defense lawyer claimed that his client had been tortured by the NDS and police officers and repeatedly stated that his confession was taken under torture. Yet the primary court did not consider it as a fact to be reflected on in its decision. During the trial, Mr. Kāmbakhsh denied writing an article against the holy religion of Islam and Prophet Mohammad.[64] No further investigation was

[61] The Law on the Structure and Authority of the Prosecutor's Office (2013) Art. 13, official gazette no 1117, clause 1.

[62] Please see Chap. 5, the Islamic Criminal Procedure.

[63] The Constitution of Afghanistan (2004) Art. 29.

[64] Parwīz Kāmbakhsh case, p. 7.

undertaken by the court to ascertain whether he was tortured or not, instead deeming his claim to be untrue.

The fourth charge against Mr. Kāmbakhsh was that he had engaged in anti-Islamic discussions with his professors and his classmates in class and had addressed questions about *women's rights* in Islam. The prosecutor's accusation that Mr. Kāmbakhsh, a third-year journalism student at Balkh University, had engaged in such actions is problematic because doing so is not a crime.

Islamic Culture is a mandatory course that all students from all departments and fields must take, and it has been included in the curricula of all universities after the Mujahedin took power. Commonly, in the Islamic Culture class, students address contemporary issues in light of Islamic principles. The professors are usually asked for solutions against the backdrop of Islamic sources for problems that the younger generations face in their daily life. This is a common activity among students and one they are even obliged to partake in. Such actions do not qualify as crimes pursuant to the definition provided in the Penal Code,[65] and accordingly the prosecutor had no authority to charge Mr. Kāmbakhsh based on these acts or demand that the court impose punishment for them.[66]

The last issue that the prosecutor raised against Mr. Kāmbakhsh was that the *shūrā-i ʿulamāʾ* (Religious Leaders' Council) of Balkh Province issued a fatwa that Mr. Kāmbakhsh had committed a serious crime that should be punished by death penalty. According to Islamic rules, blasphemy can constitute a valid reason to punish someone, but it must be proven and reliable evidence must be provided. Some Afghan scholars[67] believe that Mr. Kāmbakhsh committed apostasy, which some Islamic scholars consider as one of the *Ḥudūd* crimes punishable by death. However, a high level of proof is required to ascertain that the person has indeed converted from Islam. If there is a single sign of doubt, punishment must be rejected.[68]

5.3.1 The Mazar-e-Sharif Primary Court Decision

In the second chapter, the main principles were highlighted that could serve as indicators for an analysis of the case under investigation. This analysis will help us understand whether the required principles have been applied properly to the cases. It will discover how the Sharia principles play a role in the case of a legal lacuna in the Afghan courts' decisions regarding criminal cases.

The Mazar-e-Sharif Primary Court stated:

---

[65] Penal Code of Afghanistan (1976) Art. 27.

[66] Parwīz Kāmbakhsh case, p 8.

[67] Judge Abdul Salaam Qāḍi Zadah, former chief judge of Kabul Appellate Court and in charge judge of Kāmbakhsh case at Kabul Appellate court.

[68] Al-Bayhaqī (2003) Hadith No: 17057.

Based on the reasons and evidence provided, the court accepts the charges listed in the indictment provided by the prosecutor against Mr. Kambakhsh. Mr. Kambakhsh committed blasphemy; he used foul language and insulted Prophet Mohammad, the Holy Quran, and he printed and distributed an article, which includes insulting words against the Holy Quran, to other students at Balkh University. According to Islamic jurisdiction, he has been found guilty for the following reasons:

First, there is a consensus among all Islamic jurists and scholars that, if any Muslim insults Prophet Mohammad, he or she is not considered a Muslim and must be punished by death. According to the Holy Quran, if another Muslim is in doubt that the insulter of Prophet Mohammad is not Muslim, the Muslim in doubt must be killed because he is also considered non-Muslim (kāfir)[69] ("Then they will be accursed. Wherever they are found, they will be seized, and cut into pieces").[70]

Second, a hadith of Prophet Mohammad narrated by Ḥusayn ibn ʿAlī states that Prophet Mohammad said, "Kill those people who insult prophets, and beat those people who insult disciples and companions of the prophets." Also, Prophet Mohammad ordered his friends to kill Kaʿb ibn al-Ashraf, who insulted Prophet Mohammad. If someone insults Prophet Mohammad, or other prophets, he must be punished by death based on Ḥadd, even if he repents.[71]

Third, if someone cavils at or insults Prophet Mohammad, he shall no longer be regarded as a Muslim (he considered kāfir).[72]

Fourth, if someone insults a prophet, he becomes kāfir (non-Muslim). There is no repentance and forgiveness for those who become kāfir by insulting prophets, but there is repentance and forgiveness for those who insult Allah.[73] Fifth, for Muslims who convert from Islam, then repent and return to Islam, there is no punishment, except those who became Kāfir by insulting the Prophet Mohammad. Such persons must be punished by death, and they cannot be forgiven.[74]

Thus, Mr. Kambakhsh insulted Prophet Mohammad by using foul language and called him a murderer, an adulterer, a thief, a brigand or bandit, and an eater of lizards. Furthermore, Mr. Kambakhsh printed and distributed an article that included anti-Islamic ideas. By committing these crimes, he converted from Islam and, according to Article 130 of the Afghan Constitution and Islamic jurisdiction, we sentence him to capital punishment (death penalty).[75]

---

[69] Al-Bazāzī (1991), p. 322.

[70] The Holy Quran, Sura al-AḤzāb (33: 62).

[71] Al-Bazāzī M (1991), p. 322.

[72] Qāḍī Khān (2009) Ḥasan ibn Manṣūr Fakhr al-Dīn al-Ūzjandī al-Farghānī, Fatāwā Qāḍī Khān, Vol. 3, p 515 available at https://archive.org/details/01_20200513_20200513.

[73] In Islamic Law, generally, there are two kinds of rights: First, rights of the individuals that others must respect, and responsibility of the citizens regarding the community, which is considered as a right of the God (Allāh). The violator of the first one could be forgiven by the victim party if they forgive the wrongdoer, but the offender of the second category, who violates the right of God (Allāh) possibly be forgiven by Allah. So, since Prophet Mohammad is not alive, if someone insults him, there is no way to repent and ask for forgiveness, but if someone insults Allah, there is a chance for repent, because Allah is considered always alive. Please see Ibn ʿĀbidīn (1992a).

[74] Ibn ʿĀbidīn M (n.d.-a) Al-ʿUqūd al-Durriyya fī Tanqīḥ al-Fatāwā Ḥāmidiyya, Dār al-Maʿrifa, Beirut, vol. 1, p. 104.

[75] Parwīz Kāmbakhsh case, pp. 21–23.

The National Security Division of Mazar-e-Sharif Primary Court in Balkh Province sentenced Mr. Kāmbakhsh to death in its decision No. 63, dated January 22, 2008. The decision was accepted by the prosecutor but appealed by Mr. Kāmbakhsh. The case was sent to the Appeals Court of Balkh Province, but based on the request of the prosecutor's office and the approval of the Supreme Court, the venue was changed. According to ratification No. 830 of the Supreme Court, dated March 11, 2008, instead of the Balkh Province Appellate Court, the Kabul Province Appellate Court was authorized to render the decision regarding Mr. Kāmbakhsh's case.

5.3.2 Analysis of Mazar-e-Sharif Primary Court's Decision in Light of Sharia Principles

When a court makes a decision based on Article 130 of the Afghan Constitution, there are some conditions stated in the article that should be taken into account. First of all, the case needs to have been processed in accordance with the standards of due process of law. Second, the supremacy of the laws of the state should be considered a main principle. Third, the application of Article 130 of the Constitution should be within the limits set by the Constitution. Fourth, the decision must be in accordance with the principles of the Ḥanafī school of thought and thus properly consider the "principles of preference" and the hierarchy of the scholars and sources within the Ḥanafī school.[76] Now, we turn our attention to the decision of the Primary Court of Mazar-e-Sharif city regarding Parwiz Kāmbakhsh's case in light of the above standards and examine whether or not the decision is in line with the above norms.

There are some issues to be addressed in the primary court's decision regarding the application of Ḥanafī provisions to the case in light of Article 130 of the Afghan Constitution. First of all, the procedure of the case is examined. Second, the legal reasoning of the primary court is observed. Finally, it will be considered whether the court's decision was in accordance with the principles of the Ḥanafī school.

Based on Afghan law, the prosecutor has the duty to investigate crimes, file charges before the court, and follow up the case in court, as well as oversee the procedure for investigating the crime and implementing the final decision of the court.[77]

According to the aforementioned provisions, the act in question must fall within the definition of a crime, as provided under the Penal Code. If an act is not considered a crime, there is no legal basis for the prosecutor to investigate and file a case. Furthermore, the law states that if a case is not processed in accordance with

[76]Please see Chap. 5, the hierarchy of sources within the Ḥanafī School of thought.

[77]Law on the Structure and Authority of the Prosecutor's Office (2013) Art. 3, official gazette no. 1117.

law, the court shall issue an order to nullify the proceedings and overrule the decision. Article 289 of the Criminal Procedure Code states:

(1) Noncompliance with provisions of the law during one of the basic proceedings will result in their nullification.
(2) Basic proceedings involve observing the provisions of the law regarding the court structure, its territorial or subject matter jurisdiction, arrest, search, investigation, expert examination and the right to an attorney.
(3) In case of non-compliance with the law regarding one of the matters stipulated in paragraph (2) of this Article, the court is obligated to issue an order to nullify the proceedings and overrule the decision—even when no request has been made concerning the matter. The previous proceedings will be nullified and new proceedings according to the provisions of the law will be conducted.[78]

So when there is no legal basis to process a case in the police department and the prosecutor's office, the court should overrule the decision and issue an order regarding the nullification of the previous proceedings.

In its decision, the Mazar-e-Sharif Primary Court referred to some Ḥanafī school sources and mentioned some fatwa books, like *al-Fatāwā al-Bazāziyya* book, *Fatāwā Qāḍī Khān*, and *Radd al-Muḥtār ʿalā Durr al-Mukhtār.*[79] These are some of the Ḥanafī school books of jurisprudence. However, a set of rules has been established by Ḥanafī scholars that judges must adhere to when they make a decision on the basis of the Ḥanafī school of thought. The primary court stated that Mr. Kāmbakhsh must be punished by death because he committed a serious crime—blasphemy—and became *zindīq* and there is no chance for him to repent. According to Ḥanafī school doctrines and most Sunni schools, if someone converts from Islam, the apostate should be given time and an Islamic scholar should talk to the apostate and make him understand that he has made a mistake and should repent. If the apostate repents, there is no punishment for him and he should be set free, but in the case of *zindīq*, there is no chance to repent.[80] Since the Primary Court of Mazar-e-Sharif has used the term of *zindīq* for Parwīz Kāmbakhsh and the Kabul Appellate Court changed the classification of his crime and used the term *murtadd* (apostate), it is necessary to have a brief clarification on the terms that have been used in this regard in Islamic Jurisprudence.

In Islamic jurisprudence and theological science, there is a set of terms that carries different meanings; however, the translation of the above terms might not be much different in other languages, especially in English. In Islamic jurisprudence and theological sciences, however, there is a variety of terms, like Muslim, *mu'min*, *fāsiq*, *fājir*, *kāfir*, *mulḤid*, *mushrik*, *dahrī*, *ahl al-Kitāb*, *munāfiq*, *zindīq*, *murtadd*, that have been used to describe the status of a Muslim in terms of practicing Islam properly or whether a person is Muslim or non-Muslim. Each term has its own

[78] Criminal Procedure Code (2014) Art. 289, official gazette no. 1132.

[79] Parwīz Kāmbakhsh case, Kabul Appellate Court, pp. 21–22.

[80] The difference between *zindīq* and *apostate* is discussed further below.

characteristics and definition, and based on those characteristics, there are particular provisions in Sharia that deal with each category of person. To understand the differences between these terms, we have to define them and shed some light on jurisdictional perspectives. Therefore, different schools of thought and Islamic sects might have different definitions for these terms. What follows are the definitions that are widely accepted by Islamic scholars, especially from the Ḥanafī school.

5.3.3 Definition of Some Related Terms

There are some terms in Islamic law and other fields of Islamic sciences that look synonymous to apostasy, but having a close look at them, they carry a specific meaning. It becomes more important when we use these terms in the legal context. To avoid misunderstanding, it is necessary to provide a brief definition of these terms to distinguish the exact meaning of each.

5.3.4 Muslim and Mu'min

These are also Arabic terms and carry almost the same meaning. They refer to those Muslims who do not practice Islamic obligations in the proper way and do not respect Islamic moral values in society. Imam Abū Ḥanīfa said that when a Muslim does not perform religious prayers and obligations properly, the act is referred to as *fāsiq* or *fājir*.[81] The consequence of being subject to these categories is that the testimony of these people is not accepted in court in some cases, and the government should correct them by punishing them on the basis of *ta'zīr*.[82]

5.3.4.1 Kāfir

This is an Arabic term that refers to a person who knowingly rejects Islam and who does not believe in Allah.[83]

[81] Sharīf Al-Jurjānī A (1983), terms Fisq and Fujūr.

[82] It has been discussed in the fourth chapter with more details.

[83] 'Alī Akbar Dihkhudā Lughat Nāma-i Dihkhudā, term *kāfir*. Please see https://www.vajehyab.com/?q=%D8%AF%D9%87%D8%B1%DB%8C. Accessed 25, 07, 2019.

5.3.4.2 Dahrī

This is an Arabic term that refers to people who believe that Allah is not the creator of the universe.[84]

5.3.4.3 Ahl al-Kitāb

This is a Quranic term that refers to Jews and Christians.[85]

5.3.4.4 Mushrik

This is an Arabic term that refers to persons who not only believe that there is more than one Allah but also worship in more than one Allah.

5.3.4.5 Murtadd

(Apostate): This is an Arabic term for a Muslim who converts from Islam.

5.3.4.6 Munāfiq

It refers to those persons who do not believe in Islam but who live and behave in accordance with Islam. In other words, they are originally non-Muslims but act like Muslims.[86]

5.3.4.7 Zindīq

This is not an Arabic word. Originally, this word came from the old *Avesta*, the sacred book of Zoroastrianism. Broadly speaking, this term has almost the same meaning as *munāfiq* and, thus, refers to a person who shows himself as a Muslim but in fact does not believe in Islam.[87] There is no unanimous specific definition for this term among Islamic scholars, but it has been used in a variety of different contexts and understood to have different meanings. However, from the way in which the term has been interpreted and used, it is taken to mean someone who acts as a

---

[84] Ibn ʿĀbidīn M (1992a), p. 241.

[85] Ministry of Awqāf and Islamic Affairs of Kuwait (2008) vol. 7, p. 140.

[86] Sharīf Al-Jurjānī A (1983), term munāfiq.

[87] Al-Safārīnī (1982), p. 394.

Muslim in society but who does not believe in Islam and who seeks the opportunity to harm Muslims and the Islamic society.

Of the above terms, only *murtadd* and *zindīq* are considered serious crimes because these statuses are considered apostasy. Nevertheless, the terms *munāfiq* and *zindīq* seem alike, but there are significant differences in terms of how they are punished. Since the Primary Court of Mazar-e-Sharif city classified Mr. Kāmbakhsh's act as *zindīq*, it is important to shed light on the meaning of this term and to highlight the consequences of using this term instead of others. The Primary Court of Mazar-e-Sharif city intentionally used this term in order to prevent the accused from repenting because according to all Sunni schools, particularly the Ḥanafī school Abbasid, the apostate must be given time (3 days) to repent, except in the case of *zindīq*. Thus, it is necessary to clarify the meaning of *zindīq* and its legal status in light of Sharia.

The term *zindīq* originally came from the Persian language,[88] and some scholars believe that it refers to the followers of the *Zand* book.[89] This term was used during the Abbasid era in the second half of the second Islamic century. Some scholars believe that this term has been used for those people who show themselves as Muslims but who do not believe in Islam.[90] However, there is no agreement among Islamic scholars regarding the use of this term and its exact meaning. Some scholars believe that it means someone who rejects some basic principles of the Islamic faith, while others believe that it refers to people who do not believe in the judgment day and monotheism.[91] Other Islamic scholars believe that if someone insults one of Prophet Mohammad's disciples, he is considered *zindīq*.[92] The most common use of this term among Islamic jurists is someone who hides his anti-Islamic faith and shows himself as a Muslim by practicing Islam.[93]

This term is not found in the first class of Ḥanafī school sources (termed *ẓāhir al-riwāya*),[94] except in Imam Abū Yūsuf's book *al-Kharāj*.[95] Originally, this term drew attention from Islamic classical scholars when they were discussing whether the exhibited repentance of *zindīq* is acceptable or not.[96]

---

[88] Ibn Manẓūr M (1994); ʿAlī ibn Ibrāhīm ibn Dāwūd ibn Salmān ʿAlāʾ al-Dīn Ibn ʿAṭṭār (2011), p. 327.

[89] *Zand* is a commentary book on the Zoroastrian main book, *Avesta*. This book (Avesta) was burned, and only one-fifth of it existed and then most Zoroastrians followed the *Zand* book. Those who were followers of the *Zand* book were called *zindīq*.

[90] Al-Saffār ʿA (1992), p 286.

[91] Al-Rāzī (1999a, b) also Ibn Manẓūr M (1994); Al-Ghazālī A (1993), p. 188.

[92] Al-Sharbīnī I (2002), p. 747.

[93] Ibn Manẓūr M (1994); Ibn Taymiyya T (1995), p. 471; ʿAlī ibn Ibrāhīm ibn Dāwūd ibn Salmān ʿAlāʾ al-Dīn Ibn ʿAṭṭār (2011) Al-Iʿtiqād al-Khāliṣ min al-Shak wa-l-Intiqād, p. 327.

[94] *Ẓāhir al-Riwāya* refers to the collection of the six books compiled by Imām Mohammad al-Shaybānī, a student of Imam Abū Ḥanīfa. These six books are considered the main source of the Ḥanafī School that must be adhered to by all Ḥanafī followers.

[95] Abū Yūsuf (1999), p. 199.

[96] Al-Safārīnī (1982), p. 394.

In fact, the term *zindīq* was not known during the era of Prophet Mohammad or in the epoch of his disciples until the era of the Abbasid rulers. Ibn Taymiyya, a famous Islamic scholar, said this term has been used neither in the Holy Quran nor in the traditions of Prophet Mohammad and that it originally came from Persia. Classical Islamic scholars have talked about repenting for *zindīq* in their books. Ibn Taymiyya also stated that according to Islamic jurists (*fuqahā'*), the term *zindīq* has the same meaning as *munāfiq*, who present themselves as Muslims and perform prayers but in fact do not believe in Islam.[97]

In the course of spreading Islam to the east and its arrival in the western parts of India and China, it was faced with new customs and traditions, which existed in those regions. Most of the people in this large area, especially in ancient Afghanistan and Iran, were Zoroastrians, and there were also some followers of the Maani religion in the region. So when people from this region converted to Islam, they still believed in some principles of Zoroastrianism, and this caused some problems for the Abbasi government. In particular, the Abbasid rulers used the term *zindīq* to refer to persons who had political issues with them.[98] Thus, al-Ṭebarī—a famous Islamic scholar and historian—indicated that *al-Mahdī*, one of the Abbasi rulers, said to his son, Mūsā, that he should not be nice to the people who were considered *zindīq*. Al-Ṭebarī said a *zindīq* man has been arrested and brought to Caliph al-Mahdī in his palace. The Caliph asked the *zindīq* to repent, but he refused to do so, so the Caliph subsequently ordered that he be killed and his body be hung in a public place. He said that he was a member of a sect that first invites people to be nice and virtuous, only to later cheat people and ask them to worship two creators, the Allah of light and the Allah of darkness, instead of only one Allah. So he ordered that when his people find them, they have to kill them.[99] So it seems that the term *zindīq* has seen different meanings in different eras for different purposes, but the common meaning is that someone presents himself as a Muslim but does not believe in Islam, which is the same as *munāfiq*.

While *munāfiq* (plural: *munāfiqūn*) is a well-known term in the Quran and all of the Prophet's disciples understood what it means, neither the Holy Quran nor the Prophet Mohammad's Hadith provides any form of punishment for *munāfiq*. In other words, being *munāfiq* was not criminalized in Islam and Prophet Mohammad did not punish *munāfiq*. So, indeed, using the term *zindīq* with the same meaning as *munāfiq* by Islamic jurists has some consequences. First, *munāfiqūn* were a group of people who lived in Medina during the era of Prophet Mohammad. Prophet Mohammad knew[100] and explained the characteristics of the *munāfiq* in many hadiths, but he never prosecuted them, instead allowing them to live freely in Medina. Furthermore, there are many verses in the Holy Quran that refer to *munāfiqūn* that had already

---

[97] Al-ʿAmr (n.d.), p 333; Al-Safārīnī (1982), p. 394.

[98] Al-Saffār ʿA (1992), p. 286.

[99] Al-Ṭebarī (1959), p. 220.

[100] Al-Jaṣāṣ (2010a), p. 127.

existed during Prophet Mohammad's era, but no specific form of punishment is provided for them.

There is a famous story that a group of *munāfiqūn* built a mosque in Medina city and asked Prophet Mohammad to pray there, but the Prophet later destroyed it. Nevertheless, a mosque is a holy place in Islam. Prophet Mohammad destroyed it and converted it into a public toilet, but he did not punish the *munāfiqūn* who built it. However, they were well known,[101] and everybody knew them by name.[102] This notwithstanding, the Prophet did not punish them and did not encourage his disciples to bother them. The only punishment mentioned in the Holy Quran for this group of people is that they will go to the deepest layer of hell.[103] Even the Ḥanafī school allows Muslims to ask *munāfiqūn* for help because Prophet Mohammad asked Ibn Ubayy and his friends for help.[104]

5.3.5 Munāfiq and Zindīq

We need to have a clear understanding of these terms and to examine what the implications are if the terms *munāfiq* and *zindīq* are considered the same. How did Prophet Mohammad deal with them? Is there any punishment for *munāfiq* that should be implemented by the ruler in a Muslim community? As we go through the main sources of Sharia, the term *munāfiq* has been used several times in the Holy Quran and Prophet Mohammad's Hadiths. It was a very common term in the era of the Prophet. The Prophet and most of his disciples knew the *munāfiqūn* as persons who were acting as Muslims but who did not believe in Islam. They lived in and walked around Medina and had their own leader, called *ʿAbdallāh ibn Salūl.*[105] On one occasion, in the *UḤud* war (*Ghazwat UḤud*),[106] Prophet Mohammad even conferred with ʿAbdallāh ibn Ubayy ibn Salūl, a well-known enemy of the Prophet.[107] Even Prophet Mohammad agreed with Ibn Salūl that he should stay in

---

[101] They were 12 people and many sources introduced them by name, please see: Tafsīr Ṭebarī, (2001) vol. 14, p. 469; Ibn Kathīr (1999), p. 212; Al-Baghawī (1999), p. 93; Tafsīr Fathul Qadīr (1994) vol. 3, p 318; Al-Rāzī (1999a, b), vol. 8, p. 150; Al-Suyūṭī (1990), p. 161; Al-Ālūsī, Shihāb al-Dīn Maḥmūd ibn ʿAbdallāh Al-Ḥusaynī (1994), vol.7, p. 358; Abū Ḥayyān (1992), p. 226; Al-Jawzī (2001), p. 213; Al-Māwardī (1992), p. 142; Tafsīr Jāmi al Ahkām Qūrtubī (1964) vol.8, p. 253; Tafsīr RūḤ Maʿānī (1995) vol. 6, p. 18.

[102] Al-Jaṣāṣ (2010a), p. 128.

[103] The Holy Quran, Sura al- Nisā' (04:145) (إِنَّ الْمُنَافِقِينَ فِي الدَّرْكِ الْأَسْفَلِ مِنَ النَّارِ وَلَنْ تَجِدَ لَهُمْ نَصِيرًا).

[104] Dār al-Iftā' al-Miṣriyya, Fatāwā Dār al-Islām al-Miṣriyya (n.d.) Ministry of Auqāf of Egypt, Vol. 6, p. 61.

[105] Al-Tirmidhī (1998), Hadith No: 3650.

[106] This war *Ghazwat UḤud* happened on 23 March 625 between Muslims under the leadership of Prophet Mohammad and non-Muslims from Mecca, people under the leadership of Abū Sufyān.

[107] Ibn IsḤāq (1978), p. 324.

Medina and fight the Mecca people only if they enter Medina, but because of the insistence of some of the companions of the Prophet, he decided to go out of Medina city and fight there, though others were insisting on defeating the Mecca people outside Medina.[108]

Furthermore, even though Prophet Mohammad knew all *munāfiq* people and he introduced all of them to Ḥudhayfa ibn al-Yamān and knew every *munāfiq* in Medina, no action was taken against them.[109] It is noteworthy to narrate the story of the death of ʿAbdallāh ibn Ubayy ibn Salūl. When ʿAbdallāh ibn Ubayy died, his son came to the Prophet and informed him that his father had asked the Prophet to give him his shirt for use as a shroud for his father's body. The Prophet agreed and went to take part in his funeral ceremony and prayed for him.

The second Caliph, 'Umar ibn al-Khaṭṭāb, asked the Prophet: Are you going to attend ʿAbdallāh ibn Ubayy's funeral ceremony and ask Allah to forgive him? The Prophet said that he has the option to ask Allah for forgiveness or not, and he chose to ask for forgiveness 70 times.[110] So it means that forgiveness is permissible for *munāfiqūn*, and since it is not criminalized in Sharia, there is no provision regarding the *munāfiq* people to be punished by a court decision. Furthermore, there are many hadiths narrated by Prophet Mohammad according to which his disciples asked him for permission to kill a *munāfiq* but the Prophet declined and said Allah prevents him from killing someone who has said that "there is no Allah, except Allah", and Prophet Mohammad told them to pray.[111]

So, for the reasons above, being *munāfiq* is a serious sin but not a punishable crime that should be prosecuted and processed in court. So if the Primary Court of Mazar-e-Sharif followed the opinion of some Islamic scholars and considered *zindīq* and *munāfiq* the same, it contradicts the main principle of judgment in Sharia, particularly the Ḥanafī school of thought, that a judge must make a decision based on visible and reliable evidence, not on doubtful evidence or guess.[112]

5.4 Making a Decision Not Based on the Ḥanafī School

It is important to discuss whether the *al-Fatāwā al-Bazāziyya* fatwa book decision is in accordance with Ḥanafī school doctrines and whether a Ḥanafī judge's decision would be legitimate if it is based on another school's opinions. According to Article 130 of the Afghan Constitution, the court is only allowed to apply Ḥanafī school provisions in cases where the law itself is silent. However, the court began its legal reasoning with an opinion from a Māliki school scholar, Ibn SuḤnūn (776-854),

[108] Ibn Kathīr (1999), p. 109.
[109] Ibn ʿAbd al-Karīm M (1989), p. 706.
[110] Al-Bukhārī (2001), Hadith No: 1190.
[111] Ibn Mālik (1985), Hadith No. 375.
[112] Ibn ʿĀbidīn M (1992b), p. 365.

which is not a Ḥanafī doctrine. Although this opinion is narrated in the Ḥanafī school book, the *al-Fatāwā al-Bazāziyya* fatwa book, it is not necessary for the Ḥanafī school followers to follow it. It is very common among Islamic scholars to narrate opinions from different schools regarding the same issue to compare what scholars of different schools think, but any provision applied to a case must be in accordance with the doctrine of the school that the author follows.

The author of the *al-Fatāwā al-Bazāziyya* fatwa book made a mistake by following the idea of the Māliki scholars with regard to a case about insulting Prophet Mohammad. The Primary Court of Mazar-e-Sharif did not mention this to be an opinion from the Māliki school, which is a violation of the Ḥanafī school's main principles.

As discussed in Chap. 4, according to the Ḥanafī school principle, there are four categories of scholars with different criteria as to who can deal with legal issues in different ways based on the statuses of the scholars. Some of them have the authority to issue legal opinions independently, while others must follow the opinions of first-class scholars. These four categories are *mujtahid muntasab*, *mujtahid fī al-madhhab*, *mutabaḤḤir fī al-madhhab*, and *muqallid* (imitator).[113] The judges must respect this hierarchy of opinions[114] when they make a decision.

The Ḥanafī scholars believe that if a judge is a Mujtahid, fully qualified, and capable of exercising legal reasoning, he can make decisions based on his own opinion. If a judge is an imitator, it is his obligation to make decisions only in accordance with the preferred opinions of the Ḥanafī scholars, as collected in Imam Mohammad al-Shaybānī's *Ẓāhir al-Riwāya* books, even if the judge has a different opinion.[115] The judges must follow the principle of preference existing in the Ḥanafī school of thought and make decisions accordingly. They also believe that if a ruler orders judges to make decisions only in accordance with a specific school of thought, which is the Ḥanafī school in Afghanistan, and a judge intentionally or unintentionally fails to adhere to that order in rendering a decision, that decision shall be ineffective and must not be implemented.[116] As it is already mentioned, there are no remaining Mujtahid judges in Afghanistan—all judges nowadays are

[113] Al-Dihlawī (1995), p. 47.

[114] The first group comprises those scholars who have a certain level of knowledge and skills and who can thus infer legal opinions directly from the main sources, but within the framework established by Imam Abū Ḥanīfa, the founder of the Ḥanafī School. Imam Abū Yūsuf, Imam Mohammad al-Shaybānī, and Imam Zufar are prime examples of this category. The second group of Ḥanafī scholars – termed *al-mujtahid fī al-madhhab* –are also authorized to make preference among the opinions of the first-class Ḥanafī scholars (Imam Abū Ḥanīfa and his students). The third group of Ḥanafī scholars, *al-mutabaḤḤir fī al-madhhab*, are such who have memorized all of the opinions narrated from Abū Ḥanīfa and his direct students. This group of scholars must issue their opinion in accordance with the main sources of the Ḥanafī School and should not make any decision that goes beyond the opinions collected in the main sources of Ḥanafī doctrine. The last group comprises imitators, like current judges in Afghanistan, who must follow the Ḥanafī school doctrines without any objection or scrutiny. Please see Al-Dihlawī (1995), pp. 51–57.

[115] Ibn ʿĀbidīn M (1992b), p. 362; Al-Dihlawī (1995), pp. 81–82.

[116] Al-Ṭarasūsī (1926); Ibn Māzah M, Jindī A, Ibn Mohammad A (2004), pp. 518–520.

imitators. Consequently, according to the Ḥanafī school principle, an imitator judge must base his decisions on the main sources and preferred opinions of the Ḥanafī school doctrines. It is also a main principle that an imitator cannot go beyond his madhab and follow other madhabs.[117]

Now let us turn our attention to the decision of the Primary Court of Mazar-e-Sharif city regarding the case at hand to ascertain whether this principle was applied or not and on which sources the court relied. The Primary Court of Mazar-e-Sharif provided some legal reasoning in its decision, and it needs to be addressed whether that reasoning was in accordance with Ḥanafī principles or not.

First of all, the main concern is that the Primary Court of Mazar-e-Sharif city made a decision based on an opinion from a Māliki school scholar, Ibn SuḤnun,[118] contained in the *al-Fatāwā al-Bazāziyya* fatwa book, which is a violation of the main principle of the Ḥanafī school. Second, the judge must respect the hierarchy of the Ḥanafī school sources. Yet the *al-Fatāwā al-Bazāziyya* fatwa book is not among those main sources that a judge must base a decision on. Even the Ḥanafī scholars believe that judges should not make a decision according to an opinion found in the fatwa books unless that opinion is entirely consistent with the Ḥanafī main courses.[119] Non-Mujtahid judges must make their decisions based on the main sources of the Ḥanafī school, namely the *Ẓāhir al-Riwāya* books by Imam Mohammad al-Shaybānī.[120]

Famous Ḥanafī scholar Ibn ʿĀbidīn clearly illustrated that the opinion of the *al-Fatāwā al-Bazāziyya* fatwa book on how to treat persons who insult Prophet Mohammad is wrong and contradicts the main opinions of the Ḥanafī school and thus must not be followed. He believed that the *al-Fatāwā al-Bazāziyya* opinion conflicts with Imam Abū Yūsuf's opinion stated in his famous book titled *al-Kharāj*.[121] The *al-Fatāwā al-Bazāziyya* book's mistake was later carried over and followed by some other Ḥanafī scholars, like Kamāl ibn Hamām[122] and Mullā

---

[117] Al-Dihlawī (1995), p. 81.

[118] Mohammad ibn ʿAbd al-Salām Ibn SuḤnūn is one of the famous Mālikī school scholars. He was born in 819 in al-Qayrawān, a city in Tunisia, and died in 860 in the city of Sahil and was buried in al-Qayrawān.

[119] Ibn ʿĀbidīn M (1991) SharḤ al-Manẓūma al-Musammāt bi-ʿUqūd Rasm al-Muftī. Available via http://waqfeya.com/book.php?bid=793. Accessed 24 March 2019.

[120] The *Ẓāhir al-Riwāya* books are a collection of six books written by Imam Mohammad, a famous student of Imam Abū Ḥanīfa. These books include almost all opinions of Imam Abū Ḥanīfa and are considered a first-class source in Ḥanafī School of thought.

[121] Imām Abū Yūsuf, one of the founders of the Ḥanafī school and a famous student of Imam Abū Ḥanīfa, served as the chief justice for several years. He was the first person in Islamic history to have been named as chief justice (*Qāḍī al-Quḍāt*), and also he was the first person in Islamic legal history to have been authorized to appoint judges on behalf of the King.

[122] Mohammad ibn Hamām al-Dīn ʿAbd al-WāḤid, famous by Ibn Hamām (1388–1457) one of the famous Ḥanafī scholar and the author of Fatḥ al-Qadīr, a well-known book in the Ḥanafī School.

Khusraw,[123] in their books.[124] Overall, the *al-Fatāwā al-Bazāziyya* book's opinion is not in line with the Ḥanafī school principle.

Ibn Suhnūn believed that a person who insults Prophet Mohammad is a non-Muslim (*kāfir*) and must be killed without a doubt. If other Muslims doubt that the insulter of the Prophet is not *kāfir*, the doubting Muslims must also be considered *kāfir*.[125] This essentially implies that an individual that insults the Prophet must be killed in any case and cannot be granted mercy. If other Muslims are kind to the person and have doubts regarding his punishment, the doubters should be punished as apostates too.[126]

This opinion of Ibn Suḥnūn belongs to the Mālikī school of thought. Other schools, like Ḥanafī, Ḥanbalī, and also Ibn Taymiyya, believe that persons who insult Prophet Mohammad are apostates but that they can genuinely repent and thus be spared punishment.[127] So, according to law, a judge cannot base his decision on a school of thought other than the Ḥanafī school because the Constitution only allows the court to render a decision in accordance with the Ḥanafī school provisions in cases in which the law makes no provision.[128] Furthermore, the Ḥanafī sources clearly state that if a Ḥanafī judge who is not Mujtahid (like all current Afghan judges) makes a decision that is not in accordance with Ḥanafī school doctrines, the decision shall be deemed invalid and must not be implemented, regardless of whether the mistake in the decision was made intentionally or by accident.[129]

Furthermore, in Mr. Kāmbakhsh's case, the court's decision was also founded on some opinions taken from the *Radd al-MuḤtār* book, which states that persons who insult the Prophet shall be punished by death even if they repent. The primary court of Mazar-e-Sharif, in its legal reasoning, only mentioned the part of the discussion that is based on the Māliki school provision, but the court did not narrate the whole discussion of the *Radd al-MuḤtār* book in this regard. However, later on, the author of *Radd al-MuḤtār* clearly explained that the opinion narrated by the *al-Fatāwā al-Bazāziyya* fatwa book does not belong to the Ḥanafī school and that the opinion of its author stating that if a Muslim insults the Prophet, he must be killed in any case, whether he repents or not, is only a misunderstanding.[130]

---

[123] Mullā Khusraw (death in 1480) one of the famous Ḥanafī scholar and the author of Durar al-Ḥukkām SharḤ Ghurar al-AḤkām, a well-known book of the Ḥanafī School.

[124] Ibn ʿĀbidīn M (n.d.-b) Risāla fī al-Qawl al-Mukhtār min al-Aqwāl fī madhhab Imām Abī Ḥanīfa., p 114; Uṭwa (1994), p. 81; Risāla fī Nashr al-ʿUrf fī Bināʾ bázul AḤkām ʿalā al-ʿUrf, pp. 14–15. Available via http://waqfeya.com/book.php?bid=793. Accessed 6 March 2019.

[125] Parwīz Kāmbakhsh case, p. 22; Al-Bazāzī (1991), p. 322.

[126] Ministry of Aawqāf and Islamic Affairs of Kuwait (2008) Al-Mawsūʿa al-Fiqhiyya al-Kuwaytiyya, vol. 22, p. 184.

[127] Ministry of Awqāf and Islamic Affairs of Kuwait (2008) Al-Mawsūʿa al-Fiqhiyya al-Kuwaytiyya, vol. 22, p. 184.

[128] The Constitution of Afghanistan (2004) Art. 130.

[129] Ibn ʿĀbidīn M (1992b), p. 408.

[130] Ibn ʿĀbidīn M (1992a, b), pp. 232.

Rendering decisions that are not in line with the main sources of the Ḥanafī school is not permitted. First of all, it might contradict the preferred opinions of the Ḥanafī school, and second, it causes irregularity among the followers of the school regarding the validity of a decision. The primary court's decision contravened the main Ḥanafī sources because Imam Abū Yūsuf, the second face in the Ḥanafī school, stated in his famous book *al-Kharāj* that there are different opinions regarding apostasy. Some people believe that apostates should be given time and advised to repent, while others believe that they should be killed directly with no chance to repent.

The first group bases their views on a Hadith of the Prophet Mohammad stating that he has been ordered to fight people until they say that there is no God except Allah. Once they have said this, they and their property are safe, and Allah knows what is in their hearts.[131] There is another Hadith of the Prophet according to which he asked Usāma[132] why he killed a man who had said *kalima ṭayyiba* (give the testimony that there is no Allah except Allah).[133] Usāma responded that he did not believe him because he had only said *kalima* (given testimony) when he lost his weapon. Since believing in God is something that comes from heart, Prophet Mohammad asked Usāma "did you open his heart" and saw that he is still not believing in Allah, and he Gave Testimony (saying the "Kalima") because he was unarmed and afraid of you. Prophet Mohammad wanted to teach his companions that it is not possible to judge people's faith from their appearance.[134]

The other group relies on another Hadith of Prophet Mohammad, which states that anyone who converts from Islam shall be killed. Imām Abū Yūsuf said that if a Muslim insults, denies, or defaces Prophet Mohammad, he shall be considered an

---

[131] Al-Bukhārī (2001), Hadith No: 6924.

[132] Usāma ibn Zayd ibn Ḥāritha was one of the young disciples of Prophet Mohammad, and the Prophet really liked him. The Prophet appointed him as leader of a troupe, which also included respected disciples like Abū Bakr and ʿUmar. His father was the adopted son of Prophet Mohammad, and his mother, Umm Ayman, was the custodian of Prophet Mohammad when he was a child. When a daughter of one of the leaders from the Al Makhzumiyya tribe stole something and was about to be punished by having her hand cut off, some people came to ʿĀ'isha, wife of Prophet Mohammad, and asked her to intervene in the case. ʿĀ'isha asked why they did not ask Usāma to intervene in the case since he was very close to and highly respected by the Prophet. This shows that even ʿĀ'isha suggested that he is the right person to ask the Prophet for forgiveness.

[133] Kalima Ṭayyiba (*There is no true god (deity) but Allah, and Mohammad is the Messenger (Prophet) of Allah*) is the foundation of a Muslim belief that if a non-Muslim said that truly and with no doubt, he becomes a Muslim. In the above history, Usāma claims that since the man was unarmed and resided in Kalima because he was afraid to be killed, he did not believe in Islam.

[134] The hadith is a part of a longer hadith narrated in many books, according to which Prophet Mohammad sent a group of his disciples on a military mission. Usāma ibn Zayd came across of a non-Muslim man from the Juhayna tribe. When he saw Usāma ibn Zayd, he said "there is no God except Allah", and was then killed. When Usāma told the story to the Prophet, he asked him why he had killed him after the man had said the words. Usāma said the man had been afraid of his weapon, and that his words had not been sincere. Then Prophet Mohammad asked whether he had opened his heart and seen that his words had not been sincere. Please see Ibn al-Ḥajāj M (n.d.) Hadith No: 140.; Abū Dāwūd (2009), Hadith No: 2272.

apostate. If he repents, he should be released; otherwise, he should be killed. He also said that there is no difference between an apostate and *zindīq*, and he considered them to be the same.[135] Furthermore, in his opinion, if an apostate repents and then converts from Islam numerous times, the judge should follow the same procedure as for the first time. However, after his fourth repentance, the apostate should be beaten and then released.

Some Ḥanafī scholars believe that if a Muslim repeatedly becomes apostate, repents, and reconverts to Islam, after the first time he should be released with no punishment. If he converts from Islam for a second time and repents, he should be lashed and then released. If he coverts from Islam for a third time and then repents, he should be beaten seriously and jailed until the ruler or judge is satisfied that his repentance is sincere. If he does it again, the punishment shall be the same as for the third time and so on and so forth, but some scholars believe that in such cases, the apostate should be killed if he does not repent immediately after the fourth time.[136] If a woman converts from Islam, she should be given the opportunity to repent. In the event that she does not, she should not be killed but should be imprisoned until she repents.[137] The opinion of the author of the *al-Fatāwā al-Bazāziyya* fatwa book clearly contradicts Imam Abū Yūsuf's opinion. Obviously, the primary court should not have relied on the opinion contained in that book in the Kāmbakhsh's case as it does not constitute a Ḥanafī school doctrine.

The Ḥanafī school doctrine states that a judge is only allowed to make decisions based on a specific school that he is following. Article 130 of the Constitution is very clear in stating that when a court is faced with a case for which the law makes no provision, the alternative solution is that the provisions of the Ḥanafī school of thought must be applied. Afghan judges cannot go beyond the provisions of the Ḥanafī school and rely on other schools' opinions. Under Ḥanafī school's provisions, if a judge deviates from the school of thought the application of which he is obliged to, his decision shall be invalid and will not be implemented.[138] According to Ḥanafī school principles, judges who are Mujtahid must make their decisions according to their own inference, but if a judge is not Mujtahid, he must follow the preferred opinion of his school, a well-known rule among scholars stemming from the main sources of the school.[139]

There is another issue with the decision made by the Mazar-e-Sharif Primary Court in Mr. Kāmbakhsh's case regarding. It concerns the supremacy of the law and the applicability of the Ḥanafī school provisions. As discussed, Article 130 of the Constitution states that if there is no provision in the Constitution or other laws about

---

[135] Abū Yūsuf (1999), p. 196.

[136] Ibn ʿĀbidīn M (1992a, b), pp. 224–225; Al-Ṭarābulusī (1973), p. 191.

[137] Al-Ṭarābulusī (1973), p. 191.

[138] Ibn ʿĀbidīn M (n.d.) Majmūʿa al-Rasāʾil ibn ʿĀbidīn: Risāla fī Nashr al-ʿUrf fī Bināʾ bazul AḤkām ʿalā al-ʿUrf. Available via Waqfeya. http://waqfeya.com/book.php?bid=793. Accessed 6 March 2019.

[139] Uṭwa (1994), p. 73; ʿAlāʾ al-Dīn A (1986), vol. 14, p. 417.

the case under consideration, the court can apply Ḥanafī jurisprudence to the case. It means the Constitution only allows the courts to apply the provisions of the Ḥanafī school when there is a gap in the law regarding a case. If there is a specific legal provision to be applied to a case, the court must apply that law. However, in the Kāmbakhsh case, the primary court mentioned Article 347 of the Penal Code, along with Article 130 of the Constitution.[140] It means there is a provision in the Penal Code that should be applied to the case and there is no need to go beyond the law because Article 130 obliges the court to make a decision in accordance with law and only in case of a legal gap can the court can make a decision based on the Ḥanafī school doctrine. If the primary court mentioned a provision of the Penal Code applicable to the case, the court cannot go beyond that law. Making a decision based on the Ḥanafī school provision when a legal provision exists appears unconstitutional, and thus the Mazar-e-Sharif Primary Court violated the principle of supremacy of the law as required by the Constitution.

5.5 Punishment Based on Ḥadd Crime[141]

There is no consensus among Islamic scholars from different schools of thought as to whether apostasy should be categorized as a *Ḥadd* crime or not. There are no provisions in the Holy Quran that clearly recognize apostasy as a *Ḥadd* crime; while there is a Hadith of the Prophet Mohammad stating "kill those who change their religion,"[142] there is no consensus among the Islamic scholars that this Hadith could be the basis for considering apostasy to be a *Ḥadd* crime. Most of the Ḥanafī scholars do not consider apostasy to be a *Ḥadd* crime.

The Mazar-e-Sharif Primary Court relied on the *al-Fatāwā al-Bazāziyya* book in its decision, which states that any Muslim who insults Prophet Mohammad shall be executed based on *Ḥadd* and that repentance shall not preclude such punishment. However, there is no proof that the main sources of the Ḥanafī school are in agreement with the *al-Fatāwā al-Bazāziyya* opinion;[143] it is interesting that the court cited a book (*Radd al-Muḥtār*) as a source for its decision that does not consider apostasy to be a *Ḥadd* crime. In fact, the author of the *Radd al-Muḥtār* book says apostate is not a *Ḥadd* crime because if it is considered a *Ḥadd* crime, the punishment will not be abolished by repentance,[144] while in the case of apostate it

---

[140] Parwīz Kāmbakhsh Case, p. 17.

[141] *Ḥadd*, plural *Ḥudūd* refers to those crimes that are defined in the Quran and Sunnah with a specific punishment. Please see Kamali (2019), pp. 218–221.

[142] Al-Bukhārī (2001), Hadith No: 2794.; Al-Tirmidhī (1998), Hadith No: 1383.; Abū Dāwūd (2009), Hadith No: 3787.; Al-Nasāʾī (1986), Hadith No: 3991.; Ibn Mājah (2009), Hadith No: 2526.; Al-Tirmidhī (1998), Hadith No: 3787.

[143] Al-Bazāzī (1991), p. 322.

[144] One of the based characteristics of the *Ḥadd* crime is that the punishment for the *Ḥadd* crime must be implemented, even if the offender repents. Please see Al-Nasāʾī (1986), Hadith No: 3991.

will be forgiven if the offender repents.[145] It is not clear why the primary court cited a book that stands in complete contradiction to its own opinion. Apparently, it does not make any difference whether or not we categorize apostasy as a *Ḥadd* crime, but in reality, considering apostasy as one of the *Ḥudūd* crimes or excluded from the *Ḥudūd* crimes will lead us to a different conclusion. This difference in opinion will have a significant impact on the consequences of repenting in both cases. It means if it is considered one of the *Ḥudūd* crimes, the punishment will not be abolished by repentance, but if it is not considered one of the *Ḥudūd* crimes, the punishment could be forgiven.

To go deeper and discuss at length whether apostasy is a *Ḥudūd* crime or not would go beyond the scope of this research. Since apostasy is the core issue in Mr. Kāmbakhsh's case, it is nonetheless necessary to address that discussion in brief. Doing so will improve our understanding of how the courts in Afghanistan apply Sharia, in particular the Ḥanafī school of thought, when the state laws make no provision for a case. There is unanimity among all scholars in the Sunni schools that repentance does not preclude punishment in *Ḥudūd* crimes. For example, if a Muslim drinks alcohol or commits adultery, he will be punished even if he repents. In the case of apostasy, since the Ḥanafī school does not consider it a *Ḥadd* crime, the repentance of the apostate shall be acceptable and will preclude punishment. So the main sources of the Ḥanafī school state that if an apostate repents, he is to be let go without punishment.[146] Looking at the Islamic sources, there are many provisions in Islamic law, including the Holy Quran, the Prophet's traditions, and opinions of classical and modern scholars, that confront us with this controversial issue.

In fact, the Holy Quran and the Prophet Mohammad's traditions prevent Muslims from performing certain acts that are deemed prohibited. While some of these acts are listed as crimes with specific punishments attached, such as theft, adultery, highway robbery, etc., other acts are defined as constituting a sin or an immoral act—like backbiting or not respecting your elders—but no precise worldly punishment is stated that the courts should impose. The Holy Quran contains no specific verse that explicitly defines apostasy as a crime nor a specific form of worldly punishment for the apostate. The Holy Quran does state that apostates shall suffer painful punishment after the Day of Resurrection but does not specify the form that punishment shall take. The Holy Quran reads: "Those who have believed [become Muslim] then disbelieved [converted from Islam], then believed [for the second time], then disbelieved [for the third time], and then increased in disbelief—never will Allah forgive them, nor will He guide them to the way. Give to the hypocrites the tidings that there is for them a painful torment."[147] The Holy Quran states that Allah will gather the hypocrites and disbelievers in hell all together.[148] Obviously,

[145] Ibn ʿĀbidīn M (1992a), p. 233.

[146] Abū Yūsuf (1999), p. 213.

[147] The Holy Quran, Sura al-Nisāʾ (04:137-138) إِنَّ الَّذِينَ آمَنُوا ثُمَّ كَفَرُوا ثُمَّ آمَنُوا ثُمَّ كَفَرُوا ثُمَّ ازْدَادُوا كُفْراً لَمْ يَكُنِ اللَّهُ لِيَغْفِرَ لَهُمْ وَلا لِيَهْدِيَهُمْ سَبِيلاً (137) بَشِّرِ الْمُنَافِقِينَ بِأَنَّ لَهُمْ عَذاباً أَلِيما.

[148] The Holy Quran, Sura al-Nisāʾ (04:140) (إِنَّ اللَّهَ جامِعُ الْمُنافِقِينَ وَالْكافِرِينَ فِي جَهَنَّمَ جَمِيعاً).

there is no punishment for hypocrites in this world; even Prophet Mohammad knew all the hypocrites (*munāfiqūn*) who were living in Medina city, but the Prophet did not attempt to punish them and punishment was delayed until the justice day. So the above verses of the Holy Quran refer to people who become Muslim "believers" and then convert from Islam and become "disbelievers" possibly multiple times, but the Holy Quran only declares that there shall be punishment after the Day of Resurrection, without making mention of any worldly punishment that must be implemented by court. It is important to note that Prophet Mohammad, in his entire life, never punished anyone solely because they were apostates. It should be taken into account that although some of Prophet Mohammad's disciples converted from Islam, the Prophet did not punish them because of apostasy.[149] This serves to underline that apostasy is not classified as a *Ḥadd* crime in the Prophet Mohammad's tradition.

It is important to mention that Prophet Mohammad took the implementation of the *Ḥudūd* crimes quite seriously and never allowed anyone to intercede in the delivery of punishment to the perpetrators of such crimes. A concrete example is a theft case in which one of the respected disciples, Usāma ibn Zayd, intervened and asked the Prophet for forgiveness, but the Prophet rejected this request seriously and clearly declared that there shall be no intercession in *Ḥudūd* crimes.[150] However, some sources cite an apostasy case in which the Prophet accepted the intervention of his disciple *ʿUthmān* and forgave the apostate.

A perfect example is a case narrated by Saʿd ibn Waqqās. When Prophet Mohammad conquered Mecca, one of his disciples—ʿAbdallāh ibn Abī SarḤ—who converted from Islam, was hidden by ʿUthmān ibn ʿAffān, and he brought him to the Prophet. ʿUthmān reputedly asked the Prophet three times for forgiveness, but the Prophet did not answer and looked at the ground. Then after the third time, the Prophet accepted ʿUthmān's intercession and forgave the apostate. The Prophet then turned his face to his disciples, asking: Was there not a brave man to kill him when I three times refused to grant him forgiveness? The disciples replied that they did not know what he meant by looking at the ground and asked why he had not signaled to kill him. The Prophet replied that he shall not act as a traitor.[151] This story

---

[149] A good example is the case of one of his disciples, ʿAbdallāh ibn Abī SarḤ, who converted from Islam and escaped from Medina to Mecca, but when the Prophet took over Mecca city, he forgave him. Also, in a peace treaty between Prophet Mohammad and the Mecca leaders, it was written if a Muslim escaped from Mahammad's territory and joined Mecca people, they will be not returned to the Prophet, but if a non-Muslim joins the Prophet, he must be returned to Mecca. It shows that apostasy is not considered one of the *Ḥudūd* crimes; if it were, the Prophet Mohammad will never deal with it.

[150] ʿĀ'isha, the wife of Prophet Mohammad, narrated that a woman from a high-class family from Makhzumiiya tribe committed a theft crime. The family of the woman pressed Usāma ibn Zayd to intervene and ask the prophet to forgive her. When Usāma asked the Prophet to forgive her, the Prophet became very angry and said "are you going to intercede beyond the bounds set by Allah? The Prophet swore to God and said if his daughter Fāṭima were to steal something he would cut off her hand. Please see Al-Bukhārī (2001), Hadith No: 3216.; Ibn al-Ḥajāj M (n.d.) Hadith No: 3169.

[151] Al-Bayhaqī (1989), Hadith No: 2895.; Abū Dāwūd (2009), Hadith No: 4358.; Al-Nasāʾī A (1986), Hadith No: 4067.; Al-Ḥākim (1990), Hadith No: 4360.

clarifies that Prophet Mohammad did not consider apostasy a *Ḥadd* crime as he accepted ʿUthmān's intermediation while strongly rejecting Usāma ibn Zayd's intermediation in the abovementioned theft case.

As has already been stated, it is a central principle of the Ḥanafī school that repentance shall not preclude punishment when a *Ḥadd* crime has been committed. Since apostasy is not to be regarded as a *Ḥadd* crime, repenting plays a substantial role in that it precludes punishment. A good example is an event that occurred during the time of the second Caliph, ʿUmar. An apostate was killed without being given the opportunity to repent. ʿUmar asked Abū Mūsā al-Ashʿarī why the apostate had been killed instead of sentenced to jail for 3 days with a loaf of bread and asked to repent. Since the apostate had not been granted the opportunity to repent, the second Caliph was sad and asked Allah for forgiveness as a mistake had been made. He went on to say that he had not ordered that punishment, he had not been present, and that he had not been happy when he heard of what had occurred.[152] None of the Prophet's disciples voiced any objection to ʿUmar's words, which some scholars consider as a silent consensus (*al-ijmāʿ al-sukūtī*).[153]

One of the main principles in Islamic law is that no one, not even the Prophet, can change or abolish *Ḥudūd* punishments, and Prophet Mohammad always took a very serious stance on *Ḥudūd* crimes and never accepted anyone's intermediation. A good example is the theft case mentioned above, in which Prophet Mohammad reacted strongly when Usāma intervened in the case, but when ʿUthmān interceded in the apostasy case, the Prophet accepted his intervention and forgave the apostate. This shows that apostasy is not one of the *Ḥudūd* crimes; if it were, the Prophet would have rejected ʿUthmān's proposal and killed the apostate. Another important factor is that this happened in the last year of the Prophet's life, and there are no other hadiths in this regard to abrogate the one mentioned.

Furthermore, the Ḥanafī school's main sources do not consider apostasy to be a *Ḥadd* crime because in their books, most of the Ḥanafī school scholars excluded apostasy from the *Ḥudūd* chapter and discussed it in a separate chapter.[154] For instance, Imam Mohammad al-Shaybānī, in his book *al-Jāmiʿ al-Ṣaghīr*, did not include apostasy in the chapter of *Ḥudūd* crimes, while the book includes all the *Ḥudūd* crimes, like adultery, theft, *qadhf*, robbery, and drinking alcohol, in one chapter.[155] Moreover, the author of a famous book, *Badāʾiʿ al-Ṣanāʾiʿ fī Tartīb al-Sharāʾiʿ*, clearly said that *Ḥudūd* crimes are five and excluded apostasy from the

[152] Ibn Mālik (2004), Hadith No: 2728.

[153] Silent consensus *al-ijmāʿ* al-sukūtī refers to a case where some of the *jurists "mujtahidūn"* of a particular age give an express opinion concerning an incident, while the rest of the Muslim jurists remain silent. For further information, please see Kamali (2003), p. 248.; Rohe (2014), p. 78.

[154] Al-Sarakhsī (1993), p. 98.; MawṢilī ʿA (1973), pp. 44–45.; ʿAlāʾ al-Dīn A (1986), vol.7, p. 33; Ibn Nujaym Z (n.d.), p. 2; Al-Qūdūrī A (1997), pp. 195–204; Al-Jaṣāṣ (2010a), p. 143; Al-Jaṣāṣ (2010b), p. 5; Zaylaʿī ʿU (1896), p. 375; Al-Nasafī (2006), pp. 346–367; Al-Qūdūrī (2006), p. 5868; Al-Balkhī et al. (1893), pp. 142–188; Mullā Khusraw (n.d.), pp. 283–408; Al-Bābartī (n.d.), pp. 137–417; Ibn Hammām (1970), p. 210.

[155] Al-Shaybānī (1986), pp. 277–299.

Ḥudūd crimes.[156] Also, current Sunni schools' encyclopedias of Islamic jurisprudence do not classify apostasy as a *Ḥadd* crime.[157]

Also, modern Ḥanafī scholars believe that apostasy is not a *Ḥadd* crime. ʿAbd al-Ḥamīd MaḤmūd Ṭahmāz, in his book *Ḥanafī Jurisdiction in Modern Concept*, said *Ḥudūd* crimes are five: *adultery*, *qadhf*, *drinking alcohol*, *theft*, and *robbery*.[158] Muṣṭafā al-Zarqā' said that *Ḥudūd* crimes are five: *zinā*, *qadhf*, theft, *Ḥirāba* or *baghy*, and drinking alcohol.[159] Abū Zuhra also did not include apostasy in his categorization of *Ḥudūd* crimes.[160] Some other Islamic scholars, like ʿAbd al-RaḤīm Ṣidqī, consider apostasy as one of the *Ḥudūd* crimes, but at the same time he accepted that punishment should not be administered if the apostate repents.[161] It is one of the main principles of Ḥanafī school thinking that repenting for having committed a *Ḥadd* crime does not preclude punishment. Therefore, it is somewhat in contradiction with the main principle of the Ḥanafī school and the most reliable opinion among the majority of the Islamic schools.

Examining the legal reasoning of the Mazar-e-Sharif Primary Court on the Kāmbakhsh case, there are several issues that challenge the validity of the court's decision.

First, the decision was not made in proper accordance with the Ḥanafī school provisions because the legal reasoning of the court relied upon an idea of Ibn Suhnūn, who is a famous scholar of the Mālikī school, and not the Ḥanafī school. Article 130 of the Afghan Constitution allows the courts to make a decision in accordance with the Ḥanafī school provisions if the law makes no provision for a case. Unfortunately, the Primary Court of Mazar-e-Sharif drew on a Mālikī school doctrine, as narrated in the Bazāziyya fatwa book, rendering the decision both unconstitutional and in contravention of the Ḥanafī school provisions.

Second, according to the principles of the Ḥanafī school, judges must respect the hierarchy of the Ḥanafī sources. They must rely on the most trustworthy sources and then progress from the top to the bottom of the pyramid when making a decision. The Primary Court of Mazar-e-Sharif relied upon sources that Ḥanafī scholars forbid judges from basing their decisions on. As has already been discussed, the Ḥanafī scholars clearly state that judges must not base a decision on the fatwa books unless the same fatwa exists in the main sources. If the main sources, the *Ẓāhir al-Riwāya* books, provide a solution for a legal issue, the fatwa books must be ignored.[162] Since the Primary Court of Mazar-e-Sharif based its decision above all on the *al-Bazāziyya* fatwa book, and thus failed to respect the hierarchy of sources, the court's decision is not legally valid. In terms of punishment, Mr. Kāmbakhsh's actions were treated as a

[156] ʿAlā' al-Dīn A (1986), p. 33.
[157] Sāʿī M (2007), pp. 853–877.
[158] Ṭahmāz (2000), p. 246.
[159] Al-Zarqā' (1998), p. 673.
[160] Abū Zuhra (1998), pp. 49–51.
[161] Ṣidqī ʿA (1987), pp. 252–254.
[162] ʿUṭwa ʿA (1994), p. 65.

Ḥadd crime, while, as stated previously, the main sources of the Ḥanafī school do not consider apostasy to be a *Ḥadd* crime. There is no doubt that if a judge makes a decision that is in contravention of the main sources of the founder of the Ḥanafī school, his decision shall not be legally enforceable. In conclusion, the decision of the Mazar-e-Sharif Primary Court in the case of Mr. Kāmbakhsh is challengeable on the basis of unconstitutionality and violation of the Ḥanafī school principle.

5.6 The Decision of the Appellate Court

The Appellate Court of Kabul Province overruled the decision of the Mazar-e-Sharif Primary Court regarding Mr. Kāmbakhsh's case. The appellate court accepted the indictment of the prosecutor and believed that Mr. Kāmbakhsh had committed blasphemy by printing and distributing an article that includes insults to Prophet Mohammad and the Holy Quran. The appellate court also accepted the charge included in the prosecutor's indictment and found Mr. Kāmbakhsh guilty of committing blasphemy based on the evidence found in his room, his mobile phone, and the testimonies of his classmates and professors.[163]

One remarkable aspect of the appellate court's ruling is that it accepted the authority of the fatwa of the *ʿUlamāʾ* Council[164] of Balkh Province regarding the case. The appellate court clearly stated that the *ʿUlamāʾ* Council is a governmental institution that operates under its main office in Kabul and has a provincial office in every province. The court believed that this institution was legally authorized to issue a fatwa and defend Islam. The involvement of the *ʿUlamāʾ* Council is in accordance with Islam and supported by the government.[165] However, some members of the *ʿUlamāʾ* Council in the main office in Kabul stated that no documents exist that authorize the *ʿUlamāʾ* Council in Kabul or its other provincial offices to issue a fatwa regarding a case. They instead stated that they have monthly council meetings to deal with contemporary social issues and provide the government with an advisory opinion. The *ʿUlamāʾ* Council members do not believe that they are authorized to issue a fatwa that is binding upon the Afghan courts to serve as a basis for a court decision because the Supreme Court has its own fatwa department.[166] As mentioned earlier, the courts and the prosecutor's office can ask experts to provide

[163] Parwīz Kāmbakhsh case, pp. 22–23.

[164] The *ʿUlamāʾ* Council was established by presidential order, and all members of the council are appointed by the President. The *ʿUlamāʾ* Council has a branch in all provinces and they meet once per month, though sometimes there are delays or special meetings, depending on the agenda.

[165] Parwīz Kāmbakhsh case, p. 26.

[166] Interview with Enayatullah Baleegh and Prof. Muzafari, both members of the *ʿUlamāʾ* Council in Kabul. Dated March 16, 2019.

information or answer questions regarding a case under consideration, and the *ʿUlamāʾ* Council, according to Article 44 of the Criminal Procedure Code, could be among those institutions, but their opinion is not binding.

There are two significant points in the appellate court's decision: first, the court changed the classification of the crime from *zindīq* to apostate, and second, the punishment in the appellate court's ruling is based on *taʿzīr* rather than *Ḥadd*. These two significant issues provide more flexibility for the judges to change the primary court's decision.[167] According to Ḥanafī school's principles, in the case of *taʿzīr*, the judge has the authority to punish people differently based on their social status in society, but in the case of *Ḥudūd* crimes, judges are not authorized to change the punishment because the *Ḥudūd* crimes and their punishments are defined in the primary sources of Sharia, namely the Quran and Sunnah. Nobody, even the rulers or Prophet Mohammad himself, has the authority to change the punishment of *Ḥudūd* crimes. These two important changes have a significant impact on the appellate court's legal reasoning and ultimately resulted in a different decision. The difference between the term *zindīq* and apostate has been discussed previously.[168] This change in reasoning obviously had an impact on the punishment and left the court more room to decide differently.

The reasoning that the appellate court provided in order to nullify the primary court's decision included two parts: first, the appellate court stated that the prosecutor failed to refer to Mr. Kāmbakhsh as *zindīq* and did not punish him accordingly, and second, the definition of *zindīq*, which is used in the case, did not match the act committed by Mr. Kāmbakhsh.[169]

The law requires that the court consider the prosecutor's claims and the crimes for which the accused has been indicted. If a prosecutor has not asked for punishment for an act that is not included in the indictment, the court shall not include it in the case. If the court believes that the prosecutor has missed something, the court should refer the case back to the prosecutor's office so the indictment can be modified to be in accordance with the law.[170]

[167]Parwīz Kāmbakhsh case pp. 26–27.

[168]Please look at p. 194.

[169]Parwīz Kāmbakhsh case, p. 27.

[170]Criminal Procedure Code (2014) Art. 289, Official Gazette no. 1132: "(1) Noncompliance with provisions of the law during one of the basic proceedings will result in its nullification. (2) Basic proceedings involves observing the provisions of the law regarding the court formation, its territorial or subject matter jurisdiction, arrest, search, investigation, expert examination and the right to have an attorney. (3) In case of non-compliance with the law regarding one of the matters stipulated in paragraph (2) of this article, the court is obligated to issue an order to nullify the proceedings and overrule the decision – even though no request was made concerning the matter. The previous proceedings will be nullified and new proceedings according to the provisions of the law will be conducted."

Another problem with the primary court's decision is that Mr. Kāmbakhsh's act does not fall within the definition of *zindīq*, which refers to someone who acts as a Muslim but is actually a nonbeliever. In Mr. Kāmbakhsh's case, the story is somewhat different. By insulting the Prophet and the Holy Quran, he revealed that he was not a Muslim anymore. The term apostate refers to a Muslim who has converted from Islam to any other religion by intentionally doing or saying something that is totally against the main principles of Islam.[171] Thus, in the case at hand, the accused should be considered apostate rather than *zindīq*.

The appellate court rejected the legal reasoning of the Mazar-e-Sharif Primary Court regarding the classification of the crime Mr. Kāmbakhsh had committed and comprehensively explained that the crime committed by Mr. Kāmbakhsh was apostasy rather than *zindīq*. The appellate court stated that the primary court made a mistake in its legal reasoning and that Mr. Kāmbakhsh's case was not subject to those provisions of Sharia that the primary court had relied upon. Thus, based on Article 33 of the *Law on the Structure and Competencies of Courts of the Islamic Republic of Afghanistan*,[172] the appellate court overruled the decision of the primary court because the provisions of Sharia had not been properly implemented and the crime had been classified incorrectly. In the opinion of the appellate court, since Mr. Kāmbakhsh repeatedly said that he was sorry for what he had done and that he believed in Islam and gave his testimony of faith before the court by reciting the Kalima (the testimony),[173] he should be regarded as a Muslim. However, since he insulted Prophet Mohammad and the Holy Quran and distributed anti-Islamic and insulting propaganda, he was found guilty and, based on Article 130 of the Constitution and the provisions of Sharia and *fiqh*, his act was punishable.

The Appellate Court of Kabul Province, pursuant to Article 130 of the Afghan Constitution and the provisions of Sharia and Islamic jurisprudence, decided to punish Mr. Kāmbakhsh based on *ta'zīr* with a 20-year prison sentence starting from the moment of his arrest.[174]

[171] Concrete examples of being apostate are a Muslim not believing in one God, rejecting Prophet Mohammad as a Messenger of Allah, throwing the Holy Quran in the toilet, worshipping an idol, etc. Also, rejecting one of the unanimously accepted principles of Islam is considered apostasy; for example, if a Muslim believes that adultery or drinking alcohol is lawful (*Ḥalāl*) and fasting or praying is unlawful (*Ḥarām*), this person is also considered apostate.

[172] Law on the Structure and Competencies of Courts of Islamic Republic of Afghanistan (2005) Art. 33, official gazette no. 851: "(1) The Court of Appeals shall oversee the rulings and decisions of the lower courts, in situations according to the provisions of the related laws. (2) The Court of Appeals, while resolving cases set forth in clause 1 of this Article, shall reconsider the whole legal process. It may correct, overrule, amend, affirm, or repeal the rulings and decisions of the lower courts."

[173] There is no God but Allah, Mohammad is the Messenger of Allah.

[174] Mr. Kāmbakhsh's case, Kabul Appellate Court's Decision, p. 33.

5.7 Analysis of the Kabul Appellate Court Decision

As has already been mentioned, the appellate court based its decision on *ta'zīr* (and not *Ḥadd*) and sentenced Mr. Kāmbakhsh to 20 years of imprisonment. There are two concerns regarding this decision: first, why did the Appellate Court apply *ta'zīr* punishment? Second, as Mr. Kāmbakhsh gave his testimony of faith and repented for his mistakes, why did the Appellate Court sentence him to 20 years' imprisonment? The Ḥanafī school provisions are very clear in terms of apostasy and how it should be punished. Almost all Islamic scholars, particularly the Ḥanafī scholars, believe that an apostate should not be punished if he has repented. Even the second Caliph, 'Umar ibn Khaṭṭāb; the fourth Caliph, 'Alī ibn Abī Ṭālib; and many other classical Islamic scholars believe that it is obligatory that the apostate be offered the chance to repent and be given time to think and to recognize his own mistakes. However, some other scholars, like al-Shāfi'ī, voice the opinion that asking the apostate to repent is rather a recommendation than an obligation.[175] Consequently, giving the accused apostate time (3 days) to rethink and have a chance to repent is an accepted principle among Islamic scholars. Doing so gives the apostate time to reflect, rethink, and rectify his behavior. According to the Ḥanafī school, if he repents, he should not be punished at all.

Furthermore, the Ḥanafī scholars believe that people who insult the Prophet are apostates.[176] The Ḥanafī,[177] Ḥanbalī, and Ibn Taymiyya scholars believe that insulters of the Prophet are to be considered apostates. Thus, they can repent and reconvert to Islam within the time they are granted by the Islamic ruler or judge. However, Imam al- Shāfi'ī and Imam Mālik believe that persons who insult the Prophet must be killed even if they repent.[178] Thus, the Ḥanafī scholars state that if an apostate repents and reconverts to Islam, he should be released without punishment.[179]

Mr. Kāmbakhsh only became an apostate once as there is no evidence to prove that he had been prosecuted for apostasy before. Mr. Kāmbakhsh was before the court for apostasy for the first time, stated that he was sorry for his act, and repeatedly gave testimony in front of the court that he is a Muslim. According to the provisions of the Ḥanafī school, he should therefore have been released with no punishment since the first-class scholars of the Ḥanafī school believe that repenting precludes punishment in these circumstances. However, the chief judge of the Kabul Appellate Court said they punished him to 20 years' imprisonment based on *ta'zīr*. He and

---

[175] Sā'ī (2007), pp. 847–848.

[176] Abū Yūsuf (1999), p. 199.

[177] Al-Jaṣāṣ (2010a), p. 161.

[178] Ministry of Awqāf and Islamic Affairs of Kuwait (2008) vol. 6, pp. 184–185; Al-Jaṣāṣ (2010a), p. 141.

[179] Lajna al-Fatwā al-Islāmiyya (2009) Fatāwā al-Shabaka al-Islāmiyya, vol. 3, p. 532; 'Alā' al-Dīn, Abū Bakr ibn Mas'ūd ibn AḤmad al-Kāsānī (1986), p. 135; Abū Yūsuf Y (1999), p. 214; Al-Sarakhsī (n.d.), p. 217.

most of the Afghan judges believe that a judge has the power to punish people based on *taʿzīr* because they think that judges should be considered acting rulers in society.[180] They believe that according to Sharia principles, judges have the authority to punish people on behalf of the ruler if their act is harmful to society and the citizens.[181]

As we discussed in the second chapter, *taʿzīr* punishment is based on the principle of *siyāsa sharʿiyya*, and according to the Sharia principles, only the ruler has the authority to punish people if they act in a way that causes harm to society or the public order because it is the obligation of the ruler to keep social order and provide safety for the citizens and their properties.[182] So if a ruler fulfills his duty properly, he should have the authority to regulate some rules and punish people if they violate the rules. If a citizen acts in a way that destroys social order or public safety, the ruler can punish the wrongdoer.

It is noteworthy to say that the ruler can extend his authority to others and authorize them to act on his behalf. In this case, only the authorized officials can act on behalf of the ruler. Most Afghan judges believe that they have the authority to act on behalf of the ruler, but there is not a document to prove that the ruler authorized them to act on his behalf in terms of punishing people based on *taʿzīr* if their act is harmful to society. The only document that some of the Supreme Court judges rely upon is the official approval of the President regarding the appointment of judges.[183] The *Law on the Organization and Jurisdiction of Judiciary* defines a judge and a judicial license (*Inselak Qazaey*). Article 4 of the law says a judge is a person that has an official judicial license and adjudicates cases according to law. The law also defines the term *judicial license* as an authority that has been given by a presidential order to a qualified person to adjudicate cases.[184] None of these documents grant the judges the authority to act on behalf of the President and deal with crimes and punishment according to their own discretion. While in accordance with the Ḥanafī principles only the ruler has the authority to criminalize an act based on *Siyāsa Sharʿiyya* and punish people based on *taʿzīr* if they violate the law and harm social order and the citizens, if the ruler directly authorizes the judges to act on his behalf beyond the law, this would be acceptable. But since there is no document to demonstrate that such authority has been designated, judges cannot criminalize an

---

[180] Interview with Judge Abdul Salaam Qāḍizadha, former chief judge of the Kabul Appellate Court; Judge Deen Mohammad Gran, one of the justices of the Supreme Court; Judge Said Murad Shareefi, chief secretariat of the Supreme Court of Afghanistan; and Judge Abdul Karim Qanit, retired senior judge of the Supreme Court. Besides this, I have interviewed more than 25 judges in different courts, and all of them believe that since judges act on behalf of the ruler, they can punish people based on *taʿzīr*.

[181] Interview with Judge Abdul Salaam Qāḍizadah the former chief judge of the Kabul appellate court and Judge Said Murad Shareef, chief secretariat of the Supreme Court of Afghanistan.

[182] Ibn ʿĀbidīn M (1992a), p. 229.

[183] The Constitution of Afghanistan (2004) Art. 64, clause 13.

[184] The Law on Organization and Jurisdiction of the Judiciary Branch of Afghanistan (2013) Art. 4, clause 16 and 23.

act and punish people without law. On the other hand, the Constitution and other laws clearly say that judges must respect the law when they make a decision.[185]

It must be mentioned that the appointing of judges by the President does not mean that they can criminalize an act and punish people according to their own discretion. Obviously, all high-ranking officials in Afghanistan are appointed by the President, but it does not mean that they should not respect the law and can make decisions beyond the law. In accordance with law, all high-ranking authorities, including the President himself, must perform their duties within the limits set by law. If they act beyond the law, their act is considered a violation of law and could be punished. Making decisions not in accordance with law is unconstitutional, and decisions formulated under such circumstances must not be implemented in any case.

5.8 Conclusion

The pretrial proceedings, police, NDS, and prosecutor's office face challenges because of a lack of legal procedure and in relation to the investigation of the case. Mr. Kāmbakhsh's act is a serious crime according to Sharia, but it is not criminalized in the Penal Code or other laws of Afghanistan. According to law, the police and prosecutor's office cannot process any case where the act is not considered a crime under the law. So from this perspective, processing Mr. Kāmbakhsh's case by the police and prosecutor's department is confronted with a lack of due process of law.

Furthermore, the decision of the Primary Court of Mazar-e-Sharif city should be challenged on the basis of unconstitutionality because the primary court's decision is based on a doctrine of the Māliki school rather than the Ḥanafī school of thought. However, Article 130 of the Constitution only allows the court to make decisions in accordance with the provisions of the Ḥanafī school of thought. Also, the primary court did not respect the principle of preference, which is important for the legitimacy of the decision. The principle of preference mainly refers to the hierarchy of the sources and scholars within the Ḥanafī school. The primary court ignored the principle of preference and referred to a fatwa book in the case, which is not a reliable source in the Ḥanafī school that could be used as a basis for a judge's decision. Thus, the primary court's decision seems unconstitutional and faces a serious challenge in terms of its legitimacy based on the Ḥanafī school principles.

The Appellate Court of Kabul Province provided better analysis and legal reasoning regarding the case. The court found a mistake in the primary court's decision and changed the classification of the crime. The appellate court made its decision based on the concept of *ta'zīr* rather than *Ḥadd*, but arguably, the court's decision is beyond the limit set by law and the Ḥanafī school's principles. There is no provision in the law that states that judges can punish people based on their

[185] The Constitution of Afghanistan (2004) Art. 129.; The Law on Organization and Jurisdiction of the Judiciary Branch of Afghanistan (2013) Art. 12.

discretion. Furthermore, according to the Ḥanafī school doctrines, as the ruler has the authority to impose *taʿzīr* punishment, the appellate court's decision can also be challenged on the basis of legality. On the other hand, according to the appellate court's decision, Mr. Kāmbakhsh committed apostasy, which is not a Ḥadd crime, and the apostate has the opportunity to repent. If the apostate repents, the Ḥanafī scholars said, he should be released with no punishment even if he has repeatedly committed this act; after repentance, there would be no punishment for him.[186] Since Mr. Kāmbakhsh repeatedly and publicly repented in court, there is no reason why the appellate court should not consider his repentance and not apply the Ḥanafī school principles in this case. Overall, Mr. Kāmbakhsh's case is confronted by serious issues of legality in all stages of the process: in the pretrial proceedings as well as in the court sessions.

References

Abū al-Maʿālī Burhān al-Dīn MaḤmūd ibn AḤmad ibn ʿAbd al-ʿAzīz ibn ʿUmar ibn Māza al-Bukhārī, (2004) Al-Muhīṭ al-Burhānī fī al-fiqh al-Nuʿmānī, verified by ʿAbd al-Karīm Sāmī al-Jundī, Beirut: Dār al-kutub al-ʿilmiyya, vol.8

Abū Dāwūd S (2009) Sunan Abī Dāwūd, verified by Shuʿayb Arnūt and MuḤammad Kāmil Qara blalī. Dār al-Risāla al-ʿĀlamiyya, Beirut

Abū Ḥayyān M (1992) Al-Baḥr al-Mūḥīṭ fī al-tafsīr. Dār al-Fikr, Beirut, vol 6

Abū Yūsuf Y (1999) Kitāb Al-Kharāj, verified by Ṭāhā ʿAbd al-Raʾūf Saʿd and Saʿd Ḥasan MaḤmūd. Al-Maktaba al-Azhariyya li-Turāth, Cairo

Abū Zuhra M (1998) Al-Jarīma wa-l-ʿUqūba fī al-Fiqh al-Islāmī. Dār al-Fikr al-ʿArabī, Cairo

Al Qurtobi, Mohammad ibn Ahmad Ibn Abi Baker (1964) Tafsīr Jāmi al Ahkām Qūrtubī (1964) vol.8

Al-Sarakhsī, Muḥammad ibn Aḥmad ibn Abī Sahl (n.d.) Uṣūl al-Sarakhsī, Beirut: Dār al-Maʿrifa

Al Shawkani, Mohammad Ibn Ali, Ibn Mohammad Ibn Abdullah (1994) Tafsīr Fathul Qadīr, vol. 3,. Dār Ibn Kathīr, Damsque

Al Ṭebarī, Mohammad ibn Jarīr (2001) Jāmʿi al Bayān fī Tawīl al Quran / Tafsīr Ṭebarī, verified by Abdullh ibn Abdul Muhsen al turki, Cairo, vol.14

ʿAlāʾ al-Dīn, Abū Bakr ibn Masʿūd ibn AḤmad al-Kāsānī (1986) Badāʾiʿ al-Ṣanāʾiʿ fī tartīb al-sharāʾiʿ, Beirut: Dār al-Kutub al-ʿIlmiyya, vol. 7

Al-Ālūsī, Shihāb al-Dīn Maḥmūd ibn ʿAbdallāh Al-Ḥusaynī (1994) Tafsīr Ālūsī= Rūḥ al-Maʿānī, Verified by ʿAlī ʿAbd al-Bārī ʿAṭiyya. Dār al-Kutub al-ʿIlmiyya, Beirut

Al-ʿAmr A (n.d.) Al-Alfāẓ wa-l-Muṣṭalaḥāt al-Mutaʿalliqa bi-Tawhīd al-Rabawiyya, term *al-zindīq*, available at http://lib.efatwa.ir/41252/1/34. Accessed 06 May 2021

Al-Bābartī M (n.d.) Al-ʿInāya Sharḥ al-Hidāya. Dār al-Fikr, Beirut, vol. 7

Al-Baghawī A (1999) Maʿālim al-tanzīl fī tafsīr al-Qurʾān = Tafsīr al-Baghawī. Dār Iḥyāʾ al-Turāth al-ʿArabī, Beirut, vol. 4

Al-Balkhī et al (1893) Al-Fatāwā al-Hindiyya. Dār al-Fikr, Beirut, vol. 2

Al-Bayhaqī A (1989) Al-sunan al-ṣaghīr li-l-Bayhaqī, verified by ʿAbd al-Muʿṭiʾ Amīn Qalājī. Jāmiʿa al-Dirāsāt al-Islāmiyya, Karachi

Al-Bayhaqī AB (2003) Al-Sunan al-Kubrā, verified by MuḤammad ʿAbd al-Qādir ʿAṭā. Dār al-Kutub al-ʿIlmiyya, Beirut

[186] Al-Ṭarābulusī ʿA (1973) p. 191; Abū Yūsuf (1999), p. 214; Al-Sarakhsī (n.d.) p 217.

Al-Bazāzī M (1991) Al-Fatāwā al-Bazāziyya, published on the morgen of Al-Fatāwā al-Hindiyya = Fatāwa ʿĀlamkīriyya. Dār al-Ṣādir, Beirut, vol. 6
Al-Bukhārī M (2001) Ṣaḥīḥ al-Bukhārī, verified by MuḤammad Ẓāhir ibn Nāṣir al-Nāṣir. Dār Ṭawq al-Najāt, Beirut
Al-Dihlawī S (1995) ʿAqd al-Jayyid fī Aḥkām al-Ijtihād wa-l-Taqlīd. Dār al-FatḤ, Emirates, Al Shareqah
Al-Ghazālī A (1993) Al-Qisṭās al-Mustaqīm. Al Maktaba al-ʿIlmiyya, Damascus
Al-Ḥākim M (1990) Al-Mustadrak ʿal¯a al-ṢaḤīḤayn, verified by Muṣṭafā ʿAbd al-Qādir ʿAṭāʾ. Dār al-Kutub al-ʿIlmiyya, Beirut
ʿAlī ibn Ibrāhīm ibn Dāwūd ibn Salmān ʿAlāʾ al-Dīn Ibn ʿAṭṭār (2011) Al-Iʿtiqād al-Khāliṣ min al-Shak wa-l-Intiqād, verified by Saʿd ibn Halīl al-Zuwayrī. Ministry of Islamic Affairs, Qatar, vol. 1
Al-Jaṣāṣ A (2010a) SharḤ MukhtaṢar al-ṬaḤāwī, verified by ʿIṣmatallāh ʿInāyatallāh MuḤammad and others. Dār al-Bashāʾir al-Islāmiyya, Beirut, vol. 6
Al-Jaṣāṣ A (2010b) SharḤ MukhtaṢar al-ṬaḤāwī, verified by ʿIṣmatallāh ʿInāyatallāh MuḤammad and others. Dār al-Bashāʾir al-Islāmiyya, Beirut, vol. 7
Al-Jawzī J (2001) Zād al-Masīr fī ʿIlm al-Tafsīr, verified by ʿAbd al-Razzāq al-Mahdī. Dār al-Kutub al-ʿArabi, Beirut, vol. 3
Al-Māwardī A (1992) Al-Nukat wa-l-ʿUyūn, Tafsīr al-Māwardī. Dār al-Kutub al-ʿIlmiyya, Beirut, vol. 2
Al-Mawlā, Shahābuddīn Mahmūd Ibn Abdullah al Hussainī (1995) Tafsīr Rūḥ al-Maʿānī. Dār al-kutub al-ʿilmiyya, Beirut, vol. 2
Al-Nasafī A (2006) Kanz al-daqāʾiq, verified by Sayyid Baktāsh. Dār al-bashāʾir al-islamiyya, Beirut
Al-Nasāʾī A (1986) Sunan Al-Nasāʾī, verified by ʿAbd al-Fatāḥ Abū Ghuda. Maktaba al-Maṭbūʿāt al-Islāmiyya, Aleppo
Al-Qūdūrī A (1997) Mukhtaṣar al-Qūdūrī verified by Kāmil MuḤammad MuḤammad ʿUwayẓa. Dār al-Kutub al-ʿIlmiyya, Beirut
Al-Qūdūrī A (2006) Al-Tajrīd li-l-Qūdūrī. Dār al-Salām, Cairo, vol. 11
Al Qurtobi, Mohammad ibn Ahmad Ibn Abi Baker (1964) Tafsīr Jāmi al Ahkām Qūrtubī (1964) vol. 8
Al-Rāzī M (1999a) Tafsīr al-Rāzī, Al-Tafsīr al-Kabīr. Dār Ihyāʾ al-Turāth al-ʿArabī, Beirut
Al-Rāzī Z (1999b) Mukhtār al-Ṣuḥāḥ, verified by Yūsuf al-Shaykh MuḤammad, term *Zindīq*. Al-Maktaba al-ʿAṣriyya, Beirut
Al-Safārīnī S (1982) Lawāmiʿ al-anwār al-bahiyya. Muʾassasa al-khāfiqīn wa maktabatuhā, Damascus, vol. 1
Al-Saffār A (1992) Al-takfīr wa ḍawābiṭihi. Muʾassasa al-risāla, Beirut
Al-Sarakhsī M (1993) Al-Mabsūṭ li-Sarakhsī. Dār al-Maʿrifa, Beirut, vol. 10
Al-Sharbīnī I (2002) Kitābāt ʿAdāʾil Islām wa Munāqishātuhu. Dār al-Kutub al-Miṣriyya, Cairo, vol. 1
Al-Shaybānī M (1986) Al-Jāmiʿ al-Ṣaghīr wa Sharḥuhu al-Nāfiʿ al-Kabīr. ʿĀlam al-Kutub, Beirut
Al-Suyūṭī J (1990) Al-Dur al-Manthūr. Dār al-Fikr, Beirut, vol. 5
Al-Ṭarābulusī A (1973) Muʿīn al-Ḥukkām fī mā yataraddadu bayna al-khaṢmayn min al-aḤkām. Dār al-Fikr, Beirut
Al-Ṭarasūsī N (1926) Anfaʿ al-Wasāʾil ilā Taḥrīr al-Masāʾil. Maṭbaʿa al-Sharq, Cairo
Al-Ṭebarī M (1959) Tārīkh al-Ṭebarī. Dār al-Turāth, Beirut, vol. 8
Al-Tirmidhī M (1998) Sunan al-Tirmidhī, verified by Bashār ʿAwād Maʿrūf. Dār al-Gharb al-Islāmī, Beirut
Al-Zarqāʾ M (1998) Al-Madkhal al-Fiqhī al-ʿĀmm (Introduction to General Islamic Jurisprudence). Dār al-Qalam, Damascus, vol. 2
Dār al-Iftāʾ al-Miṣriyya, Fatāwā Dār al-Islām al-Miṣriyya (n.d.) Ministry of Auqāf of Egypt, Vol. 6
Ibn ʿAbd al-Karīm M (1989) Ausud al-Ghāba. Dār al-Fikr, Beirut

Ibn ʿĀbidīn M (1992a) Radd al-MuḤtār ʿalā Durr al-Mukhtār (Ḥāshiyya Ibn ʿĀbidīn). Dār al-Fikr, Beirut, vol.4
Ibn ʿĀbidīn M (1992b) Radd al-MuḤtār ʿalā Durr al-Mukhtār (Ḥāshiyya Ibn ʿĀbidīn). Dār al-Fikr, Beirut, vol. 5
Ibn ʿĀbidīn M (n.d.-a) Al-ʿUqūd al-Durriyya fī Tanqīḥ al-Fatāwā Ḥāmidiyya. Dār al-Maʿrifa, Beirut, vol. 1
Ibn ʿĀbidīn M (n.d.-b) Risāla fī al-Qawl al-Mukhtār min al-Aqwāl fī madhhab Imām Abī Ḥanīfa. Available at http://www.al-mostafa.info/data/arabic/depot3/gap.php?file=m001527.pdf
Ibn al-Ḥajāj M (n.d.) Ṣaḥīḥ Muslim, verified by MuḤammad Fawād ʿAbd al-Bāqī. Dār Iḥyāʾ al-Turāth al-ʿArabī, Beirut
Ibn Hammām K (1970) Shar Fatḥ al-Qadīr. Dār al-Fikr, Beirut, vol. 5
Ibn IsḤāq M (1978) Sīra ibn Isḥāq, verified by Suhayl Zikār. Dār al-Fikr, Beirut
Ibn Kathīr A (1999) Tafsīr ibn Kathīr, verified by Sāmī ibn MuḤammad Salāma. Dār Ṭayyiba li-l-Nashr wa-l-Tawzīʿ, Saudi Arabia, Riyadh, vol. 4
Ibn Mājah A (2009) Sunan Ibn Mājah, verified by Shuʿayb al-Arnūṭ. Dār al-Risāla al-ʿIlmiyya, Beirut
Ibn Mālik M (1985) Al-Muwaṭṭaʾ Ibn Mālik. Dār al-IḤyāʾ al-Turāth al-ʿArabī, Beirut
Ibn Mālik M (2004) Al-Muwaṭṭaʾ Ibn Mālik, verified by MuḤammad Muṣṭafā al-Aʿẓamī. Muʾassssa Zāyid Āl Nahyān li-l-Aʿmāl al-Khayriyya wa-l-Insāniyya, Abu Dhabi
Ibn Manẓūr M (1994) Lisān al-ʿArab, term *zindīq*. Dār Ṣādir, Beirut
Ibn Nujaym Z (n.d.) Al-Baḥr al-Rāʾiq SharḤ Kanz al-Daqāʾiq. Dār al-Kutub al-Islāmiyya, Beirut, vol. 5
Ibn Taymiyya T (1995) Majmūʿ al-Fatāwā, verified by ʿAbd al-Raḥmān ibn MuḤammad ibn Qāsim. Saudi Arabia, Madina: Majmaʿ al Malik Fahd Lil-ṭabāʾte al MaṣḤaf al Sharīf, vol. 7
Kamali MH (2003) Ijmāʿ (Consensus of opinion). In: Kamali MH (ed) Principles of Islamic jurisprudence. The Islamic Texts Society, Cambridge, pp 228–263
Kamali MH (2019) Blood money (Diya) and financial compensation. In: Kamali MH (ed) Punishment in Islamic criminal justice: a fresh interpretation. Oxford University Press, New York, Chapter 16, pp 213–224
Lajna al-Fatwā al-Islāmiyya (2009) Fatāwā al-Shabaka al-Islāmiyya, vol. 3, available at https://www.noor-book.com/en/ebook-%D9%81%D8%AA%D8%A7%D9%88%D9%8A-%D8%A7%D9%84%D8%B4%D8%A8%D9%83%D9%87-%D8%A7%D9%84%D8%A7%D8%B3%D9%84%D8%A7%D9%85%D9%8A%D9%87-%D9%84%D9%84%D8%B4%D8%A7%D9%85%D9%84%D9%87--pdf. last visited 06, 07, 2021
Law Against Terrorism Crimes (2008) Ministry of Justice, official gazette No. 952
Law on Crimes Against Internal and External Security (1987) Ministry of Justice, Official Gazette No: 649
Law on Organization and Jurisdiction of Judiciary Branch of Islamic Republic of Afghanistan (2013) Ministry of Justice, Official Gazette No: 1109
MawṢilī ʿA (1973) Al-ikhtiyār li-taʿlīl al-mukhtār. al-Maṭbaʿa al-ḥalabī, Cairo, vol. 1(2)
Ministry of Aawqāf and Islamic Affairs of Kuwait (2008) Al-Mawsūʿa al-Fiqhiyya al-Kuwaytiyya, vol. 22
Ministry of Awqāf and Islamic Affairs of Kuwait (2008) Al-Mawsūʿa al-Fiqhiyya al-Kuwaytiyya, vol. 7
Mullā Khusraw M (n.d.) Durar al-Ḥukkām SharḤ Ghurar al-AḤkām. Dār Iḥyāʾ al-Kutub al-ʿArabiyya, Beirut, vol. 5
Qāḍī Khān Ḥ (2009) Fatāwā Qāḍī Khān. Dār al-Kutub al-ʿIlmiyya, Beirut, vol. 3, available at https://archive.org/details/01_20200513_20200513
Rohe M (2014) The development of the dogmatics of Islamic law. In: Rohe M (ed) Islamic law in past and present. Brill, Leiden, Chapter 2, pp 54–93
Sāʿī M (2007) Mawsūʿa Masāʾil al-Jumhūr fī al-Fiqh al-Islāmī. Dār al-Salām li-l-Ṭibāʿa wa-l-Nashr wa-l-Tawzīʿ, Cairo, vol. 2

Shahabuddin Mahmūd ibn Abdullah al ālūsī (1995) Tafsīr RūḤ al Maʿānī / Tafsir Alusi, verified by Ali Abdulbari Attiyah, Dār al-Kutub al-ʿIlmiyya, Beirut vol. 6
Sharīf Al-Jurjānī A (1983) Kitāb al-Taʿrīfāt. Dār al-Kutub al-ʿIlmiyya, Beirut
Ṣidqī ʿA (1987) Al-Jarīma wa-l-ʿUqūba fī al-Sharīʿa al-Islāmiyya. Maktaba al-Nahḍa al-Miṣriyya, Cairo
Ṭahmāz A (2000) Al-fiqh al-Ḥanafī fī thawbihi al-jadīd. Dār al-Qalam, Damascus, vol. 3
The Constitution of Afghanistan (2004)
The Criminal Procedure Code (1974) Ministry of Justice, Official Gazette No: 268
The Criminal Procedure Code (2014) Ministry of Justice, Official Gazette No: 1132
The Holy Quran
The Interim Criminal Procedure Law (2004) Ministry of Justice, Official Gazette No: 820
The Kāmbakhsh case, p 17
The Law on the Structure and Authority of the Prosecutor's Office (2013)
The Penal Code of Afghanistan (1976) Ministry of Justice, Official Gazette No: 347.
The Police Law (2009) Ministry of Justice, Official Gazette No: 994
The Police Law of Afghanistan (2005) Ministry of Justice, Official Gazette No: 862
Unpublished Presidential Decree No. 89 (dated 4 November 2001)
Uṭwa A (1994) Qawāʿid al-Iftāʾ - Principle of verdicts- (translation by Shāh MaḤmūd Khirad). Afghan Lawyers Association, Kabul
Zaylaʿī ʿU (1896) Tabyīn al-Ḥaqāʾiq SharḤ Kanz al-Daqāʾiq. Al-Maṭbaʿa al-Kubrā al-Amīriyya, Cairo, vol. 8

Chapter 6
Selling Dog Meat Case

6.1 Introduction

In December 2014, people rallied and asked the government to punish severely those who were attending a dog meat sale in Herat city.[1] Three people were arrested while they slaughtered a street dog and cut it into small pieces, then they intended to sell the meat in the market. The primary court sentenced two of them to 13 years and one of them to 3 years in prison. Selling dog meat is not criminalized under Afghan law, but the Herat city primary court made a decision based on Article 130 of the Afghan Constitution, which allows Afghan courts to make decisions in accordance with the provisions of the Ḥanafī school of thought if the law is silent regarding a case under consideration. This case analysis will reveal how Afghan courts implement Ḥanafī school doctrines when the law is silent. Furthermore, it will also discuss the constitutionality of the decision of the court in light of Article 130 of the Afghan Constitution.

6.2 Summary of the Sale of Dog Meat Case[2]

On September 09, 1393 (November 11, 2014), Mr. X, Y, and Z, assisted by a fourth person, slaughtered a dog in their house. They cut the dog into small pieces, proceeding to take it to the market to sell. The police arrested them with the dog meat before taking it to the market. The dog meat was then sent to the forensic medicine department of Herat city public hospital for further investigation. After the investigation, the forensic medicine department specified that the dog meat is not

[1] Herat city is the center of Herat province, which is located in the west of the country. This city may be the second or third big city after Kabul, the capital of Afghanistan.

[2] The Supreme Court of Afghanistan (2015) Decision Number 640, dated 15 Aug.

L. Saeed, *Islam, Custom and Human Rights*, Interdisciplinary Studies in Human Rights 7, https://doi.org/10.1007/978-3-030-83086-1_6

suitable for eating and might cause a serious disease that cannot be diagnosed and treated in Afghanistan.[3] During the investigation, Mr. X narrated that Mr. Y and his brother-in-law, Mr. Z, slaughtered a dog in the courtyard of his house and wanted to sell its meat in the market. Mr. Y, however, argued with them and tried to stop them from doing it, but the police suddenly raided the house and arrested them. The fourth person who was with them escaped from the crime scene.[4]

Subsequently, the Religious Leaders Council of Herat Province was asked for a fatwa (nonbinding legal opinion) regarding the case. Basically, the fatwa did not touch upon the issue of selling dog meat and only talked briefly about *taʿzīr* and the authority to implement it. However, the Religious Leaders Council of Herat Province should have issued a fatwa related to the case and answered the question of the Herat Prosecutor Office directly. The council should have clearly analyzed the act of selling dog meat in light of the Ḥanafī school principals, but the council did not touch upon the case at all. To have a clear picture of the fatwa of the Herat province *ʿulamāʾ* council, it is better to provide the English translation of the fatwa to show the ambiguity and problem in the text:

> Literally taʿzīr means discipline or chastisement, but in Islamic jurisprudence it refers to unspecified punishments for some sins against right of Allah or right of human that is not included in Ḥudūd crimes. If someone harasses others, he/she must be punished by taʿzīr. A famous Islamic scholar, Zaylaʿī states that there is no specific punishment for taʿzīr crime; it depends on the wish of the ruler. If the offence is serious, the punishment will be harsh.[5] The differences between taʿzīr and Ḥadd crimes are that punishment for Ḥadd crimes is already specified, but punishment for taʿzīr crime is based on the wish of ruler. Another difference between taʿzīr and Ḥadd is that Ḥadd punishment is abolished if there is doubt, but taʿzīr punishment is applicable even with doubt. Furthermore, the punishment for the Ḥadd crime is not applicable to children, but children could be subject to taʿzīr punishments. Furthermore, there is a legal maxim in Majalla that says Damage must be prevented. Al-siyāsa (politic) is what the ruler does in favor of the society, even if there is not any obvious reason, the ruler can apply taʿzīr based on his discretion. In general, the ruler is allowed to punish wrongdoer by death penalty if a serious crime is repeatedly happened.[6]

The primary court of Herat city made its decision in accordance with Article 130 of the Afghan Constitution and, based on discretionary *taʿzīr* punishment, Mr. X and Mr. Y were found guilty and sentenced to 13-year imprisonment beginning from the date of arrest. Also, Mr. Z was sentenced to 3 years in prison according to Article 130 of the Afghan Constitution and based on *taʿzīr*. Furthermore, the court instructed the police department to arrest the individual who escaped from the crime scene as

[3]The case does not precisely say that the health department examined that meat and then gave their opinion, but their opinion is very general and talks about the harms caused by being in touch with dogs and other wild animals. They did not say that the meat of the dog, which was slaughtered by the accused, caused such a problem.

[4]Dog's meat case, pp. 1–2.

[5]Mohammad Kāmil ibn Muṣṭafā ibn MaḤmūd al-Ṭarābulusī (1905) Al-Fatāwā Al-Kāmiliyya. Available via https://archive.org/details/alf-alk. Accessed 05, 05,2021.

[6]Dog meat case, pp. 46–47.

soon as possible. The accused disagreed with the decision of the primary court and asked for an appeal.

The appellate court of Herat province affirmed the decision of the primary court of Herat city.[7] However, the prosecutor disagreed with the appellate court's decision and claimed that the accused knowingly and intentionally collected dogs from the villages, slaughtered them, and then sold the dog meat to the Muslim people. Furthermore, the forensic medicine department of Herat city public hospital also stated that the accused committed a serious crime and put many people's lives in danger. Besides this, the Islamic council issued a fatwa that selling dog meat to Muslims is a punishable crime. So the punishment given by the court is not severe enough in relation to the crime committed. Based on a mistake in the applicable law, the prosecutor disagreed with the primary court's decision and appealed to the Herat Provincial Appellate Court.

6.3 Analysis of the Sale of Dog Meat Case

The Herat primary court decided the case under Article 130 of the Constitution and punished the accused based on *taʿzīr*. In fact, the consumption of dog meat by Muslims is prohibited under the Ḥanafī school of thought,[8] but it is not criminalized in the law of Afghanistan. Nevertheless, unlike the consumption of dog meat, its sale or purchase is a controversial issue among Islamic scholars. So before looking analytically at the decision of the court, it is necessary to review some issues related to the dog and its meat in light of Sharia, specifically according to the Ḥanafī school of thought. After that, we will examine the decision of the court regarding the case to see whether the decision was reached in accordance with law and the provisions of the Ḥanafī school or not. Furthermore, prior to examining the act of selling dog meat in accordance with the Sharia, particularly the Ḥanafī school of thought, it is necessary to distinguish three key points: (1) the sale of dog meat, (2) the consumption of dog meat, and (3) the sale of dogs.

It should be also noted that there are two different issues that must not be conflated: first, consuming dog meat as food by humans and, second, the sale of dog meat for different purposes. When we refer to the consumption of dog meat as being forbidden according to Sharia, this does not mean that the sale or purchase of dog meat for other purposes is also prohibited.[9] It is legitimate to sell or buy dog meat not for the consumption of humans but to feed other animals, like cats or dogs, or other predators. Therefore, the sale or purchase of dog meat is a different issue from consumption by humans.

[7] The Appellate Court of Herat Province (2015) Decision Number 418, dated 19 March.

[8] Ministry of Awqāf and Islamic Affairs of Kuwait (2008), p. 132.

[9] Al-Bukhārī (2004), p. 349.

6.3.1 The Sale of Dog Meat Within the Ḥanafī School of Thought

According to the Ḥanafī school, selling the meat of a slaughtered dog is legal. More specifically, Ḥanafī scholars, like the author of the *al-MuḤīṭ al-Burhānī* book, explains that if someone slaughters his dog, it is legal to sell its meat, but it is prohibited to consume it.[10] It is further held that slaughtering a dog is legal for any kind of benefit. It is even advised by the Ḥanafī scholars to slaughter an ill dog that is about to die.[11] This means that there is no problem if a person slaughters a dog and sells its meat to others in order to feed their carnivorous animals, like cats and dogs. According to the Ḥanafī school doctrine, the meat of all slaughtered animals, wild and domestic, can be sold to feed other animals except pigs because it is religiously impure in nature, and thus Muslims are not allowed to gain benefit from it.[12] The Ḥanafī school scholars believe that if an animal whose meat is forbidden to be eaten (*Ḥarām*), like a wolf, lion, etc. except pig, is slaughtered, its meat is religiously clean.[13] So if the meat of a slaughtered dog is found in water, the water does not become impure and could be used for religious purposes because the dog is not religiously impure in nature.[14] The Ḥanafī scholars believe that only liquids from a dog's body such as blood, sweat, saliva, and so on are religiously impure, not all parts of a dog like skin, bone, hair, even meat if they are dry. So its skin, hair, and meat are religiously pure if it is not wet with the liquid belonging to the dog's body.[15] Thus, based on the above doctrines of the Ḥanafī school, selling slaughtered dog meat is legal and not considered a crime.

It should also be noted that killing a dog is also not a crime; it was even a recommended act in the early Islamic period. Prophet Mohammad ordered the destruction of all dogs in the city of Medina because, as he stated, "Angels will not enter a house in which a dog or image of a living thing exists." So the Prophet's companions started killing all dogs except those for hunting, safeguarding houses, farms, and herds.[16] So, according to this Hadith, killing a dog is not considered a crime in Sharia. This order was only about untrained dogs, but if someone kills a dog that is trained for hunting or security, the killer is responsible to pay for compensation.[17]

---

[10] Al-Muhīṭ al-Burhānī fī al-fiqh al-Nu'mānī, Vol. 6, p. 349.

[11] Al-Ḥaṣkafī (2002), p. 32.

[12] Ibn 'Ābidīn (1992a), p. 356.

[13] According to Sharia, all kinds of meat are not allowed to be eaten and considered not religiously clean if Muslims have them during prayer. All kinds of predators' meat are considered religiously impure and should not be kept in the pocket of a Muslim during prayer, and Muslims cannot use such meat for any other purpose unless it came from an animal that was slaughtered.

[14] Al-Sarakhsī (1993a).

[15] Ministry of Awqāf and Islamic Affairs of Kuwait (2008), p. 129.

[16] Ibn al-Ḥajāj (n.d.), Hadith No: 3928.

[17] Al-Sarakhsī (n.d.), p. 199.

According to the Ḥanafī school doctrine, if someone kills a hunting or trained dog, he must pay money as compensation to the owner of the dog.[18] However, Imam Abū Ḥanīfa stated that if someone kills even an untrained dog, he must compensate the owner of the dog, and the same fatwa is applicable to the owner of all wild animals and birds.[19] So if a person kills any wild animals or birds owned by another person, the killer must compensate the owner, even though the animal is untrained. Ibn ʿUmar[20] narrated that there is compensation if a person kills a trained dog. For example, in the case of killing a hunting dog, the killer must pay 40 Dirhams (silver coins). If a person kills a form-safeguarding dog, the owner should be compensated by a considerable amount of food, and for a dog, trained to safeguard a herd, a sheep must be paid to the owner of the dog. Also, the third Caliph, ʿUthmān ibn ʿAffān, judged in favor of a woman whose hunting dog was killed by a man, who was asked to compensate the woman in the form of 20 camels.[21] It is worthwhile to note that the Ḥanafī school scholars also allowed selling and buying trained dogs and all kinds of birds and animals, whether they are wild or domesticated.[22] These all show that a dog could be subjected to transactions and the view of the Ḥanafī scholars contrasts the common view of the Afghan citizens. The common thought in Afghanistan is that a dog is a dirty animal and should not be considered the same as other animals. It is significant to briefly discuss whether eating dog meat is prohibited in Sharia or not and, if so, whether it is the same as pig meat.

6.3.2 *Eating Dog Meat in the Sharia*

Generally, the majority of the Sunni sects believe that eating dog meat is forbidden (*Ḥarām*); however, in some narrations, Imam Mālik, the founder of the Mālikī school of thought, believed that eating dog meat is abominable (*makrūh)*, not *Ḥarām*, but many of the Mālikī school scholars have the same opinion as the majority of the Sunni scholars.[23] More specifically, there are three opinions among Islamic scholars regarding the consumption of dog meat: (1) the Shāfiʿī and the Ḥanbalī schools believe that dog is a dirty animal and all of its related parts, like meat, hair, body, saliva, and sweat are dirty; (2) the Mālikī school believes that a dog and its meat, as well as other related parts of its body, are not dirty at all; and (3) Imam Abū Ḥanīfa believed that dog meat and its saliva are dirty but that its hair and skin are not dirty if it is tanned.[24] The reason offered for this by Abū Ḥanīfa and

[18] Al-Ṭahāwī (1994), p. 18.

[19] Al-Ṭahāwī (1996), p. 213.

[20] Ibn ʿUmar is the son of the second Caliph, ʿUmar ibn KhaṬṬāb, and one of the well-known disciples of Prophet Mohammad.

[21] Al-Sarakhsī (n.d.), p. 199.

[22] Badāʾiʿ al-ṣanāʾiʿ fī tartīb al-sharāʾiʿ (1986) Vol. 11, p. 93.

[23] Ministry of Awqāf and Islamic Affairs of Kuwait (2008), p. 132.

[24] Lajna al-Fatwā al-Islāmiyya (2009) Fatāwā al-Shabaka al-Islāmiyya, vol. 58, p. 146.

Ibn Taymiyya was that there is a legal maxim that states that cleanliness[25] is the original state of all things. Therefore, if someone claims that something is religiously dirty, he has to prove that it violates the main principle by means of a text. Therefore, the saliva of a dog is religiously dirty because Prophet Mohammad's Hadith stated that when a dog licks a vessel, you have to wash it seven times with water, followed by soil.[26] Also, there is another Hadith of Prophet Mohammad in which the Prophet is said to have prohibited Muslims from eating the meat of any kind of animal that has tusks.[27] So based on these reasons, Imam Abū Ḥanīfa and Ibn Taymiyya believed that only the meat and saliva of a dog are religiously dirty, not its hair and skin if it is tanned.[28] They believed that the dog itself is not religiously impure in nature (*najis al-ʿayn*), unlike a pig, because there is no Islamic text to declare it dirty. The case of a pig is different because of its nature based on the Quranic text, which calls it naturally impure and dirty (*najis al-ʿayn*).[29] So the skin and meat of the dog are religiously clean if it is not wet because there is no text to declare them dirty; thus, it retains its original status, which is clean.[30]

Since the common belief of the Afghan people is that a dog is a dirty animal and everything belonging to a dog is impure, we thus see the impact of this public perception on the court's decision in the case under consideration. The court, in its decision, has not made any reference in the case to any source of the Ḥanafī school. The upper courts ought to review and analyze the lower courts' decisions and check their consistency with the laws,[31] And the laws authorize the upper courts to review the lower courts' decisions in order to make sure that the decision is in accordance with law.[32] However, in this case, there is no reference to any law or Ḥanafī school provision to prove the legitimacy of the lower court's decision. It seems that the common belief of the Afghan citizens regarding the dirtiness of the dog meat

---

[25]The term cleanliness in Arabic (ṯahāra: طهارة) has a different meaning from the concept in Sharia. It means that something is clean religiously, not in the context of health. For example, in the context of Sharia, alcohol is dirty (Arabic: *najis*" نجس "), but in the context of health, it is not only clean, but it even it cleans other things. Another example is pig, which is a religiously dirty animal in nature, but pig is the same as other animals outside of the context of Sharia.

[26]Ibn al-Ḥajāj (n.d.), Hadith No: 91.

[27]Ibn al-Ḥajāj (n.d.), Hadith No: 3570.

[28]Lajna al-Fatwā al-Islāmiyya (2009) Fatāwā al-Shabaka al-Islāmiyya, vol. 58, p. 147.

[29]The Holy Quran, Sura al-Anʿām, Āya # 145: "Say, in what was revealed to me, I find nothing forbidden to a consumer who eats it, except carrion, or spilled blood, or the flesh of swine- because it is impure – or a sinful offering dedicated to other than God [...]." Also, see Sura al-Baqara (2:173): "He has forbidden you carrion, and blood, and the flesh of swine, and what is dedicated to other than God [...]."

[30]Ibn ʿĀbidīn (1992b), p. 108.

[31]Law on Organization and Jurisdiction of the Judiciary (2013) Art. 47/ Art. 48, official gazette no. 1109.

[32]Law on Organization and Jurisdiction of the Judiciary (2013) Art. 54: "The appellate court reviews the lower court's decision in accordance with the law. The appellate court reconsiders all the necessary element of the case and can correct, overruled, amend, affirm, and revoke in according to the law."

provides a false legitimacy for the court's decision regarding the case. Even the Ḥanafī scholars prefer a Muslim to eat dog meat rather than other hunted animals' meat, which have *Ḥalāl* meat, during the Hajj, the annual Muslim pilgrimage to Mecca. They said in an emergency situation[33] during a Hajj ceremony that if a Muslim finds the meat of a hunted animal and the meat of a dog, the Muslim should eat the dog's meat, not the meat of the hunted animal, even though the hunted animal's meat is *Ḥalāl*. The reason behind this opinion is that in the case of the hunted animal's meat, there are two violations of Islamic principles: first, hunting is prohibited during the Hajj time, and second, killing animals is prohibited in the holy land of Mecca, except killing untrained dogs, snakes, scorpions, ravens, mice, and buzzards.[34] Killing these animals is not prohibited in the holy land of Mecca. Thus, the Ḥanafī scholars prefer eating dog meat rather than hunted animal meat in the above situation.[35] Indeed, public opinion regarding dog meat does not match the Ḥanafī scholars' opinion.

6.3.3 Sale or Purchase of Dogs Within the Sharia

Ḥanafī school scholars believe that selling and buying any kind of dog is lawful, especially if it is for safeguarding the herd of ranchers, for safeguarding farms and houses, or in the case of dogs trained for hunting.[36] The Ḥanafī scholars state that Prophet Mohammad allowed his followers to receive money from the sale and purchase of a trained dog.[37]

According to the Ḥanafī school, a dog is considered to be an asset and can be sold or bought.[38] A famous book of the Ḥanafī school, *Radd al-Muḥtār*, states that "We [the Ḥanafī School] believe that dog is considered asset and could be transacted because dog could be beneficial and people can get benefit of using it in safeguarding their properties and for hunting."[39] So according to the Ḥanafī school's principles, any benefit people can get from anything is legal if there is no contrary provision in the text of Islamic sources. Thus, gaining benefit from a dog is lawful because there is no text that prohibits it, so the sale and purchase of a dog are legal.[40]

---

[33] According to Sharia principle, if a Muslim, in an emergency situation does not find any Ḥalāl products to eat or drink and his life is in danger, the Muslim can eat and drink prohibited (*Ḥarām*) products to save their life. In the above case, in an emergency situation, if a Muslim finds two or more *Ḥarām* things, the Ḥanafī scholars made preference as to which one should be eaten.

[34] Al-Nasāʾī (1986), Hadith No: 2779, No: 2780 and No: 2781.

[35] Tafsīr Ālūsī (1994) vol. 5, p. 142.

[36] Zaylaʿī (1896), p. 328.

[37] Al-Sarakhsī (1993b, c), vol. 26, p. 176 and vol. 14, p. 80.

[38] Badāʾiʿ al-ṣanāʾiʿ fī tartīb al-sharāʾiʿ (1986) Vol. 11, p. 93.

[39] In Islamic law, some items like alcohol and pig have not considered as an asset and could not be interchangeable with Money, so if a Muslim has a pig or a bottle of alcohol, and someone destroyed them, there is no compensation.

[40] ʿAlāʾ al-Dīn (1986), p. 52; Ministry of Awqāf and Islamic Affairs of Kuwait (2008), p. 127.

It is also necessary to mention that killing dogs owned by other people requires compensating the owner of the dog, who gains benefit from the dog, like patrolling his house, safeguarding his herd, etc. ʿAbdallāh ibn ʿUmar, one of the disciples of Prophet Mohammad, adjudicated a case where a person killed a hunting dog, requiring him to compensate the owner of the dog with 40 coins of silver (*Dirham*).[41] Also, ʿUthmān, the third Caliph of Mohammad, adjudicated a case regarding a man who killed a woman's hunting dog, ordering him to compensate her with 20 camels.[42] These kinds of cases prove that a trained dog has value and that there might arise a need for compensation if someone kills it. After a brief discussion about dogs and the issues relating to their meat in light of Sharia, it is time to examine the court's decision with respect to the dog meat and find out to want extent the decision has conformed with law and the Ḥanafī school provisions.

6.4 Analysis of the Legality of the Court's Decision

The primary court of Herat city made a decision regarding a case based on Article 130 of the Afghan Constitution, without referring to any provision of the Ḥanafī school of thought. This means that the court has not mentioned any provision of the Ḥanafī school to support the legitimacy of its decision. This is important because the Constitution of Afghanistan[43] and the *Law on Organization and Jurisdiction of the Judiciary Branch*[44] imposed an obligation on the courts to state a specific reason and provision of the law regarding the case when they are making decisions. When they make a decision in light of Article 130 of the Afghan Constitution, they have to consider the Ḥanafī provisions as law, so they must refer the case to the specific provisions of the Ḥanafī school, but there is no provision of the Ḥanafī school referenced in the primary court decision. And although the decision of the primary court of Herat city did not mention any provision of law or the Ḥanafī school, it was affirmed by the appellate court of Herat province, and the Supreme Court affirmed the appellate court's decision as well. The primary court of Herat city only mentioned Article 130 of the Afghan Constitution in its decision with no reference to specific provisions of the Ḥanafī school; thus, it will now be examined how Article 130 of the Afghan Constitution was applied in this case.

[41] Al-Bābartī (n.d.), p. 466.

[42] Al-Sarakhsī (1993c), vol. 14, p. 80.

[43] The Constitution of Afghanistan (2004) Art. 129: "In issuing a decision, the court is obligated to state the reason for its verdict [. . .]."

[44] Law on Organization and Jurisdiction of the Judiciary Branch of Islamic Republic of Afghanistan (1392) Art. 12, official gazette No: 1109: "The court is obligated to state the reason of its verdict within the text of the decision [. . .]."

6.4.1 The Prosecutor's Indictment and the Primary Court's Decision

The prosecutor submitted the indictment to the primary court of Herat city with a charge of killing a dog with the intent to sell its meat to the people of Herat city. The prosecutor listed the below reasons to support his claim against the accused persons.

6.4.2 Confession

The first reason put forward by the prosecutor is that Mr. X and Mr. Y confessed that they slaughtered a dog, cut it into small pieces, and intended to sell it to the people of Herat city. It must be noted that both of them were addicted to narcotic drugs and wanted to earn money to fund their addictions. The court said: "Mr. Z is also guilty because he knew Mr. Y for three months and was arrested from the crime scene." However, Mr. Z denied his involvement in the case. The only reason that the court found him guilty and sentenced him to three years of imprisonment was that he is also addicted to drugs and had known Mr. Y for three months.[45]

6.4.3 Views of Experts

The prosecutor, to prove their claims based on the harmfulness of the dog meat, asked the public health department of Herat province for their opinion regarding the case. The health department stated that being physically in touch with dogs may cause a variety of diseases and listed some of these diseases.[46] The health department also mentioned that the treatment for some of these diseases is very complex and sometimes impossible to administer within Afghanistan.

6.4.4 Fatwa of the Religious Leaders Council of Herat Province

The in-charge prosecutor of the case claimed that he has approval from the Sharia perspective regarding the case; he requested a fatwa from the *Herat Religious Council (shūrā-i ʿulamāʾ)* regarding the case and included a hard copy of that inquiry

[45] Selling dog meat case in Herat Primary Court, 24, 10, 1393, p. 47.

[46] Selling Dog Meat case, Primary Court of Herat City, pp. 47–48, and first and second pages of the prosecutor indictment of the prosecutor.

in the file. If we look closely at the fatwa of the Council of Religious Leaders of Herat province, they have not provided an answer to the direct question regarding the case in light of the Ḥanafī doctrines. The *ʿulamāʾ* council only talked about the concept of *taʿzīr* and the persons authorized to apply it in a Muslim community. There is not even a single word regarding the case or the alleged actions of the accused.

Indeed, in Afghanistan, it is the duty of the Supreme Court to issue a fatwa regarding how such cases should be dealt with under Sharia.[47] However, the prosecutor's office asked the *ʿulamāʾ* council of Herat province for a fatwa regarding the case. Presumably, the prosecutor relied upon the provision of Article 44 of the Criminal Procedure Code, which provides:

(1) ……..
(2) The judicial police officer, prosecutor's office and courts are obligated to identify the type of investigation and other matters in their request to the experts.
(3) The prosecutor's office and courts can consider the views of other people who have the requisite expertise, knowledge and experience pertaining to the issue, in addition to the experts who provided views and are registered with the courts.[48]

Since the law opens a wide door for the judicial police, prosecutor, and courts to ask experts to have their views regarding the case, they asked Herat province religious leaders for their fatwa.

The court said: "Therefore, the court chamber of the public security of the primary court of Herat city, based on the above reasons, in accordance with Article 130 of the Afghan Constitution, made a decision and sentenced Mr. X and Mr. Y to 13 years imprisonment. The court also found Mr. Z guilty in this case and sentenced him to 3 years imprisonment. All these punishments were based on the discretionary *taʿzīr* punishment."

6.5 Analysis of the Court's Decision

Now, the Herat primary court's decision will be analyzed in light of Afghan law and the Sharia provisions in order to see whether this case should be subject to Article 130 of the Afghan Constitution or not. Even if it ought to be subjected to Article 130 of the Afghan Constitution, which provision of the Ḥanafī school is applicable to this case, if any? Furthermore, it will be examined if there is a provision in the law regarding the case or if the law is silent about the case and therefore the Ḥanafī

[47]The Supreme Court of Afghanistan has a department of *iftāʾ* (*Riyāsat al-Iftāʾ*) to issue a fatwa (nonbinding legal opinion) for the courts, governmental institutions, individuals, and Afghan consulate offices outside the country upon their official request. Even if a foreigner becomes a Muslim, after collecting the necessary information, this department shall issue a certificate for the new Muslim person. Please see the Supreme Court of Afghanistan, accessed via http://supremecourt.gov.af/fa/page/634/640 on May 4, 2017.

[48]Criminal Procedure Code (2014) Art. 44, official gazette No: 1132.

school provisions must apply based on Article 130 of the Afghan Constitution. There are some issues with the primary court's decision that should be taken into consideration.

6.5.1 Unconstitutionality

Article 130 of the Constitution requires the courts to first look at the Constitution and the laws as to whether or not there is a provision related to this case. If there is no provision in the laws, the court can make a decision in accordance with the provisions of the Ḥanafī school of thought. Although there is no specific provision of law expressly pertaining to the selling of dog meat, upon a close look at the laws, there may be some provisions that could apply implicitly to the case under consideration. For instance, Article 480 of the Afghan Penal Code states:

> A person who acts fraudulently against someone, with whom he has made a contract, in the cases mentioned below, shall be sentenced to medium imprisonment, not exceeding two years and shall be fined an amount not exceeding ten thousand Afghanis:
>
> 1. In quantity, number, measure, weight, scale, and percentage of composition.
> 2. Delivering another good for what has already been agreed upon.
> 3. In quality, basic characteristics, and useful ingredients.
> 4. Type and source of good.[49]

The case could be subject to this article: in particular, sections 2, 3, and 4 seem more related to the case. Rally in Islamic law, and it is the case in Afghanistan, that the sale and purchase of goods are based on a verbal contract, without any document exchange. So, the goods must match the characteristics and type of materials, which is common among the people in the Market and both parties verbally agreed upon. In a society like Afghanistan, common sense would dictate that the people must sell *Ḥalāl* meat in the market because more than 99% of the Afghan population is Muslim. The common culture in the market is that all the goods must be *Ḥalāl*, but the accused intended to deliver and sell dog meat instead of mutton or goat meat to the people. This means they intended to deliver a product that has a different characteristic from the type and source of meat sold in the market, that is, the common *Ḥalāl* meat. Since they intended to sell dog meat, this could be subject to Article 29 of the Penal Code, which talks about the initiation of a crime:

> (1) Initiation of a crime is the starting of an act with the intention of committing a felony or misdemeanor, but whose effects have been stopped or offset by reasons beyond the will of the doer.
> (2) ......

In this case, the accused persons intended to cheat the people by selling dog meat instead of goad or sheep meat. They have started to commit an act that breaks the

[49]The Penal Code of Afghanistan (1976) Art. 480.

law; thus, the case could be subject to the above article. Since Article 480 of the Penal Code states that the punishment for the initiator of such a crime *shall be sentenced to medium imprisonment, not exceeding two years and shall be fined an amount not exceeding ten thousand Afghanis*, this crime is categorized as a misdemeanor because the Penal Code said:

> Misdemeanor is a crime whose doer is sentenced to imprisonment of more than three month up to five years, or cash fine of more than three thousand Afghanis.[50]

Obviously, the punishment for the initiator of a crime is different from the one who is fully involved and has accomplished the crime. The Penal Code says:

> Punishment for initiating misdemeanor shall not exceed one half of the maximum punishment prescribed for the crime itself in the law, unless the law has stipulated otherwise.[51]

So according to the above provisions of the law, the case should be subject to the law, and the punishment, based on Article 31 of the Penal Code, cannot be more than 1 year of imprisonment because the accused persons were at the starting phase of the criminal act and could be punished not more than one-half of the maximum punishment for the crime itself, which is 2 years of imprisonment. Applying Article 480 of the Penal Code to the case would be more constitutional and legitimate and represent due process of law rather than making a decision to punish persons with 13 years in prison without basis in any provision of law or Sharia. The decision of the court should be considered unconstitutional because it conflicts with Articles 27,[52] 129,[53] and 130[54] of the Afghan Constitution.

Article 27 of the Constitution accepts the principle of legality of crime and punishment and declares no punishment without law, but in the above case the courts have not referred the case to any provision of the law and punished the accused without any support from law. Also, Article 129 of the Constitution declares the obligation of the court to state the reason for its decision. It means the court must provide legal reasons for the decision that has been made, but in the above case there is no reference to any provision of law or the Ḥanafī school of thought. So the court decision lacks a specific provision of law that could be the basis for its verdict. Furthermore, the court decision violates Article 130 of the Constitution, which

---

[50] The Penal Code of Afghanistan (1976) Art. 25.

[51] The Penal Code of Afghanistan (1976) Art. 31.

[52] "No deed shall be considered a crime unless ruled by a law promulgated prior to commitment of the offense. No one shall be pursued, arrested, or detained without due process of law. No one shall be punished without the decision of an authoritative court taken in accordance with the provisions of the law, promulgated prior to commitment of the offense."

[53] "In issuing a decision, the court is obligated to state the reason for its verdict. All final decisions of the courts shall be enforced, except for capital punishment, which shall require Presidential approval."

[54] "In cases under consideration, the courts shall apply provisions of this Constitution as well as other laws. If there is no provision in the Constitution or other laws about a case, the courts shall, in pursuance of Ḥanafī jurisprudence, and, within the limits set by this Constitution, rule in a way that attains justice in the best manner."

declares that the court must apply the provisions of the Constitution and the laws to the case under consideration. If the law is silent about a case under consideration, the court shall apply the provisions of the Ḥanafī school of thought. As discussed, the case is subject to Article 480 of the Penal Code, but the court made a decision in light of Article 130 of the Constitution with no reference to law provisions or the Ḥanafī school doctrines.

6.5.2 Violation of the Law

The second issue is that in accordance with Article 129 of the Afghan Constitution[55] and Articles 12 and 13 of the *Law on Organization and Jurisdiction of the Judiciary*,[56] the courts are obligated to state their legal reasoning for their verdicts. Unfortunately, the decisions of the courts in all stages of the proceedings, in the primary and appellate courts as well as in the Supreme Court, there was a distinct lack of legal reasoning to support the verdict. The primary court of Herat city only mentioned Article 130 of the Constitution in its decision, which is not related to sentencing the accused to 13-year imprisonment. The article only allows the court to make decisions based on the Ḥanafī school of thought provisions. There is no hint in Article 130 of the Constitution that someone should be punished or that a decision could be reached without giving any legal reasoning. The court must state that in light of Article 130 of the Afghan Constitution and based on specific provisions of the Ḥanafī school of thought, the court reached its decision. However, the courts, at every stage, failed to provide single legal reasoning based on the Ḥanafī school provisions to prove the legality of the decision.

In addition, the affirmation by the Supreme Court and the Appellate Court of Herat province of the primary court's decision is also contrary to the law because Article 47 of the *Law on Organization and Jurisdiction of the Judiciary* states:

> If the Supreme Court, during the reviewing the case under the consideration, finds that the lower court make decision not in according to the law or there is mistake in the application or glossing the law, the lower court decision must be revoked and send back to the lower court to make a decision in according to the law.[57]

Furthermore, one of the powers of the appellate courts is reviewing the lower courts' decisions, and they can revoke, overrule, or affirm a lower court's decision in

[55] The Constitution of Afghanistan (2004) Art. 129: "In issuing a decision, the court is obligated to state the reason for its verdict [. . .]."

[56] Law on Organization and Jurisdiction of the Judiciary (2013) Art. 12/ Art. 13, Ministry of Justice, official gazette No: 1109.

[57] Law on Organization and Jurisdiction of the Judiciary Branch of Islamic Republic of Afghanistan, (2013) Art. 47, official gazette No: 1109.

accordance with law.[58] Since the primary court's decision contradicts the provision of the Constitution and law, the appellate court of Herat province ought to have revoked the primary court's decision and sent it back to the primary court in order for it to reach a legitimate decision.

Furthermore, the Herat health department's view is also very general and talks about the possibility of some harm and disease derived from being physically in contact with dogs or some other animals, referring precisely to predators. The health department did not examine the meat and never indicated that the meat of the dog that was slaughtered by the accused had any health implications. The health department's opinion does not provide any substantive link to the case and presents a very general view. This view may be true but does not speak to the specific facts of the case. If we consider the health department's opinion as a reason for the court to make a decision, any person, particularly a butcher, who has a dog in his house could be prosecuted and punished because of the potential health problems associated with having physical contact with dogs or other domesticated predators.

As mentioned above, the fatwa of the Council of Religious Leaders (*shūrā-i ʿulamāʾ*) of Herat province bears no relevance to the case. The entire fatwa talks generally about the definition of *taʿzīr* and who has the power to apply *taʿzīr* punishments and briefly explained the differences between *taʿzīr* and *Ḥadd* crimes. There is no reference to slaughtering a dog and the sale of its meat to people in accordance with the Ḥanafī school of thought. The *ʿulamāʾ* council ought to provide enough information regarding the case in light of the Ḥanafī school doctrines and clearly state the opinion of Ḥanafī scholars in relation to the specific facts of the case. All these factors challenge the legitimacy of the courts' decisions in all steps of the proceedings, in the primary and appellate courts as well as the Supreme Court.

6.6 Conclusion

The Herat City Primary Court's decision regarding the selling dog meat case has considerable legal problems. Indeed, the common thought regarding the dirtiness of dogs in Afghan society appears to have had a significant impact on the court's decision. The Herat city citizens, along with the association of the butchers of Herat province, demanded severe punishment for the three accused of the case. They believed that selling dog meat is a violation of Islamic principles and warned that if the government does not punish them, they will act strongly against them. The people's reaction to the case was very serious, and they even asked for capital

[58] Law on Organization and Jurisdiction of the Judiciary Branch of Islamic Republic of Afghanistan, (2013) Art. 54, official gazette No: 1109.

punishment for the accused people, as demonstrated by their comments regarding the news.[59]

As discussed, the courts did not consider the act of the accused as a crime in accordance with law or Sharia, but it seems that the court evaluated that act as a severe violation of the moral and cultural standards of the Afghan society. The courts, without any legal justification, sentenced them to 13 years of imprisonment, which contradicts the accepted principles of the legal system of Afghanistan and Islamic Sharia. There are some notable issues associated with the decision of the court that should be taken into account.

First, as mentioned above, the decision of the primary court does not match the requirements set by Articles 27, 129, and 130 of the Constitution. Furthermore, it is not in accordance with the laws, particularly Articles 2 and 3 of the Afghan Penal Code and Articles 12 and 13 of the *Law on Organization and Jurisdiction of the Judiciary*. Apparently, due to the lack of legal provisions applicable to the specific fact of the case, the court reached a decision in light of Article 130 of the Afghan Constitution. However, when placed under closer scrutiny, the case is subject to Article 480 of the Penal Code, which is about acting fraudulently and cheating people in terms of the quality, basic characteristics, useful ingredients, and type and source of goods.[60] So it is also considered a violation of law, not only Article 130 of the Constitution.

Furthermore, Article 129 of the Afghan Constitution[61] as well as Articles 12 and 13 of the *Law on Organization and Jurisdiction of the Judiciary*[62] state that the court must provide legal reasoning for its decision; however, there is no legal reasoning provided in the decisions in all stages of the court proceedings regarding the case. The only provision mentioned in the decision of the court is Article 130 of the Constitution, which does not have any relationship with the case, and there is no mention of punishment in the text of Article 130 at all.

Also, Article 27[63] of the Constitution and Articles 2 and 3 of the Afghan Penal Code accept the principle of legality of crime and punishment and declare that there shall be no punishment without law, but the court sentenced the accused without a

[59] Persons who are selling dog meat should be punished. Please see Afghanistan Media Network, accessed via http://www.afghanpaper.com/nbody.php?id=84737 on September 11, 2015. Even a law professor at Herat University states that if he were to be a judge in that case, he will sentence the accused by capital punishment.

[60] The Penal Code of Afghanistan (1976) Art. 480.

[61] The Constitution of Afghanistan (2004) Art. 129: "In issuing a decision, the court is obligated to state the reason for its verdict [. . .]."

[62] Law on Organization and Jurisdiction of the Judiciary Branch of Islamic Republic of Afghanistan (2013) Art. 12/ Art. 13, official gazette No. 1109.

[63] No act shall be considered a crime unless declared by a law promulgated prior to the commission of an offense. No one shall be pursued, arrested, or detained without due process of law. No one shall be punished without a decision of a competent court taken in accordance with the provisions of law, promulgated prior to the commission of an offense.

legal basis. Thus, based on the above reasons, the Herat city primary court's decision is unconstitutional.

Punishing the accused for an act that is not a crime under the law or in Sharia does not have any legal basis in the entire legal system of Afghanistan. Since the appellate court and the Supreme Court also did not respect the provisions of the Constitution and other laws, the decision of the courts regarding the case in three stages remains problematic and is contrary to the necessary due process of law guaranteed in Article 27 of the Afghan Constitution.

References

Abū al-Maʿālī Burhān al-Dīn MaḤmūd ibn AḤmad ibn ʿAbd al-ʿAzīz ibn ʿUmar ibn Māza al-Bukhārī, (2004) Al-Muhīṭ al-Burhānī fī al-fiqh al-Nuʿmānī, verified by ʿAbd al-Karīm Sāmī al-Jundī, Beirut: Dār al-kutub al-ʿilmiyya, vol 6

ʿAlāʾ al-Dīn, Abū Bakr ibn Masʿūd ibn AḤmad al-Kāsānī, (1986) Badāʾiʿ al-ṣanāʾiʿ fī tartīb al-sharāʾiʿ, Beirut: Dār al-Kutub al-ʿIlmiyya, vol 5

ʿAlāʾ al-Dīn, Abū Bakr ibn Masʿūd ibn AḤmad al-Kāsānī, (1986) Badāʾiʿ al-ṣanāʾiʿ fī tartīb al-sharāʾiʿ, Beirut: Dār al-Kutub al-ʿIlmiyya, vol 11

Al-Ālūsī, Shihāb al-Dīn Maḥmūd ibn ʿAbdallāh Al-Ḥusaynī, 1994. Tafsīr Ālūsī= Rūḥ al-Maʿānī, Verified by ʿAlī ʿAbd al-Bārī ʿAṭiyya, Beirut: Dār al-Kutub al-ʿIlmiyya, vol 5

Al-Bābartī M (n.d.) Al-ʿInāya Sharḥ al-Hidāya. Dār al-Fikr, Beirut, vol 9

Al-Ḥaṣkafī M (2002) Al-Durr al-Mukhtār Sharḥ Tanwīr al-Abṣār wa Jāmiʿ al-AbḤār. Dār al-Kutub al-ʿIlmiyya, Beirut, vol 7

Al-Nasāʾī A (1986) Sunan Al-Nasāʾī, verified by ʿAbd al-Fatāḥ Abū Ghuda. Maktaba al-Maṭbūʿāt al-Islāmiyya, Aleppo

Al-Sarakhsī M (1993a) Al-Mabsūṭ li-Sarakhsī. Dār al-Maʿrifa, Beirut, vol 11

Al-Sarakhsī M (1993b) Al-Mabsūṭ li-Sarakhsī. Dār al-Maʿrifa, Beirut, vol 26

Al-Sarakhsī M (1993c) Al-Mabsūṭ li-Sarakhsī. Dār al-Maʿrifa, Beirut, vol 14

Al-Ṭahāwī A (1994) Sharḥ Maʿānī al-Āthār. ʿĀlam al-Kutub, Beirut, vol 5

Al-Ṭahāwī A (1996) Mukhtaṣar Ikhtilāf al-ʿUlamāʾ, verified by ʿAbdallāh Nazīr AḤmad. Dār al-Bashāʾir al-Islāmiyya, Beirut, vol 2

Criminal Procedure Code (2014) Ministry of Justice, Official Gazette No: 1132

Ibn ʿĀbidīn M (1992a) Radd al-MuḤtār ʿalā Durr al-Mukhtār (Ḥāshiyya Ibn ʿĀbidīn). Dār al-Fikr, Beirut, vol 5

Ibn ʿĀbidīn M (1992b) Radd al-MuḤtār ʿalā Durr al-Mukhtār (Ḥāshiyya Ibn ʿĀbidīn). Dār al-Fikr, Beirut, vol 2

Ibn al-Ḥajāj M (n.d.) Ṣaḥīḥ Muslim, verified by MuḤammad Fawād ʿAbd al-Bāqī. Dār Iḥyāʾ al-Turāth al-ʿArabī, Beirut

Lajna al-Fatwā al-Islāmiyya (2009) Fatāwā al-Shabaka al-Islāmiyya. vol 58, available at https://www.noor-book.com/en/ebook-%D9%81%D8%AA%D8%A7%D9%88%D9%8A-%D8%A7%D9%84%D8%B4%D8%A8%D9%83%D9%87-%D8%A7%D9%84%D8%A7%D8%B3%D9%84%D8%A7%D9%85%D9%8A%D9%87-%D9%84%D9%84%D8%B4%D8%A7%D9%85%D9%84%D9%87%2D%2Dpdf last visited 06, 07, 2021

Law on Organization and Jurisdiction of the Judiciary Branch (2013) Ministry of Justice, official gazette No: 1109

Ministry of Awqāf and Islamic Affairs of Kuwait (2008) Al-Mawsūʿa al-Fiqhiyya al-Kuwaytiyya, vol 35

The Appellate Court of Herat Province (2015) Decision Number 418, dated 19 March

The Constitution of Afghanistan (2004) Ministry of Justice, Official Gazette No: 818

The Holy Quran
The Penal Code of Afghanistan (1976) Ministry of Justice, Official Gazette No: 347
The Supreme Court of Afghanistan (2015) Decision Number 640, dated 15 Aug
Zaylaʿī ʿU (1896) Tabyīn al-Ḥaqāʾiq SharḤ Kanz al-Daqāʾiq. Al-Maṭbaʿa al-Kubrā al-Amīriyya, Cairo, vol 11

Chapter 7
Donkey Skin Cases

7.1 Introduction

This chapter analyzes the Kunduz city court's decision regarding two donkey skin cases, in which the court punished the accused by imprisonment, including the truck driver, and confiscated his truck because they were carrying ten bags full of donkey skins from Mazar-e-Sharif city to Kunduz city. However, the trade and use of donkey skin is not a crime neither in the law nor in Sharia. The court made a decision based on Article 130 of the Afghan Constitution and an opinion of the Supreme Court High Council upon an inquiry regarding the case.

In fact, the Supreme Court criminalizes an act that is not considered a crime in the law and Sharia. The main reason in the Supreme Court's opinion is that transferring donkey skins is an immoral act and there is no common usage of donkey skin in Afghanistan. The court decision will be analyzed in light of Ḥanafī school doctrines and the law of Afghanistan. Initially, the status of the trade and use of donkey and its meat and skin will be discussed based on Afghan law and the doctrines of the Ḥanafī school, and then the chapter will shed light on the Supreme Court's opinion issued regarding the case and the court decision will be analyzed accordingly. Furthermore, the confiscation of the truck will be discussed based on the provisions of the law and Ḥanafī school of thought. In conclusion, it will be assessed whether or not the court made a decision in accordance with the law and Sharia, particularly the Ḥanafī school provisions.

L. Saeed, *Islam, Custom and Human Rights*, Interdisciplinary Studies in Human Rights 7, https://doi.org/10.1007/978-3-030-83086-1_7

7.2 Summary of the Cases

There are two cases in the Kunduz province courts regarding capturing donkey skins while they were being transported from the city of Mazar-e-Sharif to Kunduz city.[1] The first case is dated November 11, 2015, and the second is dated March 29, 2017. The primary court of Kunduz city made a decision ordering the destruction of all the donkey skins in both cases and punishing the accused with short-term imprisonment and a 30,000Af fine and confiscated the truck and 240 sacks (1200 kg) of wheat flour, together with the donkey skins loaded in the truck, which are all private legal property.

The trade of donkey skin is legal, and there are not any provisions in the Afghan laws and Sharia, namely in the Ḥanafī school of thought, that prevent the trade of donkey skin, but it is not common in Afghanistan to use or trade donkey skin for any purposes. When the court received the cases, they sent an inquiry to the Supreme Court because there is no provision in the law regarding the case. The High Council of the Supreme Court issued an opinion regarding the case, and because the law lacks any provision applicable to the case, the primary court of Kunduz city made a decision based on Article 130 of the Afghan Constitution and the opinion of the Supreme Court concerning the case.

In this chapter, first of all, I will shed light on the trade of donkey and its meat and skin (there is no issue to be discussed regarding wheat flour from a legal perspective)[2] and then analyze the Supreme Court's opinion. After that, the case will be examined in light of Sharia principles to assess their status in view of Islamic law.

7.3 Trade of Donkey and Its Skin and Consumption of Its Meat in Sharia

Before looking deeply at the case, there are three issues that could be clarified in light of Sharia, particularly in accordance with the Ḥanafī school of thought. First is the selling and purchasing of donkeys, second is the consumption of donkey meat, and third is the selling and buying of donkey meat and skin.

There is no doubt that selling and purchasing donkeys are legal in accordance with Sharia, and there is no single source in the Ḥanafī school of thought stating that selling donkeys is prohibited.[3] However, sometimes jurists discuss whether extra tools like the rein and line, which are usually attached to a domestic donkey, are

---

[1]Kunduz city is the center of Kunduz province, which is located in the northeast of Afghanistan.

[2]There is no issue on the wheat flour from a legal perspective, but it was confiscated because the donkey skins were hidden under the wheat flour sacks, and the court considers them as a tool for committing a crime because the sacks were used to hide the donkey skins. Page 2 of the donkey skin case was penned by Mr. Nawāb, dated April 29, 2017.

[3]Al-Shaybānī (1983), p. 756.

included in the deal when selling a donkey, even without mentioning it.[4] Most Ḥanafī scholars believe that if a person buys a donkey, its rein and line are not included if it is not mentioned in the contract, and the buyer should return the rein and line and keep the donkey.[5] So it shows that selling and buying donkeys are permissible without any doubt.

However, many Ḥanafī scholars are of the view that eating the meat of a donkey is prohibited in Islamic Sharia.[6] There are several narrations from Prophet Mohammad stating that eating domestic donkey meat is not permissible.[7] However, there is no issue at all regarding eating wild donkey meat.[8] Almost all Sunni scholars believe that eating wild donkey meat is permissible (*Ḥalāl*), and there are several prophetical narrations regarding the permissibility of eating wild donkey meat.[9]

With respect to the use and trade of donkey skin, there is a general principle in Sharia that allows the use and trade of animal skins for different purposes. This principle is derived from the prophetical narration "Whichever animal skins be tanned, they grow pure or clean (*ṭāhir*)."[10] Based on this Hadith, the Ḥanafī scholars unanimously believe that the skin of all animals, domestic and wild, becomes pure when it is tanned, except the skin of humans and pigs.[11] The first one is an exception because it is an offense against human dignity to use his skin for any purpose. The second exception is because of the pig's impureness in nature.[12] The Ḥanafī scholars also believe that it is legal to sell or purchase donkey skin; if someone destroys or blemishes it, he must pay compensation to the owner of the skin.[13] So, in conclusion, in accordance with the Ḥanafī school principle, the use and trade of donkey skin are legal.

---

[4] Zaylaʿī ʿU (1896a), p. 318.

[5] Ibn Nujaym (n.d.), p. 318.

[6] Ministry of Awqāf and Islamic Affairs of Kuwait (2008a), vol. 5, p 318.

[7] ʿAlāʾ al-Dīn, Abū Bakr ibn Masʿūd ibn AḤmad al-Kāsānī (1986a, b), p. 38; Al-Bukhārī (2001), Hadith No: 4217.

[8] Al-Sarakhsī (1993a), vol.11, p. 233.

[9] Al-Bukhārī (2001), Hadith No: 5492.

[10] Al-Nasāʾī (1986), Hadith No: 3609; Ibn Mājah (2009), Hadith No: 1193.

[11] Ibn Abī Bakr (1999), p. 24.

[12] Badr al-Dīn al-ʿAynī A (2000a), p 418./ Mawṣilī ʿA (1973) Al-ikhtiyār li-taʿlīl al-mukhtār. Al-Maṭbaʿa al-ḥalabī, Cairo, vol. 2, p. 16.

[13] Al-Samarqandī (1966), p. 281.

7.4 Pretrial Activities

According to law, the police have the power to arrest someone if he acts illegally,[14] but the trade and transportation of donkey skins is not an illegal act under the law of Afghanistan. Furthermore, stopping and arresting people without due process of law is unconstitutional because the Constitution guarantees the right to travel and settle in any part of the country:

> Every Afghan shall have the right to travel and settle in any part of the country, except in areas forbidden by law. Every Afghan shall have the right to travel outside Afghanistan and return, according to the provisions of the law. The state shall protect the rights of the citizens of Afghanistan outside the country.[15]

When police officers stopped the truck that was carrying the donkey skins and arrested the driver and the owner of the skins, they violated the provision of the Constitution because there is no legal basis for their actions to stop and arrest people.

Also, constitutionally it is the duty of the state to protect and ensure the safety of capital investment and private businesses and provide facilities to develop trade in accordance with law:

> The state shall encourage, protect as well as ensure the safety of capital investment and private enterprises in accordance with the provisions of the law and market economy.[16]

Furthermore, the Law on Blocking Contraband says that the police have the authority to search for contraband and arrest the trafficker.[17] However, this law defines contraband as goods exported or imported without tax or goods produced, imported, exported, traded, or transported illegally.[18] The law provides further clarification for the illegal goods and says that the production, import, export, trade, keeping, and transportation of illegal goods are prohibited.[19] Thus, in accordance with the above provisions of the Constitution and the law, the trade and transportation of donkey skin is not criminalized. Moreover, the trade and transportation of donkey skin are legal under Sharia.

Generally, the police's act of arresting the accused and expropriating donkey skin is considered unconstitutional and against the law because the police violated the rights of citizens to *travel and settle*, which is guaranteed in the Constitution. Additionally, the act of the police is in violation of Article 10 of the Constitution, which placed an obligation on the state to protect and ensure the safety of capital

[14]For more details please look at Chap. 5.

[15]The Constitution of Afghanistan (2004) Art. 39.

[16]The Constitution of Afghanistan (2004) Art. 10.

[17]Law on Blocking Contraband (2000) Art. 2, official gazette no. 793. Access via http://moj.gov.af/Con tent/files/Pages/OfficialGazetteIndex_D-header.htm. Accessed 05, 12, 2020.

[18]Law on Blocking Contraband (2000) Art. 3, clause 1, official gazette no. 793. Access via http://moj.gov.af/Con tent/files/Pages/OfficialGazetteIndex_D-header.htm. Accessed 05, 12, 2020.

[19]Law on Blocking Contraband (2000) Art. 3, clause 2, official gazette no. 793. Access via http://moj.gov.af/Con tent/files/Pages/OfficialGazetteIndex_D-header.htm Accessed 05, 12, 2020.

investment and private enterprises. Furthermore, the act of transporting donkey skin is not considered a crime under Afghan law or in Sharia; thus, the police's action in the case under consideration does not have a legal basis under the law of Afghanistan and in Sharia.

7.5 The Prosecutor's Office

The assigned prosecutor of the case claimed that Mr. X (the driver) was arrested while he was smuggling 1000 donkey skins. The prosecutor used the term "smuggle," which refers to the trade or transportation of illegal goods. However, donkey skin is not considered an illegal good under the law or Sharia. The prosecutor, in the indictment, charged the accused persons based on the following reasons: (1) the arrest of Mr. X, who had donkey skins loaded in his truck; (2) the confession of Mr. X that he was told that these are skins of cows and should be transported from Mazar city to Kunduz province; (3) the report received by the police about it; (4) the confession of the accused that he delivered 61 sacks of skins and gave them to Mr. Amin Burut (without clarifying what kind of skin); (5) the confession of Mr. Z that he works in the transportation company; (6) the information provided by Mr. X that he was intending to deliver the skins to Mr. Amin's address; and (7) the confession of Mr. Y that he works as a guard or porter. The prosecutor claimed that based on the above reasons and according to Supreme Court Opinion No. 805, dated January 8, 2016, and Article 130 of the Constitution, the court should punish the accused persons harshly.

The prosecutor charged the accused based on circumstances that are not considered a crime under the law, like arresting an accused who has possession of donkey skins, confessing that he had been arrested because of the possession of such skins, the police receiving a prior report regarding the transportation of the skins, the accused confessing that he is working for a transportation company or working as a guard, and others. I will examine the indictment of the prosecutor in light of the provisions of the law to reveal whether it matches the requirement set by law or not.

First of all, as it is mentioned in Chap. 3, constitutionally, the prosecutor's office is responsible for investigating crimes and filing a case against an accused in court, and the law regulates the procedure for the processing of criminal cases.[20] Legally, it is the duty of the prosecutor to prepare a registry after the primary investigation and include in the registry information regarding the criminal incident, the method of performing the crime, the date of the commission of the crime, and the place where the crime was committed.[21] Also, the prosecutor must indicate the specific article of the law in which the committed act has been considered a crime as well as the

[20] The Constitution of Afghanistan (2004) Art. 134.

[21] Criminal Procedure Code (2014) Art. 3, clause 7, official gazette no. 1132.

applicable punishment.[22] The law also says that the prosecutor shall prepare an accusation letter, which is defined below:

> Accusation letter: written document which is, as a result of investigation, prepared by the relevant prosecutor mentioning proof, reasons and law articles to which the crime and specific punishment has been determined based on which the trial of the accused person is requested.[23]

This provision of the law clearly says that the prosecutor must mention the reasons and the article of the law being violated, with the specific punishment. It means if a prosecutor accuses someone, the act must be criminalized by law and the law has provided specific punishment for such act. The prosecutor must not investigate and prosecute someone if no criminal act has occurred. In case there is a crime committed, the prosecutor may investigate, and based on the result of the investigation, he can write an indictment, asking the court for punishment. The law provides that the indictment shall be written as follows:

> Indictment: written demand for punishment of the accused person by the prosecutor from an authorized court which mentions the type of crime, characteristics of the accused person, incriminating evidence, legal description of the crime and the law articles specifying the punishment for the specific crime and other claim conditions.[24]

Based on the above provisions of the law, the indictment shall be composed of specific items, like a legal description of the type of crime committed, incriminating evidence, and the specific punishment provided by the law for the offense. But looking carefully at the indictment of the prosecutor and the reasons listed by him reveals that it lacks legal basis and did not provide any rule that would give legitimacy to the indictment. None of the activities that the prosecutor listed as bases for the charge in the indictment are illegal. Since the act of transporting and trading donkey skin is not a crime according to law and Sharia, the prosecutor's office findings regarding the case lack a legal basis and are challenged by illegality.[25]

On the other hand, the defense lawyer made a good argument, challenging the prosecutor to prove that the trade and transportation of donkey skin are illegal. He claimed that there is no provision in the laws or Sharia to prove that his client's act is illegal, but the court made a decision and punished the accused based on Article 130 of the Constitution and the Supreme Court's opinion.

---

[22] Criminal Procedure Code (2014) Art. 3, clause 10, official gazette no. 1132.

[23] Criminal Procedure Code (2014) Art. 3, clause 14, official gazette no. 1132.

[24] Criminal Procedure Code (2014) Art. 3, clause 15, official gazette no. 1132.

[25] For more details please look at Chap. 5.

7.6 Analysis of Kunduz Primary and Appellate Court Decisions

The primary court of Kunduz city found the accused guilty of trafficking donkey skins. The decision of the primary court was affirmed by the appellate court of Kunduz province. The court's decision is based on the following: first, Supreme Court Opinion No. 805, dated January 8, 2016, regarding the donkey skin case; second, Article 130 of the Constitution; third, Article 119 of the Penal Code; and fourth, the opinion of the chamber of commerce of Kunduz province. To have a clear understanding of the decision of Kunduz's primary and appellate courts regarding the case, it is necessary to analyze all the legal reasons for the courts to rely upon them.

7.7 Analysis of the Supreme Court's Opinion

This opinion was issued by the research and studies department and approved by the High Council of the Supreme Court in response to the inquiry of the secretariat of the General Attorney Office. The opinion states that the trade of donkey skin is prohibited and its transportation is considered a punishable act. The Supreme Court's opinion provides the following legal reasoning:

- The majority of the Sunni scholars, particularly the Ḥanafī scholars, believe that eating donkey meat is prohibited (*Ḥarām*); thus, this prohibition implies the restraint on the use and selling of donkey skin.
- The Holy Quran has indicated the specific use of donkeys by saying: *And the horses, and the mules, and the donkeys-for you to ride, and for luxury.*[26] This means that the Quran limits the use of donkeys only for riding and as pack animals. The Quran does not mention any use for its skin for any purposes.
- *Istiḥsān* and *sadd al-dharāʾiʿ* are two of the secondary sources of Islamic law, but Ḥanafī scholars rely only on the first one; *sadd al-dharāʾiʿ* is not considered a source in the Ḥanafī school. Based on these two sources, the Supreme Court cannot infer that the transportation and sale of donkey skin are illegal because there are many texts that clearly indicate that the use and trade of donkey skin are legal.
- Custom (*ʿurf*) is also a source that could be relied on. In Afghanistan, it is not a common custom to use donkey skin for any purpose or for export. Based on the custom, selling donkey skin is unacceptable and against social-ethical norms. It is considered an unclean act if someone sells donkey skin in Afghan society.

[26] The Holy Quran, Sura al-NaḤl (16: 08) وَالْخَيْلَ وَالْبِغَالَ وَالْحَمِيرَ لِتَرْكَبُوهَا وَزِينَةً وَيَخْلُقُ مَا لَا تَعْلَمُونَ.

- To stop this abominable act and prevent using donkey skin as a criminal tool, the Supreme Court research and studies department proposed that any kind of use and trafficking of donkey skin must be prohibited in the country.
- In respect of the inquiry regarding the donkey skin case, we say, based on the above reasons and in light of Article 130 of the Constitution, that the doer could face prosecution for the act of transporting donkey skins, and the court shall issue an order to destroy all the donkey skins. Furthermore, the police and prosecutor deportments must do further investigation regarding the use of the meat of those donkeys and find out how they have been used.

These are the main points in the Supreme Court's opinion. We will examine the points made by the Supreme Court regarding the case to see whether it is in line with the law and the Ḥanafī school's principles or not.

In respect of the first reason, it is true that eating donkey meat is prohibited according to the majority of Sunni schools.[27] This prohibition is limited only to domestic donkeys; wild donkey meat is permissible (*Ḥalāl*), and there is no prohibition against it.[28] In a hadith, it is narrated that Prophet Mohammad ate the meat of a wild donkey.[29]

The Supreme Court's opinion states that since the majority of Islamic jurists prohibited consuming donkey meat, it signifies that the use of donkey skin is also prohibited (*Ḥarām*).[30] Mr. Mālikzai, the head of the research department at the Supreme Court, said: "It is a general principle that if consumption of any animal meat is prohibited, use of its skin is also prohibited."[31] However, he has not provided any source for such a principle. In fact, the secretary of the High Council of the Supreme Court, Judge Shareefi, disagrees with him in this regard. He said: "Not necessarily if eating animal meat is prohibited, selling of its skin is also prohibited."[32] I also have done research in the Ḥanafī main sources but could not find anything that proves Mr. Mālikzai's argument. In contrast, there are many sources, especially in the Ḥanafī school, showing that the use and trade of all kinds of animal skin are permissible, regardless of whether or not the consumption of their meat is prohibited. The only exception is the skin of humans and pigs, the first one on the ground of its dignity and the second one because of its impure nature (*najis al-ʿayn*).[33]

---

[27] Ministry of Awqāf and Islamic Affairs of Kuwait (2008a), vol. 5, p. 211.

[28] Al-Sarakhsī (1993a) Al-Mabsūṭ li-Sarakhsī. Dār al-Maʿrifa, Beirut, vol.11, p. 232.

[29] Al-Bukhārī (2001), Hadith No: 2854.

[30] Opinion of the Supreme Court regarding the case of donkey skin, dated 18 Jan 2017.

[31] Interview with Mr. Nesar Ahmad Malikzai, the head of the Research and Study Department of the Supreme Court of Afghanistan. Dated Aug. 15, 2017.

[32] Interview with Judge Murad Ali Shareefi, Secretariat of the High Council of the Supreme Court. Dated 15 Aug 2017.

[33] Al-Marghīnānī ʿA (n.d.), p. 25; ʿAlāʾ al-Dīn, Abū Bakr ibn Masʿūd ibn AḤmad al-Kāsānī (1986a, b), p. 85.

Furthermore, in accordance with the Ḥanafī school doctrine, selling donkey meat is permissible but not for human consumption as food. The author of the book *Al-Muhīṭ al-Burhānī* stated that if a person slaughters his donkey, it is legal to sell its meat because it could be used for different purposes, like feeding other animals, such as dogs, cats, etc.[34] Thus, according to the Ḥanafī school doctrine, it is legal to buy or purchase a slaughtered donkey meat, including its skin, which could be used for multiple purposes if the skin is tanned.

The second reason of the Supreme Court regarding the prohibition on the use of donkeys beyond the limits stated in the Holy Quran is highly debatable. A verse in the Holy Quran states: *horse, mule and donkey is created for riding and carrying stuff.*[35] But it does not mean that the other uses of these animals are prohibited. If we limit the use of donkeys as it is stated in the Holy Quran, why is horse meat permissible (*Ḥalāl*) and why did the Prophet eat it?[36] Furthermore, all Sunni schools believe that eating horse meat is permissible.[37] Only Imam Abū Ḥanīfa believed it is offensive (*makrūh*), but his famous students, Imam Abū Yūsuf and Imam MuḤammad, said it is permissible (*Ḥalāl*) without any doubt.[38] Imam Abū Ḥanīfa believed that eating horse meat is disallowed because of two reasons: first, there are narrations from Prophet Mohammad that contradict the eating of horse meat,[39] and second, horses have played a significant role in the holy war "jihad," so if eating horse meat is permissible, there will be a shortage in the number of horses, and this may have a negative impact on Muslim warriors in the battlefield.[40] On the other hand, there is a general legal maxim that says "things in principle are permissible (*mubāḤ*)."[41] This is the strongest ruling that most Islamic scholars agree to. Based on this principle, everything is permissible unless there is a reason to forbid it. If someone claims that something is prohibited (*Ḥarām*), he must prove it based on trusted evidence.

The Supreme Court has not provided any proof for its argument that the use of donkeys must be limited only to what the Quran mentioned, while during the Prophet's era he and his disciples had gone beyond that limitation and ate horse meat.[42] There is even another hadith reporting that Prophet Mohammad was praying while he was riding a donkey on one of the streets of Medina.[43] It means the Prophet

[34] Abū al-Maʿālī Burhān al-Dīn MaḤmūd ibn AḤmad ibn ʿAbd al-ʿAzīz ibn ʿUmar ibn Māza al-Bukhārī (2004a), p. 349.

[35] The Holy Quran, Sura al-NaḤl, Āya 8.

[36] There is a narration that Asmāʾ, daughter of Abū Bakr said, we slaughtered hours during the Prophet Mohammad era, and we eat it. Please see ʿAlāʾ al-Dīn, Abū Bakr ibn Masʿūd ibn AḤmad al-Kāsānī (1986a, b), p. 38.

[37] Ministry of Awqāf and Islamic Affairs of Kuwait (2008b), vol. 35, p. 211.

[38] ʿAlāʾ al-Dīn, Abū Bakr ibn Masʿūd ibn AḤmad al-Kāsānī (1986a, b), p. 38.

[39] Id., pp. 38–39.

[40] Al-Ghaznawī ʿU (1986), p. 174; Badr al-Dīn al-ʿAynī A (2000a, b), p. 598.

[41] Al-Sarakhsī (1993b) Al-Mabsūṭ li-Sarakhsī. Dār al-Maʿrifa, Beirut, vol. 24, p. 77.

[42] ʿAlāʾ al-Dīn, Abū Bakr ibn Masʿūd ibn AḤmad al-Kāsānī (1986a, b), p. 38.

[43] Zaylaʿī ʿU (1896b), p. 177.

had gone further than the limit set by the Holy Quran because the Quran did not mandate praying while riding on a donkey.

In respect of the usage of *istiḤsān*[44] and *sadd al-dharāʾiʿ*, it would be good to shed light on the meaning of these terms and briefly clarify when they could be used. Literally, *istiḤsān* means to consider something better, but in Islamic jurisprudence it has been used in two situations: first, it refers to a deviation of a mujtahid from an accepted principle of analogy and making an exception;[45] second, a mujtahid prefers one of two reasons based on his knowledge and specific reason, not personal will.[46] The other kind of *istiḤsān* is to make an exception from a general maxim because of public interest and to avoid difficulty.[47] The reason is that the implementation of the main principle makes it difficult to go against public interest, so the jurists prefer to make an exception. It is not based on a jurist's will to choose any option that he wants, but he must provide proof for choosing to make an exception.

In addition, the Supreme Court's opinion based on *sadd al-dharāʾiʿ* is problematic. This term is composed of two words: one is *sad*, and another is *al-dharāʾiʿ*. Literally, the term *sadd* means blocking, and *al-dharāʾiʿ* refers to tools,[48] but in Islamic juridical concept it is translated into "blocking the means."[49] In Islamic jurisprudence, *sadd al-dharāʾiʿ* is defined as a legal act that results in an illegal act.[50] The jurists believe that if a legal act leads to something illegal, the legal act itself is prohibited.[51] It is noteworthy to mention that the main condition in the usage of sadd al- dharāʾiʿ is that the outcome of the act must be illegal (*Ḥarām*) and against public interest. If the result of the act is not illegal (*Ḥarām*), there is no reason to rely on *sadd al-dharāʾiʿ*. In the Supreme Court's opinion, there is no reason to rely on *istiḤsān* or *sadd al-dharāʾiʿ* because the trade of donkey skin is not against public interest and there is no reason to prove that it causes any harm to the citizens. Furthermore, using, selling, and purchasing donkey skin is legal in the Ḥanafī school

[44] An example of *istiḥsān* is buying something based on an order. Principally, it is not legal to buy something that does not exist, like when someone ordered and paid for a shoemaker to make him a pair of shoes or boots. Based on Islamic jurisprudence, it is not legal to buy something that is not physically available, but based on istiḥsān, it is legal to do so. Ibn Hammām (1970), p. 114.

[45] Al-Zuḥaylī (2006), p. 247.

[46] Al-Sarakhsī (1993c) Uṣūl al-Sarakhsī. Dār al-Maʿrifa, Beirut, vol. 2, p. 201.

[47] Al-Bukhārī ʿA (n.d.), p. 3.

[48] Al-Fayyūmī al-Ḥamawī A (n.d.), p. 207.

[49] Rohe (2014), p. 91.

[50] Al-Zuḥaylī (2006), p. 279.

[51] Ibn Qayyim al-Jawziyya A (2002), p. 108; Rohe (2014), p. 91.

of thought, and this occurred during Prophet Mohammad's era[52] and later on, so why would there be a reason to make the trade of donkey skin illegal?[53]

Issuing an opinion based on *istiḤsān* and *sadd al- dharāʾiʿ* is appreciated because it would be an ideal situation if the Supreme Court analyzes cases in light of Sharia principles and provides answers to the lower courts regarding newly arising issues where the law is silent about them. The only concern is that these opinions must not be against the norms and standards existing in Sharia. One of these norms is that "*ijtihād* is not permissible when there is text."[54] It means if a text provides clarification regarding a case, there is no room for *ijtihād*. Since in relation to the donkey skin case there is a prophetical tradition stating that all skins of animals become pure if they are tanned, the concept of the text must be applied without excuse, and there is no room for the Supreme Court to make it illegal.

The Supreme Court also relied on customary law (*ʿurf*), which is widely accepted among Islamic jurists, especially the Ḥanafī school of thought. However, looking at the case, it does not meet the requirements necessary to make a decision based on customary law. Generally, there are two main conditions that must be respected regarding the concept of *ʿurf*.[55] First, the custom must be common among the majority of the people in a society, and second, it should not be against the principle of Sharia and particularly the text of the Holy Quran and the Prophet Mohammad's Hadith.[56]

The Supreme Court's argument based on *ʿurf* is not acceptable because there is a text of Hadith that said: "Whichever animal skins be tanned, they grow pure or clean (*ṭāhir*)."[57] On the other hand, if it is not common among Afghans to use donkey skin, it does not mean that it is illegal. There might be a variety of customs that are practiced in other Islamic societies, though not in Afghanistan, but it does not mean that whatever is not common among Afghans should be considered illegal. Based on the above reasons, the Supreme Court's opinion regarding the case did not respect the main principle of Sharia, which says that "things in principle are permissible (*mubāḤ*),"[58] and contradicts the doctrines of the Ḥanafī school.

The Supreme Court's argument that the use or export of donkey skin is not common in Afghanistan and is an immoral act in Afghan society is debatable. First of all, the main principle in Sharia is that everything is permissible unless the law or

---

[52] There is a narration that Prophet Mohammad wanted to use water from a leather bottle, which was made from donkey skin to make ablution. Somebody told him the leather bottle is made of dead donkey skin; the prophet said was not there anyone to make it tannin? It means, when the donkey skin becomes tan, it is legal to use it. Please see Abū al-Maʿālī Burhān al-Dīn MaḤmūd ibn AḤmad ibn ʿAbd al-ʿAzīz ibn ʿUmar ibn Māza al-Bukhārī (2004b), p. 195.

[53] Ibid.

[54] لَا مساغ للِاجْتِهَاد فِي مورد النَّص " Al-Zarqāʾ (1989) legal maxim no. 13, p. 147.

[55] Rohe (2014), pp. 87–90.

[56] Al-Zuḥaylī (2006), p. 268.

[57] It is a *Ḥasan* (good) hadith al-Tirmidhī said, see: Al-Tirmidhī (1998), Hadith No: 1728.; Ibn al-Ḥajāj M (n.d.), Hadith No:105.

[58] Al-Sarakhsī (1993b) Al-Mabsūṭ li-Sarakhsī. Dār al-Maʿrifa, Beirut, vol.24, p. 77.

Sharia prohibited it. On one hand, if an act is not common in a society, it does not mean that it must be prohibited. On the other hand, it has been a permissible act among Muslims since Prophet Mohammad's era, and Muslims have used the donkey skin for multiple purposes. Since there are several provisions in Sharia regarding donkey skin, it shows that the usage of donkey skin was common among Muslims.

The Supreme Court also mentioned that donkey skin could be used as a tool for criminal purposes, which sounds a little strange, but during an interview with Judge Shareefi,[59] it was revealed that it was a political decision because NDS officials informed them that insurgents use donkey skin against government security forces. They do this by covering mines with donkey skin, and mine detectors cannot find them. Mr. Amin,[60] an expert in landmine matters, rejects this and said there is no proof that donkey skin has such capability.

The Supreme Court also claimed that the use or export of donkey skin is not common in Afghanistan and is considered an immoral act in Afghan society. This is also a violation of criminal law principles because the immorality of an act is not a reason for the court to consider it a crime. There are many activities that are not illegal but are not common and maybe people consider them immoral, but the court cannot punish people if they perform such acts. For example, in many cities, especially in remote Afghanistan, driving a car by a woman is not common and people do not like it if a daughter or a young woman of their family drives a car publicly on a street, but since driving is not a crime under the law or in Sharia, a court cannot punish her because of that act. Thus, though using donkey skin is not common in Afghan society, it is legal in accordance with law and the Sharia principle, so considering it as a crime is a violation of criminal law principles.

In consequence, to stop and prevent this act from being a common practice among Afghans, the trade and transportation of donkey skin was considered a crime by the Supreme Court. This will also prevent people from using donkey skin for criminal purposes.[61] The Supreme Court believes that using donkey skin for any purpose must be prohibited because it offends the ethical norms of Afghan society. However, from the Sharia perspective, there is no basis for the Supreme Court's opinion to prohibit the trade of donkey skin or to criminalize it.

From a legal perspective, the Supreme Court has no power to criminalize an act that is not considered a crime under the law or in Sharia, particularly in the Ḥanafī school of thought. Also, legally, the Supreme Court is not authorized to order the destruction of the donkey skins. Constitutionally, the Supreme Court has the power to check the conformity of the laws with the Constitution,[62] but it is not authorized to

[59] Judge Murad Ali Shareefi, general secretariat of the High Council of the Supreme Court.

[60] Mohammad Amin has worked for several demining companies since 1997. Currently, he gives training for the Afghan National Army (ANA) engineering unit about landmines.

[61] To be sued by insurgents that they cover explosive materials and land mines and they could not be discovered if these objects were covered by donkey skin.

[62] The Constitution of Afghanistan (2004) Art. 121: "At the request of the Government, or courts, the Supreme Court shall review the laws, legislative decrees, international treaties as well as international covenants for their compliance with the Constitution and their interpretation in accordance with the law."

act as a legislature and criminalize a legal act because such act is unconstitutional.[63] The Supreme Court must respect the principle of separation of powers, which is one of the main principles under the Afghan Constitution.

Also, it is unconstitutional to order to destroy the donkey skins because the Constitution clearly states the following:

> Property shall be safe from violation. No one shall be forbidden from owning property and acquiring it, unless limited by the provisions of law. No one's property shall be confiscated without the order of the law and decision of an authoritative court. Acquisition of private property shall be legally permitted only for the sake of public interests, and in exchange for prior and just compensation. Search and disclosure of private property shall be carried out in accordance with provisions of the law.[64]

The donkey skins are legal property of the citizens of Afghanistan, and there is no provision under the law or in Sharia that recognizes the skins as illegal goods, so any order against the owner of the skins or for the destruction of the skins does not have a legal basis in the Afghan law and Islamic Sharia.

7.7.1 Applying Article 119 of the Penal Code

The primary court of Kunduz city, based on Article 119 of the Penal Code, issued an order to confiscate the truck and the wheat flour, which are private property of the driver and a businessman. The court believed that the truck and wheat flour have been used as a tool to transfer the skins from Mazar city to Kunduz city because the Penal Code says:

> The court can in cases where the law has not anticipated confiscation as a punishment, order confiscation of goods obtained through commitment of crime or used during commitment or procured for use in the commitment of crime.[65]

There are several issues mentioned in the above article that must be taken into account: first, the article used the word "can," which means it is optional for the court to order confiscation as a punishment. Since the transportation of donkey skin is not a crime at all, the court must not issue an order regarding the confiscation of the truck as punishment. Second, this article talks about smuggled goods that are already criminalized under the law. It is not about something that is not illegal either in the

[63] The Constitution of Afghanistan (2004) Art. 95: "The proposal for drafting laws shall be made by the Government or members of the National Assembly or, in the domain of regulating the judiciary, by the Supreme Court, through the Government. Proposals for drafting the budget and financial affairs laws shall be made only by the Government."

[64] The Constitution of Afghanistan (2004) Art. 40.

[65] The Penal Code of Afghanistan (1976) Art. 119.

law or in Sharia. Third, the article clearly uses the term *crime*, which the second chapter of the Penal Code clearly explains, as well as the elements of a crime. The Penal Code states that a crime is composed of three elements: material,[66] moral (contemplative),[67] and legal.[68] The material element of a crime is defined below:

> An act or omission of an act contrary to the law, such that the act should result in a criminal effect and a cause relationship be established between the act and the effect, in the material element of crime.[69]

So the basic thing is that the act must be contrary to law and must lead to a criminal offense.

The Penal Code defines moral (contemplative) element as a criminal intention:

> Criminal intention refers to impelling the will of the doer to commit an act which produced the crime, such that it should result in the effect of the intended crime or the effect of another crime.[70]

Finally, the legal element of a crime is defined as follows:

> The legal element of crime is the description of criminal acts and their punishments in the law.[71]

So it means that an act must be criminalized by law and its punishment also described under the law.

The police and the prosecutor, along with the courts, must conduct an exhaustive investigation of cases and make sure that an act is composed of all the three elements. An act is considered a crime if all the three elements exist. If one of these three elements is not present in an act, it is not a crime and must not be punished. Now, if we look at the donkey skin case, the act of transporting donkey skin lacks all the three elements. Firstly, the Transportation of donkey skins is not an illegal act. Secondly, the act of transportation of donkey's skins does not impel the will of the truck driver to commit any crime. Finally, the transportation of donkey skin is not criminalized under the law, and there is no punishment provided by law for such act. Furthermore, the use and trade of donkey skin is legal in Sharia, and many sources in Islamic jurisprudence, particularly in the Ḥanafī school of thought, allowed the use and trade of donkey skin. So the act of transporting donkey skin is not a crime at all, either under Afghan law or in Sharia; thus, the confiscation of the truck is illegal and against the law.

---

[66] The Penal Code of Afghanistan (1976) Art. 27–33.

[67] Id., Art. 34–36.

[68] Id., Art. 37.

[69] Id., Art. 27.

[70] Id., Art. 34, clause 1.

[71] The Penal Code of Afghanistan (1976) Art. 37, clause 1.

7.7.2 *Confiscation of the Truck and Wheat Flour in Light of the Ḥanafī School of Thought*

Since the court's decision is based on Article 130 of the Afghan Constitution, which allows courts to apply the doctrines of the Ḥanafī school if there is no provision of law applicable to a case, considering the circumstances provided in the article, it is worthy to examine the court's decision regarding the confiscation of the truck in light of the Ḥanafī school principles to see whether the order of the court is in accordance with the Ḥanafī school principles or not.

Generally, the taking away of the offender's property is not supported by the Quran or Prophet Mohammad's traditions. This kind of punishment is based on *taʿzīr*. Some sources say that this kind of punishment was practiced in early Islam but was later on abolished.[72]

In the Ḥanafī main sources (*ẓāhir al-riwāya*), different kinds of *taʿzīr* (discretionary punishment) are stated, but punishment by taking the offender's property is not mentioned in these sources at all.[73] Generally, taking the property of an offender as a punishment conflicts with the Ḥanafī school principles and is not considered legal.[74] Only Imam Abū Yūsuf, the second famous personality in the Ḥanafī school, allowed it by enabling the governor to temporarily take away an offender's property as a punishment. But this, he clearly said, does not mean that the government can take away the wrongdoers' property permanently as the governor must return it afterward.[75] However, according to the Ḥanafī scholars, it is a weak opinion from Imam Abū Yūsuf and should not be implemented because there is the fear of abuse of power by the rulers to take citizens' property without any reason.[76] Since the confiscation of citizens' property as a punishment is prohibited in the Ḥanafī school of thought, the court order for the confiscation of the truck is illegal and contrary to the Ḥanafī school principle.

7.8 Conclusion

The decision of the courts in the donkey skin case should be considered unconstitutional because it violates Article 40 of the Constitution, which guarantees the protection of the property of citizens and forbids its illegal confiscation.[77] Also, it

[72] Ibn ʿĀbidīn M (1992), p. 61.

[73] Ibn Nujaym (n.d.), p. 44.

[74] Ibn ʿĀbidīn M (1992), p. 62; Ministry of Awqāf and Islamic Affairs of Kuwait (2008c) vol. 12, p. 207.

[75] Al-Zuḥaylī (2015), p 5596; Ibn ʿĀbidīn M (1992), p. 61.

[76] Ibid.

[77] The Constitution of Afghanistan (2004) Art. 40.

violates Article 27[78] of the Constitution and Articles 2 and 3 of the Penal Code, which accept the principle of legality of crime and punishment.[79] Furthermore, since the transportation of donkey skins is not a crime at all, applying Article 119 to the case and issuing an order to confiscate the truck does not have a legal basis in Afghan law.

However, the order of the Supreme Court to the police department and the attorney's office for further investigation regarding the use of donkeys' meat is considerable. Because they found thousands of donkey's skins without its meat and there was a possibility of selling donkey meat in the market for human consumption. Since eating donkey meat is prohibited in the Ḥanafī school of thought, if the donkey meat intentionally has been sold to people without telling them the truth, it is considered a crime based on Sharia principles. Furthermore, it is a crime under Afghan criminal law because the Penal Code says:

> A person who acts fraudulently against someone with whom he has made a contract, in the cases mentioned below, shall be sentenced to medium imprisonment, not exceeding two years and shall be fined an amount not exceeding ten thousand Afghanis:
>
> 1. In quantity, number, measure, weight, scale, and percentage of composition.
> 2. Delivering another good for what has already been agreed upon.
> 3. In quality, basic characteristics, and useful ingredients.
> 4. Type and source of good.[80]

The above article deals with any fraudulent act committed by one party to the other in the case of a verbal contract between a seller and a buyer. Also, a butcher is responsible for selling legal and *Ḥalāl* meat to people, but selling donkey meat that is *Ḥarām* and illegal is considered fraud and a violation of the terms of the contract. Based on the above article, selling donkey meat is legal, and the butcher's act is subject to the above article, especially parts 2, 3, and 4.

Unfortunately, neither the primary court of Kunduz city nor the appellate court of Kunduz province followed this order in their decisions, and there is no report available that the police department and the prosecutor's office followed up on this.

[78]The Constitution of Afghanistan (2004) Art. 27: "No deed shall be considered a crime unless ruled by a law promulgated prior to commitment of the offense. No one shall be pursued, arrested, or detained without due process of law. No one shall be punished without the decision of an authoritative court taken in accordance with the provisions of the law, promulgated prior to commitment of the offense."

[79]The Penal Code of Afghanistan (1976) Art. 2: "No act shall be considered crime, but in accordance with the law."; The Penal Code of Afghanistan (1976) Art. 3: "No one can be punished but in accordance with proof of the law which has been enforced before commitment of the act under reference."

[80]The Penal Code of Afghanistan (1976) Art. 480.

References

Abū al-Maʿālī Burhān al-Dīn MaḤmūd ibn AḤmad ibn ʿAbd al-ʿAzīz ibn ʿUmar ibn Māza al-Bukhārī (2004a) Al-Muhīṭ al-Burhānī fī al-fiqh al-Nuʿmānī, verified by ʿAbd al-Karīm Sāmī al-Jundī, Beirut: Dār al-kutub al-ʿilmiyya, vol.6

Abū al-Maʿālī Burhān al-Dīn MaḤmūd ibn AḤmad ibn ʿAbd al-ʿAzīz ibn ʿUmar ibn Māza al-Bukhārī (2004b) Al-Muhīṭ al-Burhānī fī al-fiqh al-Nuʿmānī, verified by ʿAbd al-Karīm Sāmī al-Jundī, Beirut: Dār al-kutub al-ʿilmiyya, vol. 5

ʿAlāʾ al-Dīn, Abū Bakr ibn Masʿūd ibn AḤmad al-Kāsānī (1986a) Badāʾiʿ al-ṣanāʾiʿ fī tartīb al-sharāʾiʿ, Beirut: Dār al-Kutub al-ʿIlmiyya, vol. 5

ʿAlāʾ al-Dīn, Abū Bakr ibn Masʿūd ibn AḤmad al-Kāsānī (1986b) Badāʾiʿ al-ṣanāʾiʿ fī tartīb al-sharāʾiʿ, Beirut: Dār al-Kutub al-ʿIlmiyya, vol. 1

Al-Bukhārī M (2001) Ṣaḥīḥ al-Bukhārī, verified by MuḤammad Ẓāhir ibn Nāṣir al-Nāṣir. Dār Ṭawq al-Najāt, Beirut

Al-Bukhārī ʿA (n.d.) Kashf al-asrār ʿan uṣūl fakhr al-islām al-bazdawī. Dār al-Kitāb al-Islāmiyya, Cairo, vol. 4

Al-Fayyūmī al-Ḥamawī A (n.d.) Al-Misbāḥ al-Munīr fī Gharīb al-Sharḥ al-Kabīr. Al-Maktaba al-ʿIlmiyya, Beirut, vol. 1

Al-Ghaznawī ʿU (1986) Al-Ghurra Al-Munīfa fī Taḥqīq baʿḍ Masāʾil al-Imām Abī Ḥanīfa. Muʾassasa al-Kutub al-Thaqāfiyya, Beirut

Al-Marghīnānī ʿA (n.d.) Al-Hidāya: Sharḥ fī Bidāyat al-Mubtadā. Dār Iḥyāʾ al-Turāth al-ʿArabī, Beirut, vol. 1

Al-Nasāʾī A (1986) Sunan Al-Nasāʾī, verified by ʿAbd al-Fatāḥ Abū Ghuda. Maktaba al-Maṭbūʿāt al-Islāmiyya, Aleppo

Al-Samarqandī A (1966) ʿUyūn al-masāʾil, verified by Ṣalāḥ al-Dīn al-Nāhī. Maṭbaʿa Aʾsaʿd, Baghdad

Al-Sarakhsī M (1993a) Al-Mabsūṭ li-Sarakhsī. Dār al-Maʿrifa, Beirut, vol.11

Al-Sarakhsī M (1993b) Al-Mabsūṭ li-Sarakhsī. Dār al-Maʿrifa, Beirut, vol. 24

Al-Sarakhsī M (1993c) Uṣūl al-Sarakhsī. Dār al-Maʿrifa, Beirut, vol. 2

Al-Shaybānī A (1983) Al-ḥujja ʿalā ahl al-madīna, verified by Mahdī Ḥasan al-Jilānī al-Qadīrī. ʿĀlam al-kutub, Beirut, vol. 2

Al-Tirmidhī M (1998) Sunan al-Tirmidhī, verified by Bashār ʿAwād Maʿrūf. Dār al-Gharb al-Islāmī, Beirut, vol. 5

Al-Zarqāʾ A (1989) Sharh al-Qawāʿid al-Fiqhiyya. Dār al-Qalam, Damascus, legal maxim no. 13

Al-Zuḥaylī MM (2006) Al-Wajīz fī Uṣūl al-Fiqh al-Islāmī. Dār al-Khayr li-l-Ṭibāʿa wa-l-Nashr wa-l-Tawzīʿ, Damascus, vol. 1

Al-Zuḥaylī W (2015) Al-Fiqh Al-Islāmī wa Adillatuhu. Dār al-Fikr, Damascus, vol. 7

Badr al-Dīn al-ʿAynī A (2000a) Al-Bināya SharḤ al-Hidāya. Dār al-Kutub al-ʿIlmiyya, Beirut, vol. 1

Badr al-Dīn al-ʿAynī A (2000b) Al-Bināya SharḤ al-Hidāya. Dār al-Kutub al-ʿIlmiyya, Beirut, vol. 11

Criminal Procedure Code (2014) Ministry of Justice, Official Gazette No: 1132

Ibn Abī Bakr M (1999) Al-Maʿānī al-Badīʿa fī Maʿrifat Ikhtilāf Ahl al-Sharīʿa. Dār al-Kutub al-ʿIlmiyya, Beirut, vol. 1

Ibn ʿĀbidīn M (1992) Radd al-MuḤtār ʿalā Durr al-Mukhtār (Ḥāshiyya Ibn ʿĀbidīn). Dār al-Fikr, Beirut, vol. 4

Ibn al-Ḥajāj M (n.d.) Ṣaḥīḥ Muslim, verified by MuḤammad Fawād ʿAbd al-Bāqī. Dār Iḥyāʾ al-Turāth al-ʿArabī, Beirut

Ibn Hammām K (1970) Shar Fatḥ al-Qadīr. Dār al-Fikr, Beirut, vol. 7

Ibn Mājah A (2009) Sunan Ibn Mājah, verified by Shuʿayb al-Arnūṭ. Dār al-Risāla al-ʿIlmiyya, Beirut

Ibn Nujaym Z (n.d.) Al-Baḥr al-Rāʾiq SharḤ Kanz al-Daqāʾiq. Dār al-Kutub al-Islāmiyya, Beirut, vol. 5

Ibn Qayyim al-Jawziyya A (2002) Iʿlām al-Muwaqqiʿīn ʿan Rabb al-ʿĀlamīn. Dār Ibn al-Jawziyya, Saudi Arabia, vol. 3
Mawṣilī ʿA (1973) Al-ikhtiyār li-taʿlīl al-mukhtār. Al-Maṭbaʿa al-ḥalabī, Cairo, vol. 1, 2, p 16
Ministry of Awqāf and Islamic Affairs of Kuwait (2008a) Al-Mawsūʿa al-Fiqhiyya al-Kuwaytiyya, vol. 5
Ministry of Awqāf and Islamic Affairs of Kuwait (2008b) Al-Mawsūʿa al-Fiqhiyya al-Kuwaytiyya, vol. 35
Ministry of Awqāf and Islamic Affairs of Kuwait (2008c) Al-Mawsūʿa al-Fiqhiyya al-Kuwaytiyya, vol. 12
Rohe M (2014) The development of the dogmatics of Islamic law. In: Rohe M (ed) Islamic law in past and present. Brill, Leiden, Chapter 2, pp 54–93
The Constitution of Afghanistan (2004) Ministry of Justice, Official Gazette No: 818
The Holy Quran
The Penal Code of Afghanistan (1976) Ministry of Justice, Official Gazette No: 347
Zaylaʿī ʿU (1896a) Tabyīn al-Ḥaqāʾiq SharḤ Kanz al-Daqāʾiq. Al-Maṭbaʿa al-Kubrā al-Amīriyya, Cairo, vol. 5
Zaylaʿī ʿU (1896b) Tabyīn al-Ḥaqāʾiq SharḤ Kanz al-Daqāʾiq. Al-Maṭbaʿa al-Kubrā al-Amīriyya, Cairo, vol. 1

Chapter 8
Final Conclusion

8.1 Summary and Overview

This book examines the role of Sharia in the decisions of the Afghan courts on criminal matters. This study has tried to answer the following key questions: (1) How Afghan courts apply Sharia principles, especially the doctrines of the Hanafi School of Thought in criminal matters in the case of legal lacuna? (2) What are the limits imposed on courts when they apply Hanafi School's doctrines under Article 130 of the Constitution? (3) Will the process of the case and decision of the court explicitly or implicitly violates the basic rights of the citizens and particularly the human rights principles? Articles 130 of the 2004 Constitution of Afghanistan allows courts to use the doctrines of Hanafi School in certain cases, but there are several conditions for applying this Article to a case. These conditions challenge the courts applying this Article in a criminal case. Interestingly, there is no consensus among the Supreme Court judges and legal experts regarding the application of Article 130 in criminal cases.

The book has two sections. The first section comprises four chapters, which mostly provide theoretical bases for better understanding the role of Sharia in the Afghan legal system. The second section is dedicated to real-world case studies, showing the practical implementation of Hanafi School's doctrine in criminal matters in the light of Article 130 of the 2004 Constitution of Afghanistan.

The first chapter of the first section provides a brief historical background on the position of Islam in Afghan society, particularly its role in the Afghan legal system. It also shed light on the meaning of "Sharia" in the context of Afghanistan, which carries a different meaning from that of most of the other majority Muslim population countries.

Chapter 2 provides an analytical view of Article 130 of the Afghan Constitution and describes the pluralistic legal system of Afghanistan. Furthermore, this chapter explores the uniqueness of the Afghan legal system and introduces briefly the different players on the legal ground and their impacts on the court's decisions.

L. Saeed, *Islam, Custom and Human Rights*, Interdisciplinary Studies in Human Rights 7, https://doi.org/10.1007/978-3-030-83086-1_8

Furthermore, it sheds light on the structure of the judiciary of Afghanistan and provides the answer to the question: who becomes a judge in Afghanistan?

Chapter 3 analyzes Article 130 of the 2004 constitution of Afghanistan from different perspectives. It discusses the language of the text and the historical background of the Article. Furthermore, it discusses the source of the Article and examines the question: when did it appear in the Afghan Constitutions?

Chapter 4 discusses the implementation of Article 130 of the Constitution in practice and the norms and standards that must be considered when a criminal case has been processed. The chapter examines a variety of standards, such as the principle of legality from the perspective of Afghan law and Sharia, and suggests that these norms must be reflected when a case has been processed, whether according to Afghan Criminal Procedure Law, or Islamic Criminal Procedure. In addition, the chapter analyzes the concept of taʿzīr (discretionary punishment) and its practice by Afghan judges. Besides that, for a better understanding of the usage of the Hanafi doctrines to the cases, the principle of preference and the hierarchy of sources and dominating opinions among the Hanafi school scholars have been investigated.

The second section analyzes some real cases that Afghan courts have made decisions on by applying the provisions of the Hanafi fiqh under Article 130 of the 2004 Constitution. This section is composed of three cases study, each examining in detail a separate case in which courts applied the provisions of the Hanafi fiqh based on Article 130 of the 2004 Constitution. These cases are from different regions of the country that could represent the role of Sharia in Afghanistan.

The first case study analyzes a blasphemy case of Mr. Parwīz Kāmbakhsh, a 3rd-year journalism department's student at Balkh University, who was convicted by capital punishment by the primary court of Mazar-e-Sharif city of Balkh province. The appellate court of Kabul province overruled the decision and sentenced him to 20 years in prison, and the Supreme Court affirmed this decision. This case provides a real example of how courts applying the Hanafi school doctrines in practice and highlights the challenges that the application of Hanafi fiqh might cause.

The second case study examines the decision of Herat city primary court in a case regarding selling dog meat. A couple of individuals were sentenced to 13 years in prison because they were possibly selling dog meat in the market. The appellate court of Herat province and the Supreme Court affirmed the decision of the primary court. In this case, the courts sentenced the accused persons for an act—selling of dog meat—that was not a crime under the laws of Afghanistan and the Hanafi Scholl principle as well.

The last case study is from Kunduz city primary court regarding the transportation of donkey skins from Mazar-e-Sharif city to Kunduz city. The primary court of Kunduz city punished the accused with short-term imprisonment, and 30,000 Afghanis fine, and confiscation of the truck and 240 sacks (12,000 kg) of wheat flour, which were shipping with the donkey skins loaded to gather in the truck. The appellate court and the Supreme Court both affirmed the decision of the primary court. Like the dog meat case, this case is also interesting because transportation of donkey skins is not a crime under the laws of Afghanistan and the Hanafi School of Thought as well. The chapter also discusses the trade of donkeys and their meat and skin in light of the provisions of the Hanafi fiqh to clarify the legal status of donkey skins from a Sharia perspective

8.2 Major Findings

This study revealed that customs and ethical norms in Afghan society play a significant role in court decisions. In all cases in this study, the reaction of people impacted the court's decision. And in most of these cases, the act is not a crime according to state law and Sharia. However, because of custom and popular opinion against the act and the demand for severe punishment, the courts have convicted people absent a legally recognized crime.

It is important to note that in most cases, Sharia serves as the basis for the custom and ethical norms in Afghanistan. In all three cases reviewed in this dissertation, the reaction of the people and the court's decisions are rooted in the Sharia principles. For instance, apostasy is a serious crime under Sharia; also, selling dog meat for human consumption is prohibited in Islamic Sharia. Additionally, the consumption of donkey meat is not allowed according to the Ḥanafī school of thought.

In light of these principles, which already exist in the context of Sharia, the court issued an inquiry to the *ʿulamāʾ* council of related provinces and the Supreme Court's research and study department to get their thoughts on these issues. In response to those inquiries, the Balkh and Herat provinces' *ʿulamāʾ* council and the Supreme Court issued an opinion based on the Sharia principles. Seemingly, the Supreme Court's opinion regarding the donkey skin case is a simple epiphenomenon of the prohibition of eating donkey meat according to Ḥanafī doctrine. In conclusion, in many cases in Afghanistan, custom plays an important role in society, but a deeper study reveals that most customs and ethical norms have roots in Sharia principles. So Sharia is the main player; however, in some cases, Sharia principles are not reflected directly in decisions, but they have been performed through customs or standards set by laypeople.

Findings based on interviews showed that most judges believe that they are authorized to punish people based on *taʿzīr* (discretionary punishment) even if the act is not criminalized. Most Afghan judges believe that based on the concept of *taʿzīr*, they are authorized to apply any kind of punishment to someone if they think the act is worthy of punishment. The punishment ranges from asking the accused to show up in court to capital punishment, depending on the judge's discretion. This means that judges can criminalize an act in specific circumstances and then punish the actor based on his discretion.

The cases studied in this dissertation exemplified serious violations of the Constitution, Afghan laws, and the Sharia provisions, particularly the Ḥanafī school of thought. In most of these cases, courts have not referred to any provision of law or the provisions of the Ḥanafī *fiqh*, which is unconstitutional and against the law.

This research discovered that it is a common understanding among Afghan judges and legal experts that apostasy is one of the *Ḥudūd* crimes; thus, both the 1976 Penal Code and the 2017 Criminal Code clearly state that the code regulates *taʿzīrī* crimes, and the perpetrators of *Ḥudūd*, *qiṣāṣ*, and *diya* shall be punished based on Ḥanafī jurisprudence. As mentioned before, a common misunderstanding in Afghanistan leads the drafting committee and the legislature to exclude apostasy from the Penal codes and consider it as a *Ḥudūd* crime. So this research will help the legislature to regulate apostasy crimes in the Penal code because according to the findings in this dissertation, based on the Ḥanafī school of thought, apostasy belongs to the category of *taʿzīr* crimes, not *Ḥudūd* crimes, and it could be regulated by the Penal code.

One of the significant findings of this study is the lack of judges who are well trained in Sharia principles, particularly the Ḥanafī school of thought. As the case studies show, with the exception of Parwīz Kāmbakhsh's case, in all other cases, there is not a single provision of the Ḥanafī school that has been used by the courts regarding the case. Even in other cases, like the selling of dog meat and donkey skins, the decisions contradict the Ḥanafī school's principles.

There is a disagreement among Afghan legal experts and judges, even among the Supreme Court justices, about whether Article 130 of the Afghan Constitution should be applied only to civil cases and not to criminal cases. However, this study has not found a single civil case in which a decision has been made based on Article 130 of the Afghan Constitution, but Article 130 of the Constitution is widely applied to criminal cases. In most cases wherein Article 130 has been applied, the act that was punished by the courts is not a crime either under the law or in Sharia. Furthermore, there are several clauses in the text of Article 130 that must be considered when it is applied to a case, but courts, regardless of the norms and standards accepted in the laws and even Sharia, first criminalize an act and then punish them. While Article 130 does not refer directly to criminal cases, its historical background of proves that it is about noncriminal cases.

Furthermore, this research found that Article 130 of the Afghan Constitution only authorizes the courts to apply Article 130 to a case if the law is silent about it, but this dissertation found that the police and the prosecutor's office arrested and charged people based on Article 130, which is a serious violation of the Afghan laws because the use of Article 130 is constitutionally limited only to the courts and does not extend to the police and the prosecutor's office. So arrests by the police and charges by prosecutors based on Article 130 of the Constitution should be considered unconstitutional.

8.3 Recommendations

To strengthen the rule of law and obey fair trial standards and bring justice, the Supreme Court should pay attention to the following points:

- Because Islamic law, especially the Ḥanafī school of thought, plays a significant role in both state law and customary law, it is vitally important that Afghan judges have enough knowledge regarding the doctrines of the Ḥanafī school. A lack of knowledge leads judges to make decisions that are, in most cases, unconstitutional or contradict the Ḥanafī school principles. Based on the recommendation of the founder of the Ḥanafī school, Imam Abū Ḥanīfa, judges should take a year-long sabbatical to take time for research and study in order to gain background knowledge. Without this time away from their duties, judges would not have sufficient time for research and study.[1] Imam Abū Ḥanīfa's idea resembles the concept of the Continuing Legal Education Program for lawyers in many countries, especially in the US. Such programs enable judges to update their legal knowledge. To effectuate this in Afghanistan, the Supreme Court should start a capacity-building program for judges.

- Afghan judges should enhance their knowledge of Sharia, especially the Ḥanafī school of thought. The findings in this dissertation, based on interviews with judges, show that there is a common misunderstanding among judges about the concept of *taʿzīr*. Afghan judges believe that they are authorized to punish people under the concept of *taʿzīr* even if the act is not a crime, deciding on a punishment based on their discretion. However, such decisions have no root in Sharia; in addition, such a belief constitutes a serious violation of the principle of legality respected in both Sharia and state laws. So to avoid any misunderstanding in this regard, the Supreme Court should review its curriculum in Stage Course and update it based on the needs of the modern judiciary system and include subjects that could enhance judges' knowledge in this regard.
- It would be useful for courts to develop closer relationships with the Law and Sharia faculties to engage judges with research and publication and connect professors and students to practical work. It would help judges keep updated with new developments in different fields of law and also help law and Sharia professors to enhance their practical skills. Through this kind of engagement, both parties will benefit from each other and help courts operate properly.
- Another important finding is the lack of independence of judges. According to Sharia principles, international fair trial standards, and Afghan laws, courts must be impartial and independent when making a decision regarding a case. The judges' decisions must not be influenced by the political-social sphere but must be based on law. The cases studied in this research proved that almost all of the decisions were taken under the sphere of influence, such as political[2] or social pressure.[3] The Supreme Court must provide some regulation to protect judges from any kind of influence and guarantee their impartiality. If judges violate these

[1] Al-Ḥalabī (1973), p. 219.

[2] For instance, the decision on the blasphemy case of Parwīz Kāmbakhsh was made with, as many people claimed, high-ranking politicians being involved; thus, the case was not tried in the Balkh province appellate court and was transferred to Kabul because of the involvement of the governor of Balkh province (Kāmbakhsh family claimed). After the final decision of the appellate court and the affirmation of the Supreme Court, no punishment was implemented and Kāmbakhsh was smuggled out of the country by Mr. Carl Bildt, the Swedish foreign minister, via a Swedish government airplane. For more details, please read the blasphemy case of Parwīz Kāmbakhsh.

[3] Another case was about the selling of dog meat in Herat city, which was followed by several days' demonstrations in the city asking for capital punishment for the accused. The people gave warning that if the accused will not be punished severely, they will kill them when they are released. The court made a decision imposing a 13-year imprisonment, which is unconstitutional and contradicted the law and Sharia principles. For more details, please read the selling dog meat case.

rules, there must be some consequence or punishment from the upper court against the violators.

- One of the key recommendations of this research addresses the Supreme Court. The court should publicize its decisions and make them accessible to the people through its website. Currently, it is very difficult to have access to cases that were handled by the Afghan courts at different levels.[4] Having access to court decisions will help other knowledgeable persons in the field to read the case and write some comments about them. This will help the quality of the judgments in the country because when the Afghan judges know that their decision would be reviewed by others, they will try to make a provisional decision based on a good analysis of law according to the facts of the case.
- The concept of the supremacy of the Constitution and the laws in the legal system of Afghanistan must be considered when judges make a decision. The Constitution clearly provides: "In issuing decision, the court is obligated to state the reason for its verdict..."[5] Afghan courts, in most of the cases analyzed in this research, have not referred to any provision of the law or the Ḥanafī school of thought, which is a serious violation of the Constitution and the laws. Unfortunately, the Supreme Court has affirmed all of these cases. Besides weak knowledge of the judges in public law, particularly in the constitutional law field, one of the main reasons could be the high number of cases (more than 4000 cases in the criminal law chamber of the Supreme Court waiting for review)[6] and less than five councilor judges to review all the cases. If the quantity of cases is very high and there are less than five counselor judges, it will have a huge impact on the quality of work. One of the justices revealed that he decided on 83 cases in less than one hour.[7] So the Supreme Court should adopt a sufficient mechanism of review and increase the number of well-trained staff to lessen the workload and enhance the quality of work of justices.
- For better observation, the Supreme Court should establish an efficient online electronic system that would connect lower courts from all over the county to the Supreme Court. This system will provide facilities to observe the lower court sufficiently and receive reports from them from time to time. It will also help the lower courts to easily communicate with and receive guidance from the Supreme Court. In the two cases that are studied here, *selling dog meat* and *the*

Also, the donkey skin case in the northern city of Kunduz was mainly made based on an opinion from the Supreme Court, which contradicts Sharia, the Constitution, and state laws. For more details, please read the case.

[4]According to my personal experience, the most difficult part of this research was access to the cases. There were two things that helped me get copies of the cases related to my study: one is personal relationships, and the second is an official order from Chief Justice Halim. Although I have such an order from the highest authority in the judiciary in Afghanistan, if I did not have personal relationships with some people, I would not have gained access to the cases.

[5]The Constitution of Afghanistan (2004) Art. 129.

[6]Interview with one of the Justices of the Supreme Court, dated March 2015.

[7]Interview with one of the Justice of the Supreme Court, dated August 2016.

transportation of donkey skins, if such a system of communication existed at the time those cases were ongoing, the outcome would have been different. Furthermore, having such a system will also save time.

In applying such a mechanism, the main challenge would be the lack of skill training of the judges with such a system because many of the judges are not familiar with how to use a computer. However, six months to one year of training would be enough to make the judges able to use computers. The most efficient way of training would be the ToT (Training of Trainees) approach. The training programs could be started in Kabul and the big cities in six different zones and then extended to other provinces. Also, learning these skills could be included in the curricula of Law and Sharia faculties and the Supreme Court Stage program as well.

8.4 Conclusion

This dissertation has shown how some acts that are disfavored by Afghan society are prosecuted as crimes—even when they are not defined as crimes under Sharia or Afghan law. This finding illustrates society's tremendous influence over Afghan courts. Afghanistan has a pluralistic legal system, and there are three main players: Sharia, state law, and customs, which have been practiced in the legal field. Also, though theoretically Sharia is considered the foundation for the other two sources of law, state law has superiority as it is to be applied to all cases.[8] However, in practice, the customs and standards accepted by laypeople have played a main role in the Afghan courts' decisions in the case of a legal lacuna.

Afghanistan has a dual legal educational system: the Sharia faculty and the Law and Political Science faculty. The Sharia faculty mostly focuses on Islamic main sources, like the Quran and Hadith, and Islamic jurisprudence in Arabic classical texts, along with some law courses, which highly echo the Egyptian style, particularly the al-Azhar University's style. On the other hand, the main focus of Law and Political Science faculties is on the western-style law education system and the use of textbooks in local official languages. With the example of Afghanistan, this dissertation has shown how diverse educational backgrounds and different interpretations of Sharia and Islamic principles lead to a different conclusion. Furthermore, this study demonstrates how the lack of well-trained staff in the justice sector, especially in the judiciary, can lead courts to make unconstitutional and illegal decisions.

By analyzing the history of Article 130 of the Afghan Constitution and having a critical view on it, this study was able to draw attention to the Afghan legal scholars'

[8]The Constitution of Afghanistan (2004) Art. 130: "In cases under consideration, the courts shall apply provisions of this Constitution as well as other laws. If there is no provision in the Constitution or other laws about a case, the courts shall, in pursuance of Ḥanafī jurisprudence, and, within the limits set by this Constitution, rule in a way that attains justice in the best manner."

and judges' misuse of the article and the consequences of using it in criminal cases. Through interviews with legal scholars and judges, including most of the Supreme Court justices and the chief justice, it was revealed that the negative impact of the use of Article 130 of the Constitution in criminal cases became a hot topic among Afghan judges and legal scholars. This discussion paved the way for a provision in the new Penal Code that prevents the use of Article 130 in criminal cases.[9]

This dissertation also showed how a misunderstanding of some Islamic legal concepts and procedures leads courts to make decisions that are unconstitutional and contradict both state law and Sharia principles. Findings based on interviews in this dissertation revealed that almost all judges believed that in accordance with Sharia, they could punish anyone based on *taʿzīr*. Also, weak knowledge regarding Sharia and the legal principles and standards among the Afghan judges misleads courts into going beyond their jurisdiction and making decisions that contradict the law and Sharia.

This dissertation's major focus is on the case studies that could provide an answer to the main question of the research. By analyzing these cases, this dissertation has tried to illustrate how Sharia plays a significant role in court decision-making in the case of a legal gap. The main argument that Sharia, particularly the Ḥanafī school of thought, is the foundation of state law and customary law in Afghanistan has been confirmed by analyzing these cases. The Sharia principles sometimes display themselves through provisions of law or through customs and norms that the majority of people find acceptable. Thus, a superficial study of the cases showed that the customs and standards set by laypeople have influenced the decisions of the courts, but a deep analytical view discovered that the significant role of Sharia in the court decisions has been played through customs because the reaction of the people and the opinion of the Supreme Court have roots in Sharia. For instance, blasphemy and apostasy are considered crimes in Sharia. Also, the strong reactions of the Herat city people against the selling of dog meat have roots in Sharia, too, because dogs have been considered dirty animals and eating dog meat is strictly prohibited (*Ḥarām*) according to the majority of Islamic schools of thought, particularly the Ḥanafī school of thought. However, selling dog meat not for human consumption is legal in accordance with the Ḥanafī school principles.[10] Also, eating donkey meat is prohibited in accordance with the Ḥanafī school doctrines; however, using donkey skin is allowed, though the Supreme Court issued an opinion differently. Thus, the

[9]The New Penal Code (2017) Art. 7: "(1) Crime specification and punishment determination based on analogy is not permissible. (2) Criminalization and implementation of punishment for an action is not permissible unless the act is considered a crime in this law and a punishment has been determined for it."

[10]In many interviews and discussions with Supreme Court judges including justices, they believe that selling dog meat is prohibited because eating dog meat is prohibited. Even during a meeting with Vice-President of Afghanistan, who is a famous legal scholar with a religious study background and in charge of the justice sector in the current government, he clearly said that selling dog meat is a crime and the actor should be punished. They don't go to the details, which are available in the main sources of the Ḥanafī School and just rely upon the prohibition of eating dog meat.

theory of Sharia, particularly the doctrines of the Ḥanafī school, has a significant role in the court decisions based on this case study.

In short, this dissertation provided, first, a conceptual analysis of Sharia and its role in the legal system of Afghanistan, particularly in the judiciary. Second, it also provided a valuable fact that sheds light on the weak points of the judiciary and the legal lacunae in the field of criminal justice in Afghanistan. Last but not the least, to fill the legal gaps and strengthen the due process of law in Afghanistan, this dissertation provided a list of recommendations for the Supreme Court that will help the courts ensure due process of law. Some of these recommendations open the doors for further research and study that could be done in the future.

References

Al-Ḥalabī A (1973) Lisān al-Ḥukkām fī Maʿrifat al-Aḥkām. Al-Bāb al-Ḥalabī, Cairo
The Constitution of Afghanistan (2004) Ministry of Justice, Official Gazette No: 818
The Penal Code (2017) Ministry of Justice, Official Gazette No: 1260